372.21

WITH

D0625712

Foundations of Playwork

Foundations of Playwork

Fraser Brown and Chris Taylor

 Open University Press

Open University Press
McGraw-Hill Education
McGraw-Hill House
Shoppenhangers Road
Maidenhead
Berkshire
England
SL6 2QL

email: enquiries@openup.co.uk
world wide web: www.openup.co.uk

and Two Penn Plaza, New York, NY 10121-2289, USA

First published 2008
Reprinted 2009
Second reprint 2009
Copyright © Authors and contributors 2008

A catalogue record of this book is available from the British Library

ISBN-13: 978-0-33-522291-9 (pb) 978-0-33-522292-6 (hb)
ISBN-10: 0-33-522291-9 (pb)   0-33-522292-7 (hb)

Library of Congress Cataloging-in-Publication Data
CIP data applied for

Typeset by Bookens Ltd, Royston, Herts.
Printed in Great Britain by Ashford Colour Press Ltd.

All royalties from this book go to:
Aid for Romanian Children
whose summer camps for Roma children

The McGraw-Hill Companies

Contents

PART 2
The play environment

PART 3
The playing child and the practising playworker

PART 4
Playwork values, ethics and professional practice

PART 5
Special feature

PART 6
Play links, relating and communicating

PART 7
Working with professional diversity

PART 8
Contributing to the management and development
of play settings

PART 9
Legislation and rights

PART 10
Research and methods

Appendices

List of contributors

The Editors

Dr Fraser Brown is Reader in Playwork at Leeds Metropolitan University, and lecturer on the BA (Hons) Playwork degree. For ten years he was Director of the playwork training agency *Children First*, and previously held advisory posts with Playboard and the NPFA. He spent three years on an adventure playground in Runcorn, and managed a range of projects for the North West Play Association. For two years he was District Leisure Officer in Middlesbrough. His publications include *The Venture: A Case Study of an Adventure Playground* (2007); *Playwork: Theory and Practice* (2003); *Working Together: A Playwork Training Pack* (1989), and *School Playgrounds* (1990). He has spoken throughout the UK and around the world about his research into the effects of therapeutic playwork on a group of abandoned children in Romania, and has recently published a journal article on the subject, 'Children Without Play'.

Chris Taylor is currently a Management Committee Support Worker at Play Association Tower Hamlets; Trustee for London Play; an Associate Lecturer with the Open University; playwork trainer and consultant. She recently wrote the Learning Outcomes for the Playwork Sector Endorsed Foundation Degree for SkillsActive, and co-wrote the SkillsActive publication *The Benefits of Play and Playwork* (2007). She worked previously as the Head of Play and Youth Work Training and Development in Islington, and was Senior Lecturer on the Dip HE Playwork course, at Thurrock College. The first eight years of her working life were spent on adventure playgrounds in Swansea, London and Manchester. She is a founder member of the Good Enough Gamester Group, committed to sharing the ideas of D.W. Winnicott with playworkers.

Contributors

Arthur Battram is a freelancer specializing in playwork, management coaching and training, creativity and innovation. He advises on community-based play developments, and provides services in information design, graphic design and publishing for public and private sector organizations. He is a graduate of UCL (Bsc.Hons Psychology '73). He was an adventure playground worker in Brighton (74–76). In 1977, he took on the Pavilion Project in Middlesbrough, a Creative Play Project. Later he was Training Officer at Bradford Area Play Association, where he developed a pioneering Playwork Foundation Programme. He then joined the

Local Government Management Board where he produced 'Creating Involvement' and the best-selling 'Navigating Complexity'. He became full time with PleXity in 2000.

Natalie Baxter has worked with children in various roles since 1988, and is a recent graduate from the BA (Hons) Playwork course at Leeds Metropolitan University. She is an outdoor play advocate and her undergraduate dissertation explored the erosion of outdoor play and the subsequent effects and implications for children, the environment and the playwork profession. She has planned and delivered outdoor and environmental play training sessions in both England and Scotland, and is currently working for Wakefield Council where she has written an inclusive Play Strategy for the district.

Joan Beattie is a freelance training consultant. Previously she was the Programme Manager for Children and Young People for SkillsActive Scotland. She has worked with children since leaving school in 1972. Initially trained as a nursery nurse, Joan has worked in a variety of settings – early years, playwork, youth work and community work in Dundee, Bristol, London, Leeds and Edinburgh. After completing a BA (Hons) Professional Studies in Playwork in 1993, she went on to become a lecturer for Early Years and Playwork in Edinburgh, the Lothians, the Scottish Borders and Fife. She has co-authored a *Good Practice Guide for Out of School Care*, and has written a Playwork Training Pack for Falkirk Council. She was formerly Chair of IPA (Scotland Branch) and is now a trustee; she is on the Board of Play Scotland and is chairperson of First 4 Kids and the Playwork Centres Network.

Paul Bonel is Director of the Playwork Unit, SkillsActive. He has been involved in playwork for over 30 years. He began as an adventure playground worker, worked on several adventure playgrounds in London and subsequently moved into education and training, before progressing to his current post. SkillsActive is a member of the Children's Workforce Network (England) and is participating fully in the development of reforms under *Every Child Matters*. This has included being at the heart of the debate around establishing a common core of skills and knowledge for the children's workforce. Paul has written two books on play and playwork: *Playing for Real* and *Playwork – A Guide to Good Practice* (with Jennie Lindon).

Steve Chan is the Deputy Head, leading on Play in the Youth & Play Service, for Wirral Council. Previously, a Play Development Officer, with the Wirral Play Council initiating play facilities Wirral wide, including coordinating the Summer Play Programme, developing 'PlaySpaces' an Outreach Play Project and delivering playwork training. Initially he worked as a peripatetic playworker, then as a Playbus Development Officer, working closely with children and local communities in developing a mobile play service; converting and designing a double-decker bus into a creative play space, serving areas with inadequate play provision. He attained a BA (Hons) in Playwork at Leeds Metropolitan University.

Tony Chilton is a freelance play consultant, having recently retired from being Play Development Officer for Play Wales. He has been involved in the promotion and development of adventure playgrounds since the 1960s. After working as a play-worker in Telford, he moved to Blacon Adventure Playground in Chester, and then became Regional Officer for the NPFA, during which time he helped to found JNCTP. Subsequently he was Principal Play Development Officer for Newcastle City Council, and Community Development Worker for the Rhyl Community Agency. He has always been involved in the training and education of playworkers, delivering courses throughout the country, including those at Newcastle Polytechnic, Mabel Fletcher CFE Liverpool, Durham Technical College, and Stockport College of Technology. He is an expert in playground safety, and his writing includes *Children's Play in Newcastle upon Tyne* (NPFA, 1985).

Amy Clutterbrook is a playworker working in the play facility at HM Prison and YOI New Hall, where she works with children in challenging circumstances. After moving to Leeds in 2003, she successfully completed a BTEC National Diploma in Performing Arts at Burnley College. She then studied the BA (Hons) Playwork degree at Leeds Metropolitan University, where she graduated in 2006. While studying, she successfully completed placements in prisons in both the UK and the USA. The American system provided a strong contrast to the British approach.

Becky Cole is currently the Research and Development Coordinator for Children's Play Services within Cardiff Council. She began her play career at the age of 21 working on a playscheme for disabled young people. She has since worked as a full-time playworker striving towards fully inclusive play projects; supporting playwork-ers, children, young people and their parents to recognize and meet children's play needs. Becky has been involved with developing three local Play Strategies across South Wales. Her present role involves researching current play issues and coordi-nating a small grant scheme supporting voluntary and statutory groups. Becky has also trained and volunteered as a children and young person's counsellor.

Issy Cole-Hamilton is Head of Policy and Research with Play England, a project of the Children's Play Council where she manages a major programme of policy development, advocacy and research. She previously held posts with the Royal National Institute for the Blind, Child Poverty Action Group, and the Children's Rights Development Unit, where she contributed chapters on children's rights to play and leisure, and to a safe and positive environment, to the CRDU publication *UK Agenda for Children*. Issy also leads on Play England's policy and research service to DCMS, involving policy analysis, commissioning and undertaking research. Publications include *More Than Swings and Roundabouts*; *Playing On: Sustaining Play Provision in Changing Time*s; *Making the Case for Play*; and *Shaping the Future: The Needs and Aspirations of Blind and Partially Sighted Children and Young People*.

Mick Conway is Play England Regional Manager. Previously, he was Policy Officer for London Play, senior playworker at Bermondsey Adventure Playground, and

Director of Hackney Play Association from 1995, and has held a number of play development posts within HPA since 1985. He co-authored the Quality in Play quality assurance system, which is now endorsed by the government's Investors in Children scheme. He was a consultant on the development of the Playwork Principles, and has contributed to many play publications including the *Guide to Preparing Play Strategies* (2005); *Playwork Theory and Practice* (2003); *Best Play: What Play Provision Should Do for Children* (2000); and *Risk and Safety in Play* (1997).

Annie Davy is a Senior Education Officer with Oxfordshire County Council. She has over 20 years experience of working in education, playwork and care in both public and voluntary sectors and in community, schools, social care, health and community learning settings. She brings a practitioner perspective from nursery education, playwork and adult education and has also worked in childcare development and inspection. She is currently completing an Integrated Masters Programme at Plymouth University with 'play' as a linking theme across various human development-based areas of study. Publications include *Playwork: Play and Care for Children 5–15*, originally published in 1995 by Macmillan, with a comprehensively rewritten fourth edition published by Thomson Learning in 2006. She has also contributed to various journals and was series editor for a series of vocationally based playwork books, the *Can Do Series* published by Thompson Learning in 2002.

Perry Else is the Course Leader for the BA (Hons) Children and Playwork course at Sheffield Hallam University. He has spent over 20 years bringing play and creativity to a variety of organizations working for children. He has presented keynote papers at many conferences, often collaborating with Gordon Sturrock; for example on 'The Colorado Paper' and 'Towards Ludogogy' (also with Wendy Russell). Perry has contributed to major playwork publications such as *Best Play and Making Sense of Play* and developed materials that are used in many training courses throughout the UK. In his spare time, he organizes the conference *Beauty of Play*.

Katherine Fisher currently works as an Early Years Teacher in North London. After completing the DipHE Playwork, she worked at two outdoor pursuit centres, where she set up and managed that part of the centre which catered for nursery-age children. She then spent a year at Bath University Sports Development and Recreation Department, working as a sports assistant helping to set up sporting events such as trials for the Commonwealth Games. Subsequently she returned to Leeds Metropolitan University to complete the BA (Hons) in Playwork. She then trained and worked as a Montessori teacher in Oxfordshire, and co-authored the *Nursery World* article 'Observation: Stop and Watch'.

Tim Gill is one of the UK's leading thinkers on childhood and an effective advocate for change. His work focuses on children's play and free time. His book, *No Fear: Growing up in a Risk-averse Society* was published in 2007. Tim has advised political parties and think-tanks representing a broad spectrum of political opinion, and has carried out consultancies for major NGOs and public bodies. In 2002, while Director of the Children's Play Council, Tim led the first ever government-sponsored review of children's play under the chairmanship of Rt Hon Frank Dobson MP. Tim's website is www.rethinking childhood.com.

Mark Gladwin is a member of the play team at Bradford Early Years & Childcare Service, where he holds lead responsibility for the district's Play Strategy. Mark began his playwork career as a play development worker at York Playspace, where he organized playschemes, a scrap store, and playwork training. He later worked for the Children's Society in Leeds, promoting children's participation in the development of quality in out-of-school childcare. Mark has a DipHE in Playwork from Leeds Metropolitan University and has lectured in playwork there. A former chair of JNCTP, he is now chairperson of a York-based playwork assessment centre and a director of Yorkshire Play. Mark has recently been awarded a Master's degree by Leeds Metropolitan University for his research on children's perceptions of risk in play.

Mike Greenaway is the Director of Play Wales, the national organization for children's play. He has been a teacher, a city farmer, a playworker on adventure playgrounds, a youth officer, an education advisor, and continues to practise playwork in his home village on the Gower Peninsular for two weeks every summer. In his current position he has been instrumental as an advisor and as a 'critical friend' to the Welsh Assembly Government in the adoption of the world's first National play policy and in planning its implementation. He is a passionate advocate for children and young people's play and therefore quality playwork.

Julie Griffith is Head of Year 7 and transition in a secondary school in Islington, having also worked in a primary school. She is keen to develop good practice around the transition process of Year 6 students. She trained as a secondary school teacher and taught for 10 years in Bristol and London. She then moved into youth work, after an enjoyable stint as a youth worker in a local youth centre. She left teaching in 1989 and moved into youth work where she set up and managed a curriculum development unit. In this role she worked with many play and youth groups in Islington, supporting them in developing their curriculum and other initiatives.

Maggie Harris is Senior Lecturer in BA (Hons) Playwork at Leeds Metropolitan University. She gained practical experience in playwork in several agencies including Cranhill Beacon Children's Centre in Easterhouse, Glasgow. While at Warwick Adventure Playground, Knottingley, she developed after-school, breakfast and holidaycare provision to run in the same space, and in the same ethos, as the established open access adventure play provision. Maggie also delivered and managed a range of successful playwork training courses at Warwick. She is a member of the Wakefield and District Play Forum which delivers play services and helped write the play strategy for Wakefield District Council. She is also a member of the Voluntary Management Committee of Warwick Adventure Playground/Community Campus.

Janine Hart is a therapeutic playworker and part-time playwork tutor. Initially trained as a nursery nurse, she practised in various childcare posts before undertaking the BA (Hons) Playwork at Leeds Metropolitan University. While at university she developed Newhall Kidz play facility at New Hall womens prison (Wakefield). She is a busy mum of five and actively campaigns for outdoor play opportunities in her local community. Through her experience of working with children of incarcerated women she has gained great experience of the benefits of therapeutic playwork in relation to attachment and loss due to imprisonment.

Vicki Hunt is a Senior Play Development Worker responsible for the management of Wakefield and District Play Forum, a voluntary organization delivering a play ranger service and developing play opportunities within the Wakefield District. She liaises with local authority departments around the impact their area has on children's play opportunities, and advocating and reinforcing the benefits of including and providing opportunities for children to play. She works with a playground equipment manufacturer as an independent adviser, specifically focusing on consultation with children and communities. She is a trustee of Wakefield Prison Visits Children's Play Facility. She graduated from Leeds Metropolitan University in 2001 with a BA (Hons) Playwork.

Nick Jackson is currently the Director of Haringey Play Association (HarPA), a voluntary sector support and development agency for children's services providers in Haringey. He has extensive experience of adventure play and playwork, having worked on and managed adventure playgrounds in Islington for many years, after which he was a play development manager for Islington Play Association. He joined Haringey Play Association (HarPA) in the summer of 2004, where he led the move to newly built premises, combined with the only open access, supervised adventure playground in Haringey at Somerford Grove Community Project, which provides play opportunities for school-aged children.

Jackie Jeffrey's current activities include teaching at Middlesex University Business School and being a Director of Play Action, a company she set up to support the development of play and youth projects. The company portfolio includes a diversity of play projects and work in Durban, South Africa, to develop a youth work strategy for the region. Jackie first became a playworker at the age of 17 and has never been able to stray far from this, and includes lots of playing into the learning environment. She is currently working towards her DProf looking at the value of storytelling for the development of identity and knowledge of communities.

Eva Kane was until recently the regional manager for Fit for Play in PlayBoard Northern Ireland. She developed this Quality Award that supports outdoor and physical play in parallel, to ensuring healthy snacks in a play project. She worked in PlayBoard from 2002 but her connection with the organization goes back to when she first came to Belfast as an international volunteer in 1988. She grew up in Sweden and attended a play project herself as a child. After arriving in Northern Ireland Eva worked as a playworker in open-access provision, supported community-based play projects, assessed and internally verified NVQs in Playwork, and developed, designed and delivered Playwork training. She is presently a member of the Joint National Committee on Training for Playwork (JNCTP), and is studying for a Graduate Diploma in Playwork at the University of Gloucestershire. Her dissertation, for a Masters in Lifelong Learning, focused on playwork education and training in Northern Ireland.

Haki Kapasi is the Director of INSPIRE, a national training and development agency specializing in children's play and playwork. She is an experienced trainer and consultant in children's play, supporting organizations to develop play strategies and policies, carrying out service reviews, feasibility studies and evaluations. She also conducts action research projects. She is the author of *Playing in Parallel*; *Asian Children Play*; *I Am We Are Activities Pack*; and *Power of Play: A Guide for Community Cohesion through Play*. Haki is co-chair of the Joint National Committee on Training for Playwork and sits on the Children's Play Policy Forum.

Anna Kassman-McKerrell is Information Officer for the Children's Play Information Service (CPIS) at the National Children's Bureau (NCB), where she has been responsible for providing an information service to the play sector since 2000. Before starting at the CPIS, she worked as an Information Officer and Librarian for the Centre for Policy on Ageing, the National Institute for Biological Standards and Control, and Hackney public library service. Anna contributes to various play publications, including *Playtoday* and *Playwords*, and writes and compiles e-bulletins and factsheets on children's play. Currently, she is involved in developing a database of ongoing research on children's play. She is also a member of the Play Wales Information Service Advisory Group.

Jackie Kilvington is a 'playwork warrior' always fighting the cause of children's play. She works freelance as a playwork trainer, verifier, consultant and 'bag lady'. She has a wealth of experience working on both practical and theoretical aspects of playwork and is, among other things, currently developing a user friendly quality playwork audit for playschemes in Sheffield and researching with Ali Wood and Heather Knight the provision of affective play space.

Stuart Lester is currently Senior Lecturer in Playwork (0.5) at the University of Gloucestershire and an independent playwork trainer and advisor. Stuart has worked for many years as a playworker, mainly on Adventure Playgrounds and local community-based play projects. More recent work has centred on the design and delivery of playwork education and training opportunities at a range of levels. Stuart has also been involved in the production of a Quality Assurance scheme for play providers in Manchester, and in writing the third edition of *Training Playwork Trainers* (JNCTP, 2004).

Meynell is the Director of Meynell Games, an organization committed to creating better play opportunities. Meynell has been working with children and young people for over 30 years. He is a playworker, playwork trainer and author, and has worked in nearly every type of setting imaginable. He has worked with children and young people in many countries across three continents. Meynell is still a play-worker and can be regularly found at the Pevensey & Westham Holiday Playscheme, or out around the country taking large-scale games sessions with parachutes, balls and rings to events, festivals and gatherings.

Maureen O'Hagan MBE, recently retired, is the former Director of External Quality Assurance at the Council for Awards in Children's Care and Education (CACHE). Previous posts have included the Directorship of the Council for Early Years Awards (CEYA), Principal Lecturer in a FE College, primary school teacher, nursing sister, and nursery nurse. In the past she has run a number of summer play schemes, and been the Chair of the management committee of a voluntary aided youth club which integrated children with disabilities. Maureen is also an experi-enced author and at present has three textbooks in print and two distance learning packs. Maureen is the Vice President of the UK branch of the World Organization for Early Childhood Education (OMEP), and the UK Editor of the *International Journal of Early Childhood*.

Maureen Palmer is presently a Training Officer with Islington Council's Children's Services. Prior to becoming a trainer Maureen worked for nine years in Islington as a Play and Youth Officer. Maureen has also worked on adventure playgrounds across London since 1976. During this time she spent over ten years working on the Cornwallis Adventure Playground in Islington and has spent some time in the last few years researching the impact of that work with the adults who 'grew up' on Cornwallis. Throughout this work Maureen has sought to develop an 'overstand-ing' of health and safety as a play-focused methodology, to support playwork prac-tice and facilitate children's play.

Sue Palmer is the Head of School of Film, Television and Performing Arts at Leeds Metropolitan University. She has been involved in play development work since the 1970s. Having worked as a playworker and play development worker, she then worked for Playboard as a play forum officer. She was responsible for developing the BA (Hons) Professional Studies at Leeds Metropolitan University, and was team leader for the development of the BA (Hons) Playwork course. She has been External Examiner to the University of Northumbria's BA (Hons) Childhood Studies course, and is responsible for teaching, learning and assessment in the School of Film, Television and Performing Arts at Leeds.

Dr. Marianna Papadopoulou is an Associate Lecturer at the Open University, teach-ing courses related to Childhood and Child Development. As a BA graduate in Childhood Studies and Early Years Teaching she has worked in early years settings in Greece and in England. She has carried out two research projects with young children. The first was part of her MA course (1997) and studied children's processes of learning and development. The second, her Doctoral project, searched into children's everyday experiences in order to explore their developing understanding of the world around them and their emerging sense of self. She was awarded her PhD in 2003.

Keith Ramtahal is presently a Lecturer in Learning Difficulties and Disabilities at a college in Gloucestershire. Between 1984 and 1988 he worked on adventure playgrounds in North London. He began teaching on Access to Playwork courses in 1992 and has been a Senior Lecturer in Education at a London University. Prior to teaching in Further and Higher Education he practised for 18 years as a teacher and senior manager in schools in London and Cairo. He has taught young people from Nursery to Year 10. Keith has a professional and political interest in Equality and Diversity issues in education.

Stephen Rennie is Senior Lecturer in BA (Hons) Playwork at Leeds Metropolitan University. He has been a playleader, play organizer, development worker, and regional advisor, working for voluntary organizations, local authorities, and national bodies. He was Vice Chair of the Fair Play for Children Campaign for eight years. He has undertaken research consultancies into juvenile crime, social behaviours and playground design. In 1999 he completed his MA in Playwork Studies by researching the uses of imagined play in the development of interpersonal skills. He reads Braille, and holds qualifications in playwork, youth work and counselling.

Val Richards is a former Assistant Director of the Squiggle Foundation, and edited two monographs for Winnicott Studies. In the past she taught English and Drama in schools and higher education. She is a therapist, a supervisor, and seminar leader for trainees. At her placement in a psychiatric hospital she led a drama therapy group. She also established a project on Winnicott for Islington playworkers. Her most recent publication is: *The Who You Dream Yourself: Playing and Interpretation in Therapy and Theatre* (2005), and she has made contributions to a number of books, including *His Majesty, the Baby* (1991); *Time-sickness* (1993); *Mothers, Mirrors and Masks* (1994); *Hunt the Slipper* (1998); *If Father Could Be Home* (1998); *Article* (1999); and *Winnicott and Education* (2002).

Wendy Russell divides her working time between being a Senior Lecturer in Playwork at the University of Gloucestershire, working as an independent playwork consultant, and her own research on play and playwork. Her qualifications include BA (Hons), MEd and PGCHE. She discovered adventure playgrounds in London in 1975 and was smitten. She has since worked in face-to-face playwork, development work, research, management and mainly in playwork education and training. Her freelance work has included designing and delivering training courses from entry to degree level, and working on a range of development, strategic and evaluation projects for local authorities, the private sector and local and national voluntary organizations.

Tanny Stobart is a playwork training and policy consultant. Prior to this she was National Programme Manager – Policy UK with the Playwork Unit at SkillsActive.

She trained in graphic design and photography and teaching. She worked as a volunteer playworker on a London adventure playground. She co-directed the Wandsworth Family Workshop Unit in London and was Assistant Education Officer for the Community Education Service in Devon. She edits and co-designs *Take Ten for Play* and *Take Ten MORE*, national publications that support learners undertaking qualifications at Level 2 and 3 in Playwork.

Dr. Brian Sutton-Smith was born in Wellington, New Zealand. He was the first New Zealand educator (1949) to receive a NZU PhD educational research fellowship. He was nominated by Victoria University for a Rhodes Scholarship, but proceeded to the USA with a Fulbright Post Graduate Fellowship in 1952. Brian converted his three children's books, written while a New Zealand schoolteacher, to a life-long search for the multiple meanings of human play. He has authored or edited 43 books on play and over 300 scholarly articles, while holding professorships and academic directorships at BGSU Ohio, Teacher's College Colombia University New York, and the Graduate School of Education at the University of Pennsylvania where he is currently a Professor Emeritus.

Louise Taffinder is currently working with Leeds Youth Offending Service. Making good use of her BA (Hons) Playwork degree, Louise has worked across the globe with children in places as diverse as Canada and Romania. In Canada she worked in the Toronto Children's Hospital. In Romania, Louise worked with some of the most deprived and vulnerable children in Europe, namely the Roma communities of Transylvania. She particularly enjoys her regular voluntary work on the children's summer camps, organized by the charity Aid for Romanian Children. Louise previously worked in Leeds for a children's service known as Children in Vulnerable Accommodation (CHIVA).

Ben Tawil is North Wales Development Officer for Play Wales. He has had an active interest in childcare and playwork for over 15 years. Whilst studying at Leeds Metropolitan University for his playwork degree he developed a self-build playground with early year's children at a local nursery. On completion of the degree Ben moved across the border to Wales where he was assistant manager of The Venture adventure playground in Wrexham. He developed strong links with Play Wales supporting the development of the national strategy for playwork education and training. Ben has spoken at many conferences about his experiences on the adventure playground and regularly can be heard espousing the virtues of the self-build process. Before taking up his present post, he worked in Bradford for the Early Years and Childcare Service, taking responsibility for the development of adventure play and the management of outreach play provision.

Dr. Terry Thomas is a Reader in the School of Social Sciences, Leeds Metropolitan University. He was previously a social worker and a senior social worker (Team Leader) in various West Yorkshire local authority social services departments. At Leeds Metropolitan University he has taught on the Diploma in Social Work and was part of the team that developed the new BA in Social Work, launched in 2004.

Terry has completed work for the NSPCC, the Home Office and the Council of Europe on matters relating to child protection. He is the author of the books, *The Police and Social Workers* (1994), *Privacy and Social Services* (1995) and *Sex Crime: Sex Offending and Society* (2000, 2005).

Adrian Voce is Director of Play England. After a long career in play, residential care and special educational needs, Adrian was appointed in 1998 as the first Director of London Play. In 2004 he became Director of the Children's Play Council. Adrian is currently leading the development of Play England, a £15m, five-year project to establish and develop a strategic national play agency, with regional support and development offices across the country. Adrian has had many articles on children's play published in national journals, including *Community Care*, *Children Now* and *Green Spaces*. Most recently he was editor of *Planning for Play* (CPC/Big Lottery Fund, 2006).

Kirsty Ward has over 18 years experience of working with children in a variety of settings. She initially trained as a nursery nurse, working in the private sector before moving to the public sector in 1993. A qualified Nursery Nurse and Play Specialist, she has since gone on to attain a DipHE and BA (Hons) in Playwork at Leeds Metropolitan University in 2004. She currently works on a paediatric neurosciences ward at Leeds General Infirmary, with children who have both life-changing and life-threatening conditions. She has a particular interest in children with acquired brain injury.

Sophie Webb is a graduate of the BA (Hons) Playwork course at Leeds Metropolitan University. She is a specialist in the use of therapeutic playwork to address the needs of severely disadvantaged children. Originally she was concerned with the value of play to children in hospital, but after spending time in Romania, working with children who were abandoned at birth and spent most of their lives tied in a cot, she developed a deep interest in the power of play as a therapeutic tool. She currently works with the Scallywags project in Cornwall.

Penny Wilson works for the Play Association Tower Hamlets, (PATH) as the inclusion worker. She originally started as an inclusive playworker at the HAPA/Kidsactive/Kids Chelsea Adventure Playground. Her work at Chelsea taught her the power of all children's play and led to her reading the work of Winnicott. She was an early member of The Good Enough Playworker study group which produced resources tailored for playworkers and an illustrated booklet translating Winnicott into the language of playworkers. She continues to try to find ways to communicate with other professionals and parents the vital need for all children to play freely, without adult-imposed agendas.

Ali Wood has been living and working with children and young people in a variety of settings (youth work, community development work, foster care, children's hospital as well as playwork) but it is childrens' right to play that has been her driving passion. She has her own consultancy and writes, trains, researches, verifies and thinks a lot, which results in occasional moments of hilarity, fury or insight.

Mike Wragg is a Senior Lecturer on the BA (Hons) Playwork degree at Leeds Metropolitan University. Prior to taking up that post he worked as Head of Play Services for Stoke-on-Trent City Council, and as manager of Warwick Adventure Playground & Community Campus in Knottingley, West Yorkshire. Within that role Mike worked as a face-to-face playworker and delivered a number of playwork training courses. Previously he was Play Development and Training Officer with Bradford MDC. Mike has also been a part-time lecturer, and worked in, and managed, a number of out-of-school clubs and holiday playschemes. He is actively involved with several regional and national playwork organizations and committees.

Acknowledgements

We are very grateful for the cooperation and hard work of all the contributors to this book. Without their goodwill, it would not have been possible to complete the task. In addition we would like to acknowledge the contributions to specific chapters of the following:

Chapter 1: *The Journal of Education* for permission to quote extensively from an article that first appeared in Issue No. 35, March 2005, under the title 'Children Without Play'.

Chapter 7: Peter McCartney for contributing his playwork history knowledge and creative inspiration that provided the theme for the chapter.

Chapter 9: Penny Wilson for her additions and advice.

Chapter 12: The editor of *The Ecologist*, Harry Ram, for his contributions and for permission to reprint an edited version of a longer article that first appeared in the October 2005 issue of *The Ecologist* (www.theecologist.org).

Chapter 19: Play Wales for permission to reprint an extract from the book, *The Venture: A Case Study of an Adventure Playground* (Brown 2007)

Chapter 25: National Children's Bureau for permission to reprint brief extracts from their Highlight no. 223, *Play Theories and the Value of Play* (Brown 2006)

Chapter 26: Bridget Murphy for her playground memories and Tim Ferguson, Director of Manchester Young Lives, whose 30 years experience of playwork in the city has usefully informed this chapter.

Chapter 27: The amazing children and families who made Cornwallis what it was and is today. Jess Milne, Play Manager and Jackie Jeffrey and Frankie Drain playworkers during the 1980's. Barnard Park Adventure Playground for supporting the research and Janine Brady for sustaining Adventure Play in Islington for many years.

Chapter 38: Janine Brady, Colin Simmons and Kay Brokenshire for interviews and editorial comments.

Chapter 44: Somerford Grove Community Project and Adventure Playground and Haringey Adventure Play Association, for permissions to include the project.

Chapter 47: Joe McIver – it was great working with you – the Barnard Park Adventure Playground team particularly Jenny O'Shea. Dave Martins and the Islington Health and Safety Team and Maureen Greeno, P.A. par excellence and bedrock to the delivery of play and youth services in Islington.

Chapter 56: White Rose Initiative, first for their permission to conduct the research project, and second for their permission to report on its remarkable achievements.

Chapter 56: Dr Cornel Puscas, who at the time of the research was Director of the Sighisoara Paediatric Hospital, for permission to refer to the hospital records, and for allowing us to report honestly on the lives of the children in his hospital.

Without his support the Therapeutic Playwork Project would not have existed. We would also like to place on record the fact that the hospital has subsequently made giant strides towards changing things.

Chapter 56: *The Journal of Education* for permission to reprint an edited version of a longer article that first appeared in Issue No. 35, March 2005, under the title 'Children Without Play'.

Finally, we both want to thank our family members and friends for their patience. It can't have been easy these last few months.

Fraser wants to thank Anne, Louisa, Phil, James, Lucy and Emily, students and colleagues at Leeds Met. Chris wants to thank Ron, Sophie, Laura, Kathy, Jazza, Tylah, Sheila Fagg, Babs and Perry Tunesi, Dot Lewis, Brian Reeve and all with whom she works.

Photographic acknowledgements

Cover photographs: Waiting in Line © Anne Brown – Roma children from Cold Valley village waiting in the 'soup queue' for a hot meal provided by local volunteers, and financed by the Aid for Romanian Children charitable trust (see Chapter 40).

Busy painting © Eccleshill Adventure Playground, Bradford

Den building © The Venture, Wrescham

Dressing up © Wakefield Play Forum

Night-time in Transylvania © Tim Vernon, Aid for Romanian Children

Peeking through a tyre © Eccleshill Adventure Playground, Bradford

Plotting and Planning © Eric Butler, Islington Young Peoples Services, Barnard Park Adventure Playground

FRASER BROWN and CHRIS TAYLOR
Introduction: foundations

It's tempting to suggest this book is for everyone. It is about children and play, something that characterizes past adult experiences, and children's lives in the present. Claiming such universal appeal may be something of an overstatement, but the editors feel confident that it will be of interest to anyone working or spending time with children and young people in a diversity of working, parental or caring roles as well, of course, to playworkers.

This volume reflects the key characteristics of the Playwork Sector Endorsed Foundation Degree currently being offered at the University of Hertfordshire, Leeds Metropolitan University, the University of Brighton and, from September 2008, the University of Northumbria. Foundation degrees are strongly linked to employment, with an emphasis on work-based learning and reflective practice. These themes run through the book; also each section links directly to the specification of learning outcomes for the Playwork Sector Endorsed Foundation Degree, developed by SkillsActive and funded by the Department for Education and Skills.

While such an approach brings consistency to curriculum design, it also gives rise to concerns that it might become too prescriptive or formulaic. Therefore, when compiling this reader, contributors were asked to write broadly and free-associatively around these headings and the ingredients of the degree. This invitation was met with diversity and originality, and we are confident the contents will appeal to a wide audience. Such is the range of contributions, there is something here for everyone, from the playscheme volunteer to the full-time playworker; from the children's centre worker to the play therapist; from participants on a two-day training course, through to all levels of CACHE or NVQ; from first-year undergraduates to postgraduate students.

Geographically, the contents relate to the UK with chapters on Play in Northern Ireland, Scotland, Wales and England. There are also two chapters relating to projects in Romania, reflecting the long-standing commitment of the editor, Fraser Brown, and his wife Anne, and regular input of numerous students from Leeds Metropolitan University. All proceeds of this book go to the Aid for Romanian Children Charity, and the editors are very grateful for the generosity of all contributors.

A small act of celebratory quirkiness has informed the structuring of the book. We were delighted when Brian Sutton-Smith, one of the world's leading play theorists, agreed to make a contribution. Brian has written more on the subject of children's play than almost anyone, and his work has inspired many playwork practitioners. On receipt, we found his chapter to be rather special – a contribution right at the cutting edge of 21st-century thought about children's play. We therefore decided to make it the central chapter of the book. Chapter 28, '*Beyond Ambiguity*', explores Professor Sutton-Smith's intellectual journey since the publication of his classic text, *The Ambiguity of Play* (1997). For those familiar with his work, this chapter may well be the first you read; for others, it might work as a central transitional piece that can be visited and revisited anew, as it relates to much of the content and ideas surrounding it.

Broadly speaking, the first half of the book focuses upon the playing child and the domain of playwork – core concerns relating to the identity and methodologies of the work. The second half relates to the interface between playwork and the broader outside worlds, of theories from other professional domains, the management and development of play projects, and relating to other professions comprising the children's workforce, all within a legislative and regulatory context. The book concludes with a section on research methods and examples of current research projects.

The book starts with an introduction to '*Playwork Theory and Playwork Practice in the UK*'. Stobart overviews the state of play across the UK. A more detailed consideration of play and playwork in the four countries is provided by Beattie (Scotland); Greenaway (Wales); Kane (Northern Ireland); Voce, and Bonel (England). Cole-Hamilton examines the place of staffed provision for play, and the editors provide a theoretical overview (Brown) and specific example of play theory (Taylor); Sue Palmer examines aspects of the methodologies of playwork practice.

'*The Play Environment*' includes two chapters examining the importance of the outdoors and play (Gill, and Baxter). Lester provides a humanistic perspective on play environments, through the use of dramaturgic analogy. The section concludes with a specific focus on the nature of the relationship between risk and play and playwork (Gladwin) and a consideration of the use of Quality Assurance to enhance and sustain the quality of play environments (Conway).

'*The Playing Child and the Practising Playworker*' section begins with three thought-provoking chapters from playwork theorists: Else; Russell; and Battram, followed by an examination of the distinctive nature of playwork and the role of the playworker, in a variety of settings – the adventure playground (Tawil); after-school childcare (Harris); hospitals (Ward), prisons (Hart and Clutterbrook) and play centres (Meynell).

Long-serving play practitioners draw upon their playwork experience to inform the discussion in '*Playwork Values, Ethics and Professional Practice*'. One of the editors provides a Manchester-based view of the history of the adventure playwork tradition (Taylor) and Maureen Palmer explores her work on an adventure playground in North London. Conway draws upon more contemporary work as a member of the Scrutiny Group which holds the Playwork Principles in trust for the playwork profession (see Appendix 2). Those very principles are exposed to critique by one of the editors (Brown).

In '*Play Links, Relating and Communicating*' two chapters are given over to a consideration of the contribution of the work of D.W.Winnicott, to an understanding of the importance of playing for children's development, and emotional health (Taylor and Wilson; and Richards). Davy's contribution interestingly explores the role of rhythm in playwork, and the section is rounded off with a very practical examination of the role parents can play as play activists by Chan.

In the section entitled '*Working with Professional Diversity*' Bonel discusses the implications of the Common Core of Knowledge and Understanding, for playwork. This leads on to a consideration of the interface between playwork and related professions: with early years (Fisher, and O'Hagan); youth work (Taylor); education (Ramtahal; and Griffith); and with volunteers (Taffinder). Wragg provides a thought-provoking chapter about the role of the playworker as provocateur.

This is followed by '*Contributing to the Management and Development of Play Settings*'. First, Voce provides a consideration of national strategic positioning; second, Chilton offers a description of the perfect playwork manager; and finally life at the coal-face is explored in chapters from Harris and Hunt, Jackson, and Rennie.

The '*Legislation and Rights*' section, relating to the national context, is considered in relation to both children's rights (Cole-Hamilton) and anti-discriminatory laws that have encouraged a move towards more inclusive practice in relation to a number of issues: race (Kapasi); disability (Wilson); and gender (Papadopoulou). All contributors provide a playwork eye view, with interesting results as the remarkable chapter on Health and Safety by Maureen Palmer reveals. Child Protection is approached from a social work perspective and usefully informs the whole section (Thomas). This section is rounded off with a chapter by Kilvington and Wood, which explores the gender divide in playwork theory and theorists.

The concluding section looks at '*Research and Methods*' as described by Sue Palmer, and Jackie Jeffrey, and hopefully informs and inspires the reader to embark on their own research endeavours and future contribution to the field. It contains reference to two recent research projects (Cole; and Brown and Webb). The first Appendix, which was compiled by Anna Kassman-McKerrell of the Children's Play Information Service, provides a brief annotated bibliography of some of the most significant playwork texts.

Foundations of Playwork will take the reader to a diversity of settings, in which play can be found: the adventure playground, playcentre, playscheme, after-school club, to the parks and streets and to the outdoors. Play is also described in hospital and prison settings. The perspectives offered reflect the personalities and professional roles of the contributors. These range from playworkers on adventure playgrounds and in other settings, through to regional and national managers, development and support workers, social policy and library staff, psychotherapists, teachers in schools, further and higher education, and freelance trainers and consultants.

Such professionals and many others comprise the contemporary children's workforce. Playwork adopts an holistic view of the child, responding to whatever presents in the play setting, what turns up and is needed. This professional method seems to be attuned to contemporary discourses of childhood, and an unprecedented legislative focus upon the delivery of integrated children's services as provided through the Children Act 2004, the *Every Child Matters* agenda, and the Common Core of skills knowledge and understanding for the children's workforce. Most recently, the Time to Talk consultation by the Department for Children, Schools and Families sought a broad-based contribution to inform the subsequent publication of a ten-year Children Plan (DCSF 2007b) to achieve the outcomes of the *Every Child Matters* agenda. For the first time Playwork is seen by the government as having a clear role in that regard.

Even more encouraging, perhaps, has been the increased importance and recognition given to play by the government in recent years. In 2004 *Getting Serious About Play* was published, the result of a review of children's play in England by Frank Dobson MP. Following from this a cross-Whitehall group on play, with representation from seven government departments, the local government association, leading independent groups and the BIG Lottery Fund, has been established and meets regularly to promote play and ensure its inclusion in policy development. In 2006 *Time for Play*, produced by the Department for Culture, Media and Sport, outlines the government's interdepartmental commitments to play reflecting its increased recognition. The £155 million BIG Lottery funded Children's Play initiative was launched in 2006 to develop free, open-access play provision in areas of need. Play England has been formed to assist local authorities in their development of play strategies, and to develop a supportive national infrastructure for play. December 2007 saw the publication of *The Children's Plan: Building Brighter Futures* (DCSF 2007b), which included specific recognition of the importance of play, and committed the government to publishing a play strategy by the summer of 2008. For the first time in a government document we also saw importance given to the role of playworkers.

> The play strategy will support individuals in communities to take a professional role by providing funding to enable 4000 play workers to achieve recognised play qualifications, and within that to enable a core of professionally qualified new graduate leaders to emerge.
>
> (DCSF 2007b: 29)

Foundations of Playwork arrives at a moment of optimism for children's play and we believe will usefully contribute to the future growth and development of play environments and playwork.

Part 1

Playwork theory and playwork
practice in the UK

1

FRASER BROWN
The fundamentals of playwork

Starting with the ideas of Abernethy (1968), Benjamin (1974) and Hughes (1975), the playwork profession focused largely on adventure play. Most of its early thinking derived from the Danish architect Sorensen, who envisaged 'junk playgrounds' where children could imagine, shape and create their own reality. In *Planning for Play* Lady Allen of Hurtwood quotes correspondence between herself and Sorensen from 1947, which provides an interesting insight into his thinking:

> The object must be to give the children of the city a substitute for the rich possibilities for play which children in the country possess ... It is opportune to warn against too much supervision ... children ought to be free and by themselves to the greatest possible extent ... one ought to be exceedingly careful when interfering in the lives and activities of children.
>
> (1968: 55)

So already in 1947 it is possible to identify the germ of ideas we now take for granted: children being in control of their own play places (Hughes 1996); the value of providing enriched play environments (Brown 2003b); and the dangers of adulteration (Sturrock and Else 1998).

In the 1980s Hughes and Williams (1982) made the first attempt to develop some solid theoretical grounding for playwork practice. The decade also saw the widespread use of the SPICE acronym by playwork trainers and managers, usually misrepresenting the original concept (Brown 1989, 2003b). Playwork theory has developed substantially since then, led by writers such as Hughes (1996, 2001a, 2002a), Sturrock and Else (1998), Battram and Russell (2002), and Lester (2004). However, those writers have tended to focus on biological, psychological and evolutionary models of play and playwork to the detriment of sociological and developmental models. This chapter seeks to redress the balance, by proposing a slightly different focus.

In the book, *Playwork: Theory and Practice*, I described playwork as follows:

> Playwork may be seen as a generalised description of work that includes adventure play, therapeutic play, out-of-school clubs, hospital play, environmental design, and much more – all those approaches that use the medium of play as a mechanism for redressing aspects of developmental imbalance caused by a deficit of play opportunities.

> (Brown 2003a: 52)

This has sometimes mistakenly been taken to mean that I see play solely as part of the child's preparation for adulthood, which would of course be a ridiculous over-simplification. Play is also full of impact for the here and now. The following chapter is intended to outline the elements of play and playwork that I see as being fundamental underpinnings to our work.

Children learn and develop both while they are playing and through their play: the child's interactions with his/her environment are a fundamental part of development

It is one of the most basic assumptions of the playwork profession that, given the right conditions, children will learn and develop both while they are playing, and through their play. In many modern communities, for a variety of reasons (including the increase in traffic, parental fears and poor housing design) that process is breaking down, with the result that children are not achieving their natural state of balance (homeostasis). It is the role of a playworker to create those 'right' conditions, so that the play process can be effective. Thus, the first aim of playwork is simply to create the sort of rich environment that enables play to take place. However, we should not lose sight of the idea that children are maturing at the same time as they are playing, and so the second aim of playwork should be to create the sort of environment that enables the child to grow towards self-fulfilment, referred to by Maslow (1973) as self-actualization.

Many modern environments contain elements that act against the play process

In most cases the playworker's initial role is to analyse the child's environment in order to identify and remove any barriers to the play process. In most playwork projects there are elements of the work that have little to do with play, but which nevertheless have to be addressed; otherwise the quality of the child's play experience is likely to be restricted. For example, checking the safety of play equipment on an adventure playground is not in itself a playful activity, but most playworkers regard it as part of their role. In certain circumstances playworkers might even take it upon themselves to feed hungry children. After all it's not easy for a starving child to play. Such actions are crucial to the playwork role. This is not simply a matter of human sensitivity but also a practical necessity. If children are to benefit fully from their play, then their playworkers have to address many of their non-play problems as well. In my view that is good playwork practice.

An enriched play environment holds greater potential for child development

The playworker is also concerned with enriching the child's play environment in order to stimulate the play process. This might contain elements of scaffolding (Wood et al. 1976), or Vygotsky's (1966/1976) concept of the zone of proximal development. However, both those concepts imply a level of intervention that would not be accepted in the playwork approach. Hughes suggests that playworkers should aim for 'a low adult to child approach ratio' (1996: 51). Thus, enriching the play environment is not so much about aiding specific elements of learning, but rather adopting a holistic approach to development. There are a number of factors that playworkers have to take into account when considering how best to create such an environment. In *Playwork: Theory and Practice* I summarized these as: freedom; flexibility; socialisation and social interaction; physical activity; intellectual stimulation; creativity and problem solving; emotional equilibrium; self-discovery; ethical stance; adult–child relationships; and the general appeal of elements such as humour, colour and so on (Brown 2003b).

In their work with children playworkers should to take account of the concept of compound flexibility, the theory of loose parts, and the Portchmouth principle

There are several ways in which the play environment may be enriched. For many playworkers the most important element in their work is *compound flexibility*, that is 'the interrelationship between a flexible/adaptable environment and the gradual development of flexibility/adaptability in the child' (Brown 2003b: 53). According to Sutton-Smith the function of play is 'adaptive variability' (1997: 231). Taking these two concepts together we can infer that the role of the playworker is to create flexible environments which are substantially adaptable or controllable by the children. One way of doing this is to ensure there are lots of 'loose parts' in the play environment. When explaining his 'theory of loose parts', Nicholson suggests that 'in any environment both the degree of inventiveness and creativity, and the possibility of discovery, are directly proportional to the number and kind of variables in it' (1971: 30). Thus, a room full of cardboard boxes is more likely to stimulate creative play, than a fixed climbing frame. This concept links to Vygotsky's (1966/1976) zone of proximal development, via the Portchmouth principle. Portchmouth (1969: 7) says, 'it helps if someone, no matter how lightly, puts in our way the means of making use of what we find'. He gives the example of providing buckets and spades for children to play on the beach. There is no need to tell them what to do. The play environment contains its own play cues in such circumstances.

Playworkers need to suspend their prejudices and be non-judgemental in all their dealings with the children, that is they need to adopt an attitude of 'negative capability'

Most adults who come into contact with children bring their own agenda to that relationship. For example, teachers have an obligation to teach the national curriculum (a set of adult priorities). Doctors, social workers, even parents, invariably have their own adult priorities. The playworker is unusual in as much as s/he attempts to suspend personal prejudice, and go along with the flow of the children's needs and tastes. This brings us to the concept of 'negative capability'. The poet John Keats (1817) suggested this was a characteristic of all creative minds. He recommended the complete suspension of all prejudices and preconceptions as a prelude to opening up the creative flow of the mind. In the modern era this is reflected in the words of the jazz musician Miles Davis, who, when asked to reflect on his unique ability, explained it thus: 'You need to know your horn, know the chords, know all the tunes – then forget about all that, and just play' (in Sanjek 1990/1998: 411). The similarity between this approach to creativity, and one of the most fundamental aspects of the child–adult relationship in playwork, is explored by Fisher towards the end of chapter 35. She suggests that playworkers have to guard against entering the play environment with their own preconceptions and prejudices. Only then will they truly be there for the child. This approach requires a great sensitivity to the learning potential of the playwork setting, and means the playworker has to be prepared to stand back when others might be inclined to rush in.

Sturrock and Else (1998) take this one stage further, highlighting the dangers of playworkers bringing their own childhood-based neuroses into the setting. It is often the case that those with whom we work are socially and economically disadvantaged or emotionally vulnerable in some way. Therefore, it is absolutely essential that the adult brings no 'baggage' to the relationship. If a child begins to share a problem with the playworker, and the worker finds herself saying, 'that happened to me too', then her value to that child is doubtful. In all probability she will do more harm than good. The playworker must be there entirely for the good of the child.

Intervention is sometimes necessary but the child's agenda has to be taken as the starting point for the playworkers' interventions

Hughes suggests that both the 'content and the intent' of play should be determined by the child, and that playwork should be 'child-empowering' (1996: 22–3). In the child's daily life, play is his/her only experience of being in control of events. If playworkers are not to 'adulterate' that experience, they have to ensure that wherever possible they are following the child's agenda (Sturrock and Else 1998). It follows that in most circumstances the playworker would expect to adopt an approach of 'preparation followed by withdrawal' (Hughes 1996: 23). For the playworker in a therapeutic setting it is especially important to take the child's agenda as the starting point for interactions. Even in the case of the abandoned children in Romania, where the children required a stronger presence over a more extended period, it nevertheless remained the case that most of our interventions were a response to the specific play behaviours of each child (see Chapter 56).

Our own experience of play enables us to develop the human attributes of sympathy, empathy, affective attunement and mimesis, and so make appropriate responses to children's play cues

Adam Smith (1759/1976) suggested that human beings are innately sympathetic to each other, and that it is the human capacity for mimesis that makes this interpretation possible. Through fantasy, invention and symbolic play, humans are able to use parts of the body to describe almost anything. For example we all know what it means if a child is running round the playground yelling 'brooom, brooom', and we can easily interpret the accompanying actions. To quote Donald:

> Mimesis rests on the ability to produce conscious, self-initiated, representational acts ... Thus, mimesis is fundamentally different from imitation and mimicry in that it involves the invention of intentional representations. When there is an audience to interpret the action, mimesis also serves the purpose of social communication.
>
> (1991: 168–9)

Human beings are probably the only animals able to symbolize meaning in their actions in this way. For Trevarthen (1996) mimesis is a talent which gradually develops, and play is the catalyst. In other words, we learn how to interpret other people's play cues while we are playing. This is a skill that is fundamental to effective playwork practice (Sturrock and Else 1998).

Similarly Daniel Stern's (1985) concept of *affective attunement* may be something that we learn through our play. Stern did not suggest that. He focused instead on the mother–baby relationship, and was interested in the way mothers attune with their babies' rhythms. That makes it possible to demonstrate to the baby ways in which its actions might be further developed. For example, if an object is just out of reach, a baby may have to make a double movement in order to grasp it. The mother is likely to clap her hands twice, or make a sound 'ah-ah', in exactly the same rhythm as the baby's grasping action. This apparently simple interaction contains some very complex subtexts. The obvious message is, 'I am in tune with you', but there is a more subtle and far more powerful message, 'I can help you translate your actions into a different form'. Stern linked most of his ideas to the mother–baby interaction. However, we have evidence from the work in Romania that affective attunement can easily be achieved by an empathetic adult working with a severely disturbed child (Brown and Webb 2005).

Indeed it is my view that sympathy, empathy, mimesis, affective attunement and the sensitive interpretation of play cues, are skills and abilities that are easily absorbed and developed during play. It is doubtful whether they could be learnt in the classroom. They are all skills that are essential to the playworker.

Playwork is about creating relationships and building the child's self-esteem

One of the most significant elements of the playwork role is the way in which relationships are made with the children. If the child–adult relationship is effective, there is a good chance of not only helping children with their problems, but also raising their self-esteem generally. Roberts (1995) has attempted to apply some of Piaget's thinking about schemas to this subject. Although she focuses on the world of pre-school practice, her ideas have merit for playwork in general. She suggests that small children will develop a set of cognitive structures that favour one schema. They may be enclosers, transporters, connectors, and so on. This has implications for the way we approach specific children. For example, a child who spends most of the time throwing stones around, may simply be a 'trajectory' child who has been offered no other way of connecting with his/her basic schema. A playworker who provides a set of skittles, or a game of cricket, may be able to address the situation effectively, without recourse to disciplinary controls. Roberts makes it clear that children do not favour one schema to the exclusion of all others. Nevertheless her approach highlights the need for provision to be sensitive to the requirements of the client. In the playground setting an 'enclosing' child might be stimulated by opportunities to build dens; a 'rotater' might like the roundabout and so on. Roberts goes on to suggest that by responding to these favoured schemas we are giving the child a powerful message; in effect 'I respect the things that matter to you'. By so doing the playworker can help to build the child's self esteem.

Playworkers need to develop their own cultural awareness: macro and micro

Else (2001) suggests that, 'with knowledge based on child development' therapeutic playworkers need to have 'cultural competence' – of their own and others' cultures. This is no less true of any playworker in any setting. Else is not simply referring to the need to understand and respect the culture of a different race or religion. He is also talking about cultures within cultures. Thus, an after-school club in a big city is likely to be influenced by several cultures: the culture of the nation, the city, the local estate, the venue, the children who use that venue and so on.

Conclusion

Clearly the children's learning and development derive substantially from the playworkers' ability to create an enriched play environment that is supportive of the play process. The playworkers' use of negative capability, their suspension of judgement and prejudice, coupled with a determination to take each child's agenda as his/her own starting point, helps to create a good quality playwork environment: in other words, an environment that offers adaptability to the children, and so encourages the compound flexibility process. Through their empathy, and their ability to interpret the children's play cues effectively, playworkers are able to create strong trusting relationships, which in turn help to enhance the children's self-esteem. If such approaches were applied in a typical playwork setting in the UK, I would expect children to cope well with their immediate world, and also to develop naturally. I have seen this straightforward playwork approach work very effectively in settings as diverse as adventure playgrounds, after-school clubs, hospitals and prisons – even in Romania, with some of the most play-deprived children in the world.

2

ISSY COLE-HAMILTON
Where children play: the place of staffed provision

Given time, space and opportunity children play wherever they are. The most common play place for children today – as in the past – is the street and neighbourhood open spaces where they live, but over the past 30 years or so children's freedom to play out has become increasingly restricted. This is primarily because of their parents' and their own fears for their safety. The three most common concerns are about traffic, 'stranger danger' and bullying from other children and young people.

Staffed play provision – either static or mobile – has a crucial role to play in offering children the personal safety they and their parents seek while allowing them the freedom and excitement of being able to play in an environment which offers a variety of play experiences and choices.

Play in the streets and local neighbourhoods

Children have always played in the streets and neighbourhoods near their homes although evidence suggests they do so now less than in the past. Research for the Home Office and Department for Education and Skills conducted in 2003 (Home Office and DfES 2005) showed that 67 per cent of 8–10-year-old children never went to the park or shops on their own; and 33 per cent never played out with their friends without an adult being present. Many children do not play out as much as they would like to. For example, the Playday 2005 survey showed that 39 per cent of the 671 7–14-year-olds who were interviewed said they did not play out as much as they would like to (British Market Research Bureau 2005).

Similarly, research on housing estates in the mid-1990s found that children playing out tended to do so on the streets partly because they could more easily meet their friends there, but also because much of the time they were moving about in search of others (Wheway and Millward 1997). Two surveys carried out in 2001 found that children played out on the streets more often than anywhere else, even if this was not always their preferred play space (Child Accident Prevention Trust 2001).

As they get older children move further away from their homes to play and this has not changed significantly over time. In the early 1980s Parkinson (1985) found that, during school holidays, children played most often in the streets close to their homes but went further from home as they got older. O'Brien found that the number of primary school children who walked to school had decreased since 1990 and that there had also been a reduction in the number of children who said they travelled to school without an adult (in Greenfield et al. 2000).

Children also play on areas of land that they find interesting and exciting but which are not really there as play places. Cemeteries, waste-land, quarries, allotments, building sites and reservoirs all offer children exciting and challenging outdoor play opportunities. If there is nowhere else as interesting for them to go, they will play in these places.

Play in parks

For young people, in particular, parks are essential places to hang out and meet their friends. They see parks as relatively safe environments, compared with the streets, where they often feel they are not welcome (Greenhalgh and Worpole 1995). Good parks also offer younger children, especially in urban areas, freedom and a play space away from traffic. The green spaces, trees, plants and small animals found in parks may be the only regular access city children have to the natural environment.

Although many adults consider that parks are essentially places for children they are often worried that the parks they use may not be safe enough for their children to play in without an adult. Children are also very conscious of the poor quality of the parks near their homes. They are frequently seen as dirty, dangerous and unattractive places (Cole-Hamilton 2002).

Play in dedicated play space

Unsupervised play areas

Children's playgrounds, containing 'traditional' playground equipment, are common features in residential areas in cities, towns and villages. Recently there has been considerable interest in developing these play areas in more imaginative ways and in introducing landscaping and more natural features.

Play areas are often located in parks but also frequently in residential areas near children's homes. Children are more likely to use play areas in places where they can see and be seen. Play areas in hidden corners or a long way from busy paths and streets are less likely to be used and more likely to be vandalized. Well-used play areas are an important meeting place for parents as well as children. Cycling and skateboarding are all popular play activities and dedicated courses and ramps offer challenging and exciting play places where children and young people can develop and hone their skills.

Supervised and semi-supervised play provision

A small proportion of children have regular access to play provision staffed by skilled and trained playworkers. These open access, supervised play opportunities, in adventure playgrounds, play centres and holiday play schemes, tend to be popular with both children and parents as they offer parents the confidence that their children are both safe and enjoying themselves, and children have a wide range of play opportunities.

Recently a new type of playworker, often called play ranger, has been offering children semi-supervised play opportunities. Play ranger projects differ around the country but may work in parks, schools or local neighbourhood spaces. In most areas they work closely with the local children and communities to find out what children want to do and where they would like to be able to play. Play rangers visit areas where children want to play, make sure these places feel safe and offer children more choices by showing them games and activities they can try out.

There is little nationally available information on the extent to which children and young people use staffed play provision. Research conducted for the Home Office and DfES (2005) found that 12 per cent of 8–10-year-old children attended school holiday play schemes but this did not indicate how many of these had open access or were free of charge.

Research evaluating the Big Lottery Fund (formerly New Opportunities Fund) Better Play funding programme has demonstrated the value of staffed play provision to children and young people. Through studying in detail six very different approaches to providing supervised play opportunities and activities for school-aged children, the *Better Play* evaluation (Youlden and Harrison 2006) illustrated how the programme touched and improved the lives of many children and how staffed play provision can do much. It could:

- give children, especially those from disadvantaged communities, a wide range of experiences they thoroughly enjoy and want to repeat;
- provide children with a real alternative to playing on the streets or remaining at home isolated from their peers and relying on television or computer games for stimulation;
- increase children's access to a range of new play opportunities and experiences, offering them opportunities they would not otherwise have, which extend and challenge them physically, creatively and socially;
- increase opportunities for disabled children to play in mainstream provision allowing all those involved to benefit from the interaction between disabled and non-disabled children;
- support the development of children's self-esteem and social skills;
- contribute to children's physical health and social and emotional well-being;
- contribute to children's learning and understanding of their own and other people's cultures;
- increase children's knowledge and understanding of the natural environment;
- offer children opportunities for social interaction with children and adults they would not normally meet;

- provide play places where their parents feel confident children are safe and enjoying themselves;
- provide parents and other family members with opportunities to understand and support their children better, both in the projects and at home;
- contribute to social cohesion and friendship networks in communities;
- offer voluntary work and employment opportunities to local young people and adults.

Childcare provision and extended schools services

Increasingly, children whose parents are at work or in training spend much of their time, when not at school, in childcare provision, much of which will, in the future be provided by schools. During term time this might be at breakfast and after-school clubs and during the holidays at play schemes. People involved in providing this type of childcare have an important role in ensuring that the children they look after get good play opportunities.

3

TANNY STOBART
Playwork as a profession: distinct or extinct?

Can where you live in the UK make a difference to playworkers?

The playwork workforce in the UK is at a critical point. On the one hand, it feels like there has never been a better time, with more playworkers employed than ever before and an increasing number of posts with the word 'play' in the title. There are specific qualifications and a specialist Playwork Unit within the Sector Skills Council, SkillsActive, committed to professionalizing the sector and to the development of playwork qualifications, education and training across the UK. There is a discrete set of Playwork National Occupational Standards and a small but growing number of Further and Higher Education institutions offering degree courses specializing in play and playwork. In common with other groups working with children, playworkers feel they have a special role within the workforce. Their contribution involves supporting children (and families) in their out-of-school time and in the holidays. Recognizing that everyone working with children has responsibilities to care for them, playworkers have a very special responsibility to encourage the setting-up of play opportunities that are self-directed, freely chosen and encourage children to socialize, take decisions and develop the important skills needed in adulthood (SkillsActive 2006).

But on the other hand it feels like playwork is fighting for survival. As politicians and public officials start to put in place structures to support greater integration between different parts of the children's workforce, and develop new qualification frameworks, the comparatively small, but dedicated and enthusiastic playwork workforce feels vulnerable. Added to this vulnerability is the current fragility of children's play itself.

Increasingly there are concerns being expressed by parents and practitioners that children are being denied access to play. They worry that children's early play experiences at school (nursery and pre-school) are being manipulated into a learning ethos with an emphasis on achievements. They recognize that things are not the same as when they were young, with children today more likely to attend a homework club than play out after school, choose their own play opportunities or take any sort of risk. Older children complain there is nowhere for them to go, to 'chill out'. Generally there is a growing tendency for children to be over-scheduled (Elkind 2001) or 'wrapped in cotton wool' (Waiton and Baird 2006).

Although this is backed up by evidence such as the Government White Paper, *Choosing Health*, which noted that many children appear to have less time being physically active, because of the increase in car use and heightened concern about the potential risk of unsupervised play outdoors (DoH 2004), when it comes to implementation, recognition of the importance of play can be marginalized (DoH 2006).

In September 2006 a letter was written to the *Daily Telegraph* signed by over 100 eminent academics, practitioners and writers concerned that today's children 'still need what developing human beings have always needed ... real play (as opposed to sedentary, screen-based entertainment), first hand experience of the world they live in ...'.

Many playwork organizations are arguing for greater recognition of the vital contribution playwork can bring to services for children, and of the need to support and encourage play in children's lives. They are also concerned that children's recreation and out-of-school time is being marginalized to such an extent that children's natural propensity for play is under threat.

One factor that is making a difference to this pessimistic picture is that it is not the same across the UK. In some places there is much greater recognition of the importance of play. This is because there are separate constitutional arrangements in England, Wales, Northern Ireland and Scotland. The current government has a programme of decentralization of power and has established a Parliament and an Executive in Scotland in 1998; a National Assembly in Wales in 1999; and has put in place plans for longer-term devolution of power to regional level in England. The Belfast Agreement in 1998 paved the way for constitutional development in Northern Ireland, with a similar range of legislative and executive powers to the Scottish Parliament. After seven years of direct rule devolution was restored to the Northern Ireland Assembly in May 2007 following the election of a four-party Executive of 12 ministers.

So it now depends where you live in the country, what the structure is for the recognition of play and for play service delivery. This includes what kind of play opportunities are available locally, what kind of play services there are, and what qualifications and training opportunities will be available for playworkers.

Table 3.1 shows that although all four nations have a Children's Commissioner, a National Play Organization, and a National Childcare Strategy, there is varying commitment to the concept of a National Play Policy and Play Implementation Plan.

This means that the National Childcare Strategy is being implemented across the four nations, with a varying level of commitment to play and consequently to the culture and practice within the children's workforce.

Table 3.1 Varying commitment to play across the four nations

Nation	Is there a children's Commissioner?	Is there a National Play Organization?	Is there a National Childcare Strategy?	Is there a National Play Policy?	Is there a National Implementation Plan for play?
England	Yes	Yes: – Play England – Children's Play Council	Yes	In progress	No
Wales	Yes	Yes: – Play Wales	Yes	Yes	Yes
Scotland	Yes	Yes: – Play Scotland	Yes	In progress	No
Northern Ireland	Yes	Yes: – PlayBoard, Northern Ireland	Yes	In progress	No

In Wales there is recognition of this distinction and a commitment to play as fundamental to the whole of children's lives. The Assembly Government has adopted seven core aims for its Childcare Strategy 'to ensure that all children and young people have access to play, leisure, sporting and cultural activities' (DfTE 2005: 6). It acknowledges that 'active play is one of the best opportunities for children to have exercise and is encouraged in good quality childcare' (2005: 6). Wales is leading the way by having a *Play Policy Implementation Plan*, which clearly states the range of opportunities that are required to support children's play. This includes the development of training resources on play for both teaching and non-teaching staff in schools and producing guidance on what constitutes good play opportunities. The implementation plan is also committed to continuing 'to support the unique role of the playworker to facilitate children's play in the community' (Welsh Assembly Government 2004: 16).

There is also a strong lobby in Northern Ireland towards establishing a play policy. This is heightened by the longer-term impact of the sectarian conflict and young people being denied a wide range of opportunities for play, particularly outdoors. Territorialism, isolation and playing at home have become the norm so that children's ability to roam and explore the local environment at will has been almost completely lost (Hughes 2000). By providing children with improved play opportunities in local parks, streets and neighbourhoods, playwork is recognized as having an important role in supporting children to live together (PlayBoard 2007). PlayBoard, the national play organization in Northern Ireland is fully committed to the development of the play policy but recognizes that there is still some way to go before this is likely to be achieved. Currently, the draft policy is awaiting endorsement from the new Assembly and represents months and months of work towards a shared understanding of the value and fundamental benefits of play.

In England the government has at last responded to repeated calls for a national play strategy, and is committed to producing a document by the summer of 2008. Previously it had been resistant to such a move, and merely allocated funding via the Big Lottery Fund's programme for children's play. From that source Play England was awarded £15 million to develop a regional infrastructure. This whole issue is explored in greater depth in the Chapters by Adrian Voce and Paul Bonel.

Currently Scotland has neither a national strategy nor a lottery funded play programme. However, in the May 2007 elections the Scottish National Party (SNP) came to power with a manifesto promising to 'work with local authorities and the voluntary sector to develop an effective play strategy to increase the range of quality play opportunities for children and young people in every part of Scotland' (SNP 2007).

It is this understanding and acknowledgement of the distinctive contribution of play to children that is key. In a climate where the move towards integrated children's services is widely acknowledged as making sense; where politicians and officers like those in the Scottish Executive are identifying the way forward as seeing 'each worker as part of the wider workforce working in partnership with others to support the delivery of agreed outcomes for all children' (Scottish Executive 2007), a more unified approach is inevitable.

In the future, the titles for people who work with children may be different; they could be known as children's workers, or even social pedagogues. However, the important thing is that play remains at the centre of professional concern for these workers. Play should be considered equally alongside other outcomes. Children and young people's capacity for positive development will be enhanced if given access to the broadest range of play environments and opportunities. If this is to be achieved it will require a dedicated, skilled and competent workforce; one that understands all children and young people need to play, and that play is fundamental to the healthy development of individuals, communities and countries.

4

ADRIAN VOCE
The state of play in England

On 11 Decmber 2007 Ed Balls, Children's Secretary announced the Children's Plan to the House of Commons, detailing the dedication of £225 million government funding to create more and safer places to play and promising a wide-ranging play strategy for mid 2008. Principles underpinning the Plan include recognition of the rights of children to enjoy their childhood, to receive preventative and holistic services responsive to need and for all children to realise their potential to succeed.

This chapter and chapter 41 were written before the welcome announcement of the Children's Plan. They describe the context of events, principles and debates that, at the time, underpinned a perhaps necessarily strident, playwork perspective, on the need for a national play strategy.

A real 'state of play' report, if it were to address how, where, how often and to what effect children in England do or don't play, is a job for many researchers, academics, statisticians and analysts. Thankfully, the chapter heading is a pun (if a rather obvious one). What I am going to discuss is the current state of the policy landscape on which so much provision for children's play now depends, and how we got here over the last few decades. It has been a complex journey and this condensation of it is necessarily simplified, but I hope to draw out the key themes.

There is mounting evidence that children's access to environments offering even minimal play value has drastically diminished in just a few decades. Increasing traffic and its toll on the young; commercial and social pressures on space; fearful perceptions of the threat from strangers; real fears of bullying and crime; changed patterns of family life; and an education system narrowly focused on testable academic proficiency, have all conspired to deny large numbers of children the play lives that were traditionally taken for granted. In general, the modern economy and its effects on society has devalued children's play where it cannot be exploited for some other purpose.

This means that children's opportunities, certainly for outdoor play, have become increasingly dependent upon social policy. The response in England has been mixed. Through the '60s and '70s, voluntary and community groups mobilized to establish staffed adventure playgrounds, holiday play schemes and after-school clubs, while national and local charities began to campaign for the child's right to play and offer support to providers. This voluntary activity was largely enabled by local authority grant schemes and charitable trusts, while more and more councils themselves began to offer play services. There was a growth in supervised play provision and the genesis of a new profession: playwork, with its core ethos of honouring, enabling and engaging the child's self-directed play, and co-constructing with children the environments where playing could be most fully expressed.

The '80s and '90s saw a general reduction in community services and increased competition for local funding as grant schemes became tighter or replaced by a commissioning and contracting culture. Within the public sector as a whole, the market played a bigger and bigger role. This period also saw childcare rise steadily up the political agenda to become a major theme of social policy.

Each of these trends contributed to a decline in the kind of free, supervised, open-access play provision that had begun to thrive. Set up to compensate for the absence of green and open space or play friendly streets and estates – often in areas of high density and deprivation – play projects did not lend themselves to market forces. On the other hand, the childcare industry, driven by a national government strategy, with a clientele of working parents and employers, and programmes of start-up funding, subsidies and tax breaks, took off. The effect on free play projects, whose 'clients' were first and foremost children – with no weight to bear on the economic levers of social policy – was that many were closed, or converted to childcare as local authorities redefined their out-of-school services to meet nationally imposed targets. These were restricted, mostly, to children whose parents could pay. Play value was less important than ticking the boxes for registration under the growing regulatory framework.

Although there had been some valiant efforts in the '70s and '80s to establish a national infrastructure to support the growth of play provision to combat the decline in playable communities, in the absence of a clear national policy, this had proved difficult to sustain. By 1997, although there was central funding for the beginnings of a workforce strategy, play provision as such lacked any further policy commitments beyond an information service via a contract with the Department for Culture, Media and Sport (DCMS), held by the National Playing Fields Association (NPFA). It was hard at this point to see the decline in provision not becoming terminal.

The change of government raised hopes of a change, and so it was that the Children's Play Council (CPC) asked the new Culture Secretary, Chris Smith, to address a national conference about funding for play in 1998. Smith set some challenges: identify clear outcomes for provision, establish a vocational training structure and speak with one voice, he said, and the government will listen. Responding to these challenges, the play sector produced Best Play (NPFA 2000), identifying the outcome objectives of good provision, the characteristics of good play environments and the ethos of the play movement. A training and qualifications framework underpinned by the same values was also established (see Chapter 8), while other developments, such as the production of quality assurance models like Quality in Play (Conway and Farley 2001), further reinforced the growing professionalism and distinct ethos of the play sector.

The Secretary of State responded to these developments in two significant ways. In 1999, he awarded a contract to CPC for a policy and research programme to run alongside the information services previously provided by NPFA, and in 2001, immediately prior to the general election, he promised £200m of lottery funding for play provision across the UK.

After long delays, owing to the restructuring of lottery distributors and the decision to commission a national review before deciding how the play funding should be delivered in 2005 the Big Lottery Fund announced its Children's Play initiative for England. Based largely on the recommendations of the review, chaired by the Former Health Secretary, Frank Dobson the initiative allocated £124m to be divided among every local authority area in the country.[1] The money would only be released on the production of a play strategy – based on a clear policy and underpinning play ethos – to deliver free, local provision on which children themselves had been consulted. A further £16m was directed to a programme, *Playful Ideas*, designed to encourage innovation, another recommendation of the play review. In the third component of the initiative, £15m was awarded to CPC to grow and establish Play England, a new national structure dedicated to supporting the initiative and promoting the longer-term growth of provision.

When CPC was awarded its contract in 1999, its first task was to survey the national state of play provision from a strategic perspective. *Making the Case for Play* (Cole-Hamilton and Gill 2002a) found that provision was patchy and often insubstantial. Play services were frequently marginalized and therefore vulnerable to cuts. There was a dearth of strategic planning, with most local authorities reflecting the lack of national policy drivers. The headline recommendation of the report was for a national government play strategy, underpinned by mainstream funding.

In the sense that the report of the later play review, *Getting Serious About Play* (DCMS 2004), was specifically about lottery funding, it had proved something of a red herring in the campaign for this longer-term national play strategy. Nevertheless, in her response to the review, Culture Secretary Tessa Jowell, said that the government would be 'considering a more strategic, cross-departmental approach to play policy'.

The first outcome of this cross-government approach, *Time for Play* (DCMS 2006) was, to many in the play sector, disappointing, with Frank Dobson himself calling the document 'wishy-washy' (Children Now 2006). Although it flagged up, probably for the first time in a discrete publication, the importance that the government attaches to good play provision, it fell short of specific proposals, placing the onus on local authorities and the play sector to 'take advantage of the opportunities' presented by the funding, the new infrastructure and the range of other policy areas where play should be considered.

In July and August 2007 – partly, no doubt, as a result of the impact that the lottery programmes and Play England were having on debates about childhood – the role of good play provision and adequate playable space within the public realm were being considered, in their own right, as subjects for serious policy development by the new administration of Gordon Brown. A new Secretary of State for Children (not just Education) marked a significant shift in government thinking and the importance for play advocates was underlined when this new department assumed joint responsibility for play policy with DCMS. A government consultation on a new safeguarding strategy, *Staying Safe* (DCSF 2007b), highlighted the importance of outdoor play for children, helping them to understand risks and develop their resilience. As the government consulted on its new ten-year children's plan there were signs that more was to come. The challenge for play advocates is to help shape and substantiate policy so that it is informed by and responsive to the ethos and good practice developed on the ground. We need to develop the tools and hone the arguments to allow this growing interest to translate into a real and lasting expansion of play opportunities for children. This is a long game: developing and piloting strategic indicators; developing the evidence base; making the right campaigning moves to exert real influence on ministers. The aim is for supervised play provision to feature in future public spending rounds and for children's play needs to be factored in to key decisions about traffic, planning, housing and parks. If the lottery funding is to be more than a flash in the plan, it is a game we must win.

Notes

[1] The funding applications were solicited from the unitary or district authority for the area, but were expected to demonstrate partnership working, including, particularly, the engagement of the voluntary and community sector.

5

JOAN BEATTIE
Playwork in Scotland

Overview

Like its sister nations the playwork sector is relatively new in Scotland. It has never been a statutory provision and in the past it has depended upon volunteers. Scotland is a largely rural country and some isolated communities in the Highlands and Islands are completely excluded from accessing play opportunities. More recently the National Lottery has allowed many play settings to be established, but there is a question about longer-term sustainability. Provision for children aged 4–16 includes breakfast clubs, out-of-school provision, wrap-around care, holiday playschemes and adventure playgrounds. There is a core of experienced workers who tend to be older, and because the sector is expanding rapidly, there is an increase in inexperienced unqualified staff.

Policy drivers

There have been a number of policy initiatives in recent years that are having an impact on the sector:

- The Regulation of Care (Scotland) Act 2001 has resulted in the setting-up of the Care Commission with the responsibility for regulating and inspecting care and play services. This legislation also resulted in the establishment of the Scottish Social Services Council (SSSC) which is responsible for registering people who work with children and regulating qualification requirements.
- *Meeting the Childcare Challenge: A Childcare Strategy for Scotland 1998* was the start of a process to increase and qualify the workforce, to introduce Childcare Tax credits, to establish Childcare Partnerships and to put in place a Childcare Information Service.
- The Scottish Credit and Qualifications Framework (SCQF) was set up by the Scottish Executive, Universities Scotland, the Scottish Qualifications Authority (SQA) and the Quality Assurance Agency (QAA) for Higher

Education Scotland. It is intended to provide a new way of understanding and comparing qualifications in Scotland.

- The Children (Scotland) Act 1995, the protection of Children (Scotland) Act 2003 and the Regulation of Care (Scotland) Act 2001 introduced more stringent systems to make sure that all people who want to work with children are suitable to do so.
- A National Review of the Early Years and Childcare Workforce was undertaken by the Scottish Executive in 2006, and highlighted the need to adopt a single shared framework of roles and responsibilities for those working with children across Scotland. It is envisaged that each worker within this single children's workforce will know how their work with children complements the work others do, while understanding that they are working towards an agreed set of outcomes for all children.

Funding

There is no direct national funding for playwork although there is funding through the Scottish Executive from the Education and Early Education and Childcare departments for early years work and childcare, which includes playwork.

The National Lottery has had a major impact and allowed many out-of-school clubs to be set up. This is supposed to be 'additional' money, but there was little funding for the sector in the beginning. Now there are concerns about future sustainability. Parents are the main customers and the fees they pay are expected to cover the costs of provision. This has meant that the employees pay scales tend to be low.

Funding for training is provided by the Workforce Development Fund (from the Scottish Executive and administered by the local authorities). The key department in the Scottish Executive is the Scottish Executive Enterprise, Transport and Lifelong Learning (SEETLLD). The Enterprise Networks include Scottish Enterprise and Highlands and Islands Enterprise responsible for Local Enterprise Companies (LECs). Each LEC has its own Chief Executive and is responsible for Training and Skills Funding. Further Education funding is allocated by the Scottish Further Education Funding Council (SFEFC). In some cases funding is augmented by European Social Fund (ESF) funding. Local authorities have the discretion to spend the funds they receive and there are inconsistencies across the country depending on where you live. In rural areas training costs can be significantly higher than in towns or cities.

In the past the Scottish Executive has also funded conferences/events for the playwork sector through SkillsActive (and previously through SPRITO, the former national training organization for Playwork).

Training and qualifications: current and future provision

The level of qualification in the overall childcare sector is improving. Over 60 per cent of staff now hold childcare qualifications at the equivalent of SVQ Level III (SCQF Level 6) or above. This is the level required to register with the Scottish

Social Services Council (SSSC) as a practitioner from 2006. A further 21 per cent have qualifications below this level; while 16 per cent have no formal childcare qualifications, but more than 50 per cent of this group are working towards one. These figures are taken from Pre-school and Childcare Workforce Statistics (Scottish Executive 2006).

However, there is a high turnover of staff and because there are numerous qualifications that are acceptable for playwork positions many staff do not have the necessary playwork skills needed to work with older children and young people. There are currently only three discrete playwork qualifications available: S/NVQs in Playwork Level II, III and IV.

Scotland is leading the way in the development of the Scottish Credit and Qualifications Framework (SCQF). Its main purpose is to make the relationship between qualifications clear, to make progression and transfer between qualifications easier. It has been created to bring together all Scottish mainstream qualifications into a single unified framework for Higher Education qualifications, SQA qualifications, Higher National qualifications and Scottish Vocational Qualifications. There are 12 levels ranging from Access 1 at SCQF level 1 to Doctorate at SCQF level 12. It is being embedded throughout Scotland's education and training provision.

The SCQF development, together with the Regulation of Care (Scotland) Act 2001 and the National Review of the Early Years and Childcare Workforce 2005, is set to have a major impact on the future of playwork training and qualifications. It is expected that the main attributes of a qualifications structure will be:

- one framework for the whole sector;
- services led by degree qualified professionals;
- entry and exit points at each level;
- FE, HE and vocational routes to support flexibility and inclusion;
- recognition of prior learning;
- support for progression and Continuous Professional Development (CPD);
- support for identification of a shared skills/knowledge base across children's services.

The development will mean:

- qualifications at a number of levels;
- levels linked to SSSC registration requirements;
- bench-marking against a professional base of knowledge skills and values to allow practice in any setting;
- acknowledgement of specialisms in qualifications and CPD.

Skills needs

A key concern of workers is that the work they do is undervalued. Playwork and childcare is too often seen as a job anyone can do, requiring no skill or training. However, the workforce in Scotland is already moving towards a more professional basis. An increasing percentage of the people involved now possess a qualification for working with children, and from 2006 under the SSSC regulations all workers are required to register. This means a commitment to qualifications and CPD. For new entrants to the workforce the core skills will be important, but those skills relating to problem solving, team working and communication should also be included. IT skills will be important for working with IT-literate children.

It is expected that playworkers will need to develop all-round skills with specialisms in certain areas; sports, arts, outdoor, adventure and environmental play and possibly a greater understanding of health and nutrition. Higher-level qualifications will be needed for the new structure: Lead practitioner, Practitioner and Support Workers, and because the sector will need to attract more people to be trainers and assessors, more courses with flexible delivery mechanisms will be required.

A national partnership approach for playwork in Scotland

Putting Playwork on the Map was a four-month pilot project delivered around four locations within the Highlands and Islands in 2003. It established a new model of awareness raising and training activities, taking the central theme of Article 31 from the UN Convention on the Rights of the Child and focusing on the child's right to play. The project was delivered as two components: a visit to the local after-school clubs and the Article 31 Roadshow Seminar. It brought the children's ideas on board and promoted their rights to play at and outwith the clubs. The project raised Article 31 awareness at the seminar where children and adults were encouraged to participate as equals.

After-school visits

Of the 80 operational clubs in the region the project team managed to visit and consult with the children of nine clubs, to gain their perspectives on play, and let them guide us into their world. The results were always inspiring, sometimes chaotic, but nevertheless child-led and good fun. Tools and weapons were designed and manufactured from innocuous pieces of driftwood and bodies were painted in rainbow colours (but mainly purple!), large cardboard boxes and balls of string turned into dens that were then tried out to see if they were waterproof when the inevitable rain came. Play was explored and adult boundaries were surrendered. Of the noticeable benefits, children and playworkers had fun and further evolved positive relationships. Hearts and minds were stimulated and engaged. Grown-ups had the chance to reminisce about the days when their only thought was what to play next.

Article 31 Roadshow Seminar

Four Saturday seminars were held in Argyll and Bute, Caithness, Western Isles and Inverness and Nairn. The seminars took a Roadshow format with an array of free leaflets, promotional literature and information about play and playwork, travelling alongside our guest speakers. The project tried to combat the distance aspect of training by taking the information out to the rural communities. Playworkers networked, shared ideas and asked questions appropriate to their area. Being involved with the after-school clubs gave the project team the understanding to consider local views more accurately. The seminar, in some instances, took the form of a workshop. It brought IPA members, drama and arts practitioners, outdoor adventure play, and qualification guidance to the area. Adult attendees reflected on their own childhood experiences and learnt international skills. Child delegates wanted more joint play sessions with the adults! The seminars gave our playwork practitioners the chance to value their careers and reflect upon their fundamental role in society. Funding for this project came from Highland and Islands Enterprise and the Scottish Executive.

Current partnership working

Links have been made and joint conferences and seminars have been held between SkillsActive Scotland and Play Scotland, the Scottish Out of School Care Network, the Scottish Qualifications Authority, the Scottish Social Services Council, the International Play Association (Scotland Branch), the Out of School Care Federation and a number of Local Authorities across Scotland. In October 2006 the Scottish Implementation Plan for the UK National Strategy for Playwork Education and Training was launched at the annual Scottish Playwork conference.

A number of joint initiatives have taken place over the last few years around playwork training but unfortunately there has been no more funding forthcoming to emulate the *Putting Playwork on the Map* project. For several years now SkillsActive has held an annual Playwork Conference for playwork trainers, colleges, Childcare Partnerships, Local Authorities and key stakeholders plus an annual conference for playworkers. These focus on the latest developments in play and playwork training, while showing the playwork field that the national organizations are working together to meet the needs of the workforce and ultimately the children of Scotland.

6

MIKE GREENAWAY
Play in Wales

Prior to the establishment of the National Assembly for Wales, playwork in Wales followed a pattern similar to the rest of the UK. In 1983 the Conservative Government responded to an early day motion (EDM 1983) signed by an All Party Group of 255 MPs, and supported by the NPFA and Fair Play for Children, and established the Association for Children's Play and Recreation. Playboard, as it became known, had a UK-wide remit, and for some time made a considerable contribution to the development of play provision. However, it was apparent from early on that there were philosophical differences between the playwork sector and the government. In 1987 The Trustees of Playboard determined that the organization should be wound up in 1987, rather than comply with government requirements to change the focus of its work.

In Wales, as a result of the vagaries of four nations finance, the proportion of funding allocated by the UK government for the Welsh Office to contribute to Playboard was retained, and in 1989 passed to the Welsh Local Government Association (WLGA) to establish a body to support the development of play provision in Wales. Play Wales, as administered by the WLGA, had a limited impact upon the development of staffed play provision. It focused principally on the development and maintenance of fixed-equipment play areas – this being the nature of play provision provided by the District Councils.

The 1980s and early 1990s were not a good time for playwork in Wales. Most staffed provision that had been funded, particularly at its inception, by a range of government funding initiatives, including Urban Aid and various Manpower Services programmes, came to an end. In some areas, notably Cardiff, local authorities continued to fund playwork in the guise of adventure play and elsewhere as seasonal playscheme provision. By the mid 1990s there remained seven adventure playgrounds in Cardiff and two in North Wales.

In 1995 the Welsh Office undertook a consultation on the future funding of Play Wales. At odds with a very clear response from the field that Play Wales's funding should continue to be centrally administered, it was decided that the funding be distributed to all local authorities on a pro-rata basis, with an expectation that

Play Wales apply individually to each local authority for the respective proportion of funding. By 1996 Play Wales was in a parlous position. However, the election of a new Labour Government and the appointment of Wyn Griffiths MP as the Minister for Children in Wales provided a lifeline. In response to some focused lobbying by the All Wales Play Forum and other voluntary play associations, Wyn invited the sector to establish a new national charity that would be funded centrally by the Welsh Office. With the support of Children in Wales, the 'old' Play Wales was wound up and a new national charity, Play Wales/Chwarae Cymru, was established.

From the outset the new Assembly Government of Wales expressed a commitment to raising the profile of children's rights, and as one of its first actions, endorsed the UN Convention on the Rights of the Child (UNICEF 1991). It determined to undertake policy development on the basis of entitlement, with the responsibility for play being placed with Jane Hutt AM, the Minister for Social Services. In 1998 Play Wales was successful in securing European funding and worked with Bob Hughes, to develop *The First Claim … a framework for playwork quality assessment* (Hughes 2001b) and subsequently *The First Claim … desirable processes* (Hughes 2002b). *The First Claim* was distinctive in drawing together current understanding and theory in respect of playwork, arguably for the first time. While it was developed intentionally for an audience of playworkers, it helped shape a wider understanding of the processes of play, and how playworkers can most effectively facilitate play. It was particularly useful in sharing an understanding with a wider audience of politicians and government officials, both national and local.

In the late 1990s the UK governments were embarking upon Childcare Strategies that were clearly focused upon the economic needs of parents, rather than the play needs of children. Initially, following the lead of the UK government, play provision (often termed 'open access' after the Children Act 1989) was excluded from the Welsh Assembly Childcare Strategy (1998). This was a decision that did not represent the reality of many Welsh communities, where informal 'open-access' provision was the care provision of choice for many parents, particularly for their older children. The rationale behind this decision has been the cause of speculation, but it would appear that it was not informed by a clear policy agenda.

At this time the Welsh Assembly Government determined to deliver national strategic development through local Framework Partnerships. These were comprised of representatives from the local authorities, the voluntary sector and industry. In addition, the first substantive piece of legislation was enacted by the Assembly: *Extending Entitlement* (2000) placed for the first time in the UK a statutory duty upon local authorities to offer youth provision.

In 2000, partly as an attempt to redress the imbalance created by the Childcare Strategy, with its disproportionate focus on care rather than play, the Assembly distributed a £1,000,000 Play Grant to the newly formed Framework Partnerships. This was to support the development of new open access play provision. At the same time the Assembly commissioned a national review of children's play provision, *The State of Play* Report (Mannello and Statham 2000). Although originally intended as funding for one year, the Play Grant was continued, rising in annual value from the original £1m to £2.75m in 2002. The Play Grant was subsequently subsumed into the unified fund, Cymorth, and as such continues to be used for the development of play provision.

Initially the Play Grant was used for a range of purposes, but within a year it was recognized by most partnerships that the funding would be most effectively used strategically, to establish play development posts. Time has demonstrated that these posts have significantly contributed to coherent strategic development. The funding has also supported innovation throughout Wales, particularly with the development of outreach and detached playwork on the streets and in parks.

As well as providing an analysis of play provision in Wales, the *State of Play* Report also included a recommendation that the Assembly adopt a play policy. Play Wales, working with Children in Wales, was commissioned to draft recommendations. This work formed the basis of the Welsh Assembly Government (2002a) Play Policy which was adopted with cross-party support. The Play Policy articulates the importance of play, and gives recognition to the erosion of children's play opportunities in 21st-century Wales. It also underlines the Assembly's commitment to supporting the development of play provision that compensates for the erosion of the spaces and freedoms from which children have traditionally benefited. Significantly, it also included a commitment to develop a strategy for the implementation of the policy.

In 2005 the ministerial responsibility for play transferred from Social Services to Education, within what was to become the Children's Strategy Division, under Jane Davidson AM. It is of note that both Jane Hutt AM and Jane Davidson had experience of playwork and youth work in former careers. The Assembly established a Play Policy Implementation Group comprising representatives from all organizations with an interest in play within Wales, to draft recommendations on the content of a Play Strategy. As its work developed, representatives from all the Assembly Departments whose work had a direct or indirect impact on children's play were invited to join the group. Play Wales and Children in Wales were commissioned together to support the work of the Group and draft the Recommendations (Welsh Assembly Government 2004). The involvement of departmental representatives was very significant, with most of the recommendations to the Minister being informed directly by those upon whose area of work they would impact. The Recommendations, with cross-party support, were published for wider consultation, and in 2006 the Welsh Assembly Government Play Policy Implementation Plan (Play Strategy) was launched.

During the development of the Recommendations it had become increasingly apparent that the playwork sector would be better placed to argue its case if there were a set of philosophical principles by which play and playwork could be seen as distinct from other related areas of work. This perception was supported by findings of consultations undertaken by Sprito, now SkillsActive, the sector skills council for playwork.

In 2002 Play Wales received funding from the Assembly to lead a UK review of the Playwork Values and Assumptions. Play Wales worked with PlayEducation to produce a draft statement for consultation, and a 'scrutiny group', comprised of playworkers, each with considerable playwork experience, undertook the role of 'honest broker' in the consultation process. The resulting 'Playwork Principles' were endorsed by SkillsActive in 2004.

In 2002 the Assembly also granted additional dedicated funding to Play Wales for the development of peer-led professional endorsement of playwork training. From an early stage, it was recognized that there were areas of commonality between playwork, youth work and community development work. The close working relationships that had been established between the sectors lent themselves to the inclusion of playwork and community development work within the purview of the Education and Training Standards Committee of the Wales Youth Agency (WYA). Additionally, many of the legal relationships with the Assembly and Joint Negotiating Council were already established, which had significant benefits for the playwork sector. This development had the explicit support of the playwork sector in Wales, and was seen as a positive development in increasing the professional status and pay of playworkers. In 2005 when the functions of the WYA were subsumed into the Education Department of the Assembly, it was agreed that a 'new' Education and Training Standards 'sub-committee' of the Assembly, with responsibility for playwork, youth work and community development work be established.

Since its inception the Welsh Assembly has launched a range of initiatives that have contributed to the wider recognition of the importance of play and the development of play provision:

- The Integrated Children's Centre initiative, which included guidance that funding be used to support the development of adventure playgrounds for children up to 16 years (Welsh Assembly 2002b).
- The Foundation Phase, for children aged 3 to 8 years, which identifies the importance of play in children's learning and places a requirement on schools that 40 per cent of children's taught time will be outside in the natural environment.
- Communities First, an initiative that focuses on the most deprived communities throughout Wales, uniquely designed to be delivered from within communities rather than the usual 'top-down' model.
- Community Focused Schools, an initiative to enable the use of school premises by the wider community outside the school day.

In 2005 Play Wales, as part of the CWLWM partnership with national childcare organizations, received European funding to develop new qualifications and training materials for playwork. At the time of writing, the first phase of pilots have been successful, and it is anticipated that in due course the training will be used by staff who work in any setting where children's play may be facilitated, as well as playworkers.

Throughout the development of play policy and strategy there has been a determination to see playwork and the development of play provision as an entitlement rather than a response to a pathological view of children. The strength of the Assembly Play Policy is that it articulates a positive position – play is fundamentally important to children's development, and it is for this reason that it should be supported and funded by the State. However, it is also recognized that as a result of investing in play there are a range of 'windfall' benefits that accrue in respect of, for example, children's health and community safety.

Currently, work continues towards targets set out in the Assembly Play Policy Implementation Plan with some notable successes. The Children Act (2004), implemented in 2006, included a clause placing a statutory duty on Local Authorities to cooperate in the delivery of play provision, and it is widely antici- pated that this requirement will be strengthened in due course. In 2006 the BIG Lottery launched the £13 million Child's Play programme to support capacity building through the cross-sector development of infrastructure, and strategic projects, and Play Wales has been contracted to support the delivery of the programme. In 2007 Play Wales was awarded funds to establish a special centre dedicated to the development of playwork education and training in the country.

It is hoped that the Child's Play programme and the Welsh Assembly Play Policy Implementation Plan will significantly contribute to a paradigm shift away from the idea that provision for children's play must be limited to playgrounds with fixed equipment, impact absorbent surfacing and a fence, towards the concept where children's play is widely valued in a wide range of environments, rural and urban, adequately resourced and supported by a workforce of trained specialists, playworkers.

7

EVA KANE
Play provision in Northern Ireland

From playwork by accident to playwork by design

First of all, just a note of caution: this is not the definitive history of play provision in Northern Ireland (NI), but a personal and generalized view of it. I was accidentally thrown into playwork in Northern Ireland in the mid 1980s. Since then I have spent most of my time connected to play provision in one way or another, and I recognize that my experience has given me a particular perspective. Not only was my entry into playwork accidental, I believe the early days of play provision in Northern Ireland were also accidentally playwork.

Playwork Principle No. 3 states that 'the prime focus and essence of playwork is to support and facilitate the play process' (PPSG 2005). Play provision in the 1970s was mainly in disadvantaged urban areas. In those areas, volunteers (often mothers) provided opportunities for children to 'get off the streets'. Sometimes this was supported by community workers; some councils even employed playleaders.

In Northern Ireland the backdrop was civil unrest, and what was to become over 30 years of 'the troubles'. The main focus of play provision was to give children and young people opportunities to try new things, which were often beyond the scope of the home or the family. If funds permitted they might offer a trip to somewhere the children would otherwise never get to. Sometimes it was just a safe space in the neighbourhood. Belfast even saw a brief period of providing traditional adventure playgrounds. However, their wooden structures seemed to suffer from the same violence that surrounded them.

At this time, there was no such thing as playwork qualifications; most staff saw themselves as just 'minding the kids', and maybe that was a blessing in disguise. The children were allowed to get on with it while the volunteers had a cup of tea in the corner, unless some kids got into real bother.

Then came a time of slow professionalization: it was no longer permissible to have tea near the children! PlayBoard NI came into being in the mid 1980s. With its birth, and the introduction of the first foundation course in playwork, came specialized training for staff with few previous training opportunities. The predominantly community-based, open-access provision, mainly staffed by volunteers became supported by a growing number of voluntary organizations. Issues such as child protection, first aid and health and safety started to grow in importance and the tea-drinking staff started organizing themselves and providing activities for the children.

The first input of some serious money came in 1996 with the so called 'Peace' money (European Union Special Support Programme for Peace and Reconciliation). This allowed local communities to employ a Playworker who could coordinate and support the local volunteers. With this funding opportunity came a need to do community relations or cross-community work. New training opportunities started to flourish, most of them focusing on how to deal with children's sectarian comments and how to manage children's behaviour. There was little space for exploring the behaviour and the language in the light of the play process. At the same time there was the growth of the sector that specialized in taking children away from the urban violence. Many of the residential centres or peace organizations that grew up in Northern Ireland became the hotbed for playworkers. The realization that children often can play their way through their prejudices better than we can guide them was a lesson many learnt. For many of the staff and volunteers involved, this was hard work with huge rewards where a commitment to children and play was embedded for life.

While play provision was initially dominated by urban, open-access provision many community-based play projects now became childcare providers. Their main focus was to support women returning to work: there was a huge increase in such provision in rural areas. The resources provided by the New Opportunities Fund (NOF) lottery money and the 'Peace Funding' supported the development of 14,000 school-age childcare places by 2004. As a result, paid playwork professionals grew rapidly in numbers. Due to a lack of access to playwork qualifications outside of Belfast, people with a variety of qualifications came into the profession. The school-aged childcare part of play provision has now become dominated by staff with childcare qualifications that have learnt all about supporting children's learning through their stages of development. This new part of the childcare sector had to be incorporated into the responsibilities under the Children (NI) Order 1995 and became regulated by social workers. This period saw an emphasis on meeting the needs of the parents rather than the play needs of the children. This led broadly to a focus on care and education rather than on play.

It is estimated that the Northern Ireland playwork workforce comprises nearly 4000 staff (SkillsActive 2005b: 3). This audit is the first of its kind and it is acknowledged that it probably underestimates the size of the sector. For example, staff such as junior youth workers, wouldn't necessarily self-identify as playworkers, even though they work with school-aged children and young people with an approach that often resembles playwork.

The playwork sector has had little support to develop a training and education infrastructure and this is reflected in the workforce. Even with playwork qualifications now more available across Northern Ireland the majority of paid playworkers still come from an early years background:

93% of playworkers are women, young (60% under 30) part time workers with low pay and short term contracts ... only 35% hold a playwork qualification ... 86% ask for more training ... 25% of playworkers have to pay for training themselves.

(as detailed in Kane 2003: 58–72)

An added difficulty has been the lack of progression routes to professional qualification. Until very recently the only available route in Northern Ireland has been the NVQ. In a context with a lack of any adventure playground tradition and few play specific training and professional development opportunities for staff, play provision has been dominated by an approach that tends to structure children's time and activities, as well as minimize risk and challenge.

The light on the horizon is that the policy context for playwork in Northern Ireland is changing rapidly. For the first time government has provided funding for play provision. Groups previously funded by 'Peace' have now access to some money to ensure sustainability. The sector can also look forward to two important developments. First, PlayBoard and NIPPA – The Early Years Organization – drafted a Play Policy for Northern Ireland on behalf of the Office of First Minister and Deputy First Minister; the consultation was launched in October 2006. Second, PlayBoard has taken the lead in the partnership with SkillsActive to draft an implementation plan for a Playwork Education and Training Strategy, to be launched at PlayBoard's conference in October 2007. It is hoped that the recognition of a need for a Northern Ireland-wide play policy will mean that local government, for the first time, will have both commitment and resources for meeting children's play needs.

This is in stark contrast to the dark clouds that appear to be forming. In the training field the threat is the idea of a children's workforce, leading to the possible diminishing of the role of playwork as a profession focusing on the support of the play process. The idea of extended schools is also looming on the horizon and some play providers feel that cost-free structured after-school activities will put them at risk of closure. It will also further diminish the time for play in children's lives.

In Northern Ireland there is the added irony of extended schools effectively adding to segregation. For the last 20 years play provision has developed excellence in terms of allowing children from different backgrounds and different schools to come together in play. This investment, skill and knowledge might now be lost and play opportunities not be maximized.

With PlayBoard and its partner's ongoing work to renew the interest in play as a freely chosen, intrinsically motivated and personally directed activity, the awareness is slowly rising of children's play needs and the increased quality of play experience that a playworker can provide. In a society where play has been designed out by planners, educationalists, health and safety officers and social policy makers we are now in a period where playwork has to happen by design, rather than by accident!

8

PAUL BONEL
Playwork education, training and qualifications: looking to the future

On 14 June 2006 SkillsActive launched the first UK strategy for playwork education, training and qualifications, *Quality Training, Quality Play 2006–2011*, at the All Party Parliamentary Group on Play. The key aim of the strategy is to build a professional workforce that has the recognition and respect from government, the general public and our colleagues in other sectors. As playworkers we know the contribution playwork makes to children, young people and their families. We want others to recognize it too. The SkillsActive vision anticipates that by 2016, playwork will be a profession acknowledged as central to the provision for children and young people and the fulfilment of their individual potential. So what have been the successes that we can build on; the initiatives that will enable us to realize our vision; and the opportunities that lie before us?

Success stories

Transitional module

The Transitional Module (TM) or to give it its full name, Level 3 Award in Early Years and Child Care for Playworkers and Level 3 Award in Playwork for Early Years and Child Care Workers, has provided an eagerly awaited route between the two sectors. The TM crystallizes the essential skills, knowledge and understanding that the Level 3 practitioner needs to work in the respective disciplines, building on what they have in common. Now a building block of the Integrated Qualifications Framework, it is one of a number of joint initiatives between the Early years/Childcare and Playwork sectors.

Playwork Sector-Endorsed Foundation Degree

Following the sector's involvement in the development of the Early Years Sector Endorsed Foundation Degree, the Playwork Higher Education Committee

(PHEC), under the auspices of SkillsActive, led the way with a Foundation Degree for Playwork. With funding secured by SkillsActive from the DfES and Foundation Degree Forward, the PHEC took forward the development of learning outcomes, a statement of requirement, and a foundation degree framework for playwork. The Statement of Requirement with the SkillsActive Code of Practice ensured that Higher Education Institutions were meeting the needs of the playwork sector, and the University of Hertfordshire was the first to achieve Playwork Sector Endorsed status.

Playwork endorsement

Peer-led endorsement is a crucially important facet of the work of SkillsActive and has enabled the sector to set standards and procedures that confer a quality kite mark to training courses, qualifications, training providers, trainers and training products. From small beginnings it is now a system that is not only supported by employers and training providers in playwork but also increasingly recognized by government, funders and other agencies. It puts playwork in a strong position with the enhanced role for Sector Skills Councils, following the report by Lord Leitch in February 2007.

New National Occupational Standards

The National Occupational Standards (NOS) continue to be the building blocks for the training and qualification infrastructure in playwork. Under consistent review and scrutiny they are kept up to date with developing theory and practice in the sector. UK wide they enable the skills, knowledge and understanding of playwork to be transferable across borders. New standards at Level 4 and shared standards with Early Years/Child Care have been two innovations in recent times.

The playwork principles

Another major innovation has been the development of a brand new set of principles to provide a sound theoretical and value base for the sector (PPSG 2005). These principles are now being built into the NOS at all levels and the previous assumptions and values have been phased out.

New initiatives

Children's Workforce Network

This strategic forum in England, with its new and emerging counterparts in the other nations, is overseeing the development of workforce reform under the banner of *Every Child Matters* (DfES 2005a). With representation from all Sector Skills Councils and key professional bodies representing workers with children, young people and families, the Children's Workforce Network (CWN) has a major programme of work under way and is a key advisor in the development of the DfES

Children's Workforce Strategy. SkillsActive, representing Playwork, Sport and Leisure is a member and an active participant in a number of initiatives (see below).

Integrated Qualifications Framework

The Integrated Qualifications Framework (IQF) is set to be a major reform to the structure of qualifications for those working with children, young people and families. The design principles of the IQF incorporate transferable generic units at each level, sector specialisms that take account of the wider workforce and transferable learning routes between sectors, for example the transitional modules between playwork and early years/child care referred to earlier. The intention is for the common generic units to incorporate the common core and other skills, knowledge and understanding that are both essential and transferable. The IQF is also being developed to be fully compatible with the emerging *Qualifications and Credit Framework*, itself a major reform of all adult qualifications in England by the Qualifications and Curriculum Authority.

14–19 Diploma in Society, Health and Development

The Society, Health and Development Diploma (SH&D) is one of 17 such diplomas that are to become a national entitlement for young people in all schools in England by 2013. The SHD is in the first group to be developed and will be available from 2008. Although it would have been good to have had a line of learning just for the children's workforce, this is still an important development for the sector. It is also the first bite of the cherry, as Playwork will also form part of the 14–19 Diploma for Sport and Leisure being led by SkillsActive. The SH&D is being led by Skills for Health and areas of learning for working with children will sit alongside those for working with adults in health, care and justice. For the first time an introduction to working with children in a play setting will be available to 14–19 year olds, and the full qualification is equivalent to 3 A levels.

New opportunities

The next 5–10 years is going to be a time of great change for working with children. As well as the reforms in England there are similar new and far-reaching initiatives in Wales, Scotland and Northern Ireland and these all come on the heels of major new initiatives in every country. The great challenge for playwork is to take advantage of these reforms in building new opportunities for career development and professional status and recognition, while at the same time developing and promoting the unique and crucial nature of how the sector works with children and young people.

The landscape of what it means to be a children's worker is being redrawn at every level, with an ever increasing drive towards improved professionalism, enhanced communication between the sectors and an inter-disciplinary framework of training and qualifications up to and including higher education. The recommendations of Leitch are important for us. Sector Skills Councils have an important place in the government's drive towards 21st-century skills, employment and economic development. Playwork, as an integral part of SkillsActive, is in the frame to benefit from this and other reforms.

Playwork has made great strides forward in the last 10 years in its profile and recognition. This looks likely to continue, perhaps at a greater pace, given the recent announcement of the Children's Plan (DCSF 2007b), the proposed expansion of play settings and opportunities for children and young people, and the development of a national play strategy. Such initiatives include the training of 4000 playworkers, the consolidation of a core graduate workforce, and the introduction of playwork training for those whose work impacts the lives of children and young people, for example, highways, parks and green spaces, police, as well as colleague professions comprising the children's workforce.

Laudably the Playwork infrastructure is currently in place to meet the challenges of these new opportunities for expansion, growth and recognition.

The establishment of Play England provides a much-needed vehicle for the promotion of play and the enhancement of playwork provision at national and regional level. By assuming that mantle it also enables SkillsActive to dedicate its resources to issues of workforce development in general and education, training and qualifications in particular.

9

CHRIS TAYLOR
Playwork and the theory of loose parts

Playworker:	'I'm going to a workshop on the Theory of Loose Parts.'
Teacher:	'What's that?'
Playworker:	'It's the idea that if you give children lots of bits and pieces, sticks, wheels, ropes, water, sounds etc, they'll play, have fun and create new things.'
Teacher:	'Hmmn – and they call that a theory?'

As this teacher suggests, 'loose parts' have been a natural, ubiquitous and somewhat 'taken for granted' feature of children's play. However, in the 1970s Simon Nicholson presented his theory of loose parts, which has subsequently been used to inform playwork theory and practice. Nicholson was the son of Barbara Hepworth and Ben Nicholson, and after their divorce, for a while lived with Salvador Dali and his contemporaries. As an artist, he became disillusioned with the world of formal art, seeing it as an artificial construct, and believing that creativity resided in everyone, that all had artistic potential. His theory of loose parts, with its emphasis on community, inventiveness and creativity, articulates this.

Like all theories 'loose parts' can be seen as both a product of, and contribution to the times in which it was written. The 1970s had followed two decades of post-war reconstruction and recuperation. The period was characterized by rapid urban growth, the growing ascendancy of the car, and increasing civil unrest in inner city areas. Post-war aspirations were giving way to disillusionment in Europe and the USA. There was a pervasive sense of the need for change. For some, this was seen to lie in the collective works of self-determining groups. People could come together to create new ways of living, creating new institutions and communities. This would lead to progress and improvement. This was a time of trade union activism, community action, civil rights and the adventure play movement! The theory of loose parts in terms of its appeal to adventure play touched contemporaneous preoccupations with egalitarianism, self-governance and tempering the impacts of urbanization, with creativity and alternatives to the established order.

Nicholson saw the new adventure playgrounds described by Ward (1961) as a 'parable in anarchy' or 'a free society in miniature', as prototypes for the design and build of adult communities. Observing children at play and architects at work, Nicholson realized that children played on the playgrounds when they were being built and disappeared when they were finished. Architects were having all the fun designing and planning, but all too often the results were sterile, empty playgrounds. Children were being cheated!

Nicholson (1967) appreciated that children loved to interact with variables such as materials and shapes, smells and other physical phenomena such as magnetism and gravity, media such as gases and fluids, sounds, music and motion, chemical interactions, cooking and fire and other people and animals, plants, words, concepts and ideas, thus arguing that the key feature of effective, interesting and engaging environments must involve movement and flexibility. He saw the beach as a loose parts environment, par excellence. The ever-changing interface of land and sea, of rock pools, living and dead creatures, the noise of the surf and the seabirds and so on. Could such qualities be recreated in an urban environment?

The Theory of Loose Parts states that 'in any environment both the degree of inventiveness and creativity and the possibility of discovery are directly proportional to the number and kinds of variables in it' (Nicholson 1971: 30).

The environment is defined dynamically as a system of interactive parts and Nicholson expressed an optimistic vision of the long term impacts of loose parts play on adventure playgrounds on children's lives. 'In terms of loose parts we can discern a natural evolution from creative play and participation with wood, hammers, ropes, nails and fire to creative play and participation with the total process of design and planning of regions in cities' (1971: 31).

It's of central importance that environments contain loose parts, and are characterized by flexibility and change. Later, Nicholson became less enamoured with some adventure playgrounds, he felt they had become fixed settings, with workers reluctant to replace the play structures built in the previous decade.

Loose parts and playwork theory

Loose parts and play types

Movement and flexibility are central to play experiences, so it is perhaps unsurprising to find them in the various play types, described by Hughes (2001a, 2006). For example 'exploratory play' involves discovering and experimenting with the construction, deconstruction, reconstruction and modification of materials, for example old clocks, radios and locks, and larger play equipment, such as rope bridges and platforms. Mastery play involves the exploration and manipulation of the natural environment. For example building camps and dens, 'not only tells children it can be done, it is also recognition of the security that the natural environment can give them and ... is an important play lesson' (Hughes 2001a: 53). As Hugh suggests, loose parts are a 'formidable ingredient for enabling children to engage in play' (2001a: 229).

Compound flexibility and play and the theory of loose parts

Brown, discussing compound flexibility and child development, provides a closer focus on loose parts and creativity in the play process. He suggests that 'flexibility in the play environment leads to increased flexibility in the child. The child is then better able to make use of the flexible environment ... and moves closer to their developmental potential than would otherwise have been the case' (2003b: 56–7). Creativity is expressed through the manipulation of loose parts in the environment, and the results reflect back to the child in the process of playing out their creativity; this feeds and stimulates a forward momentum in the spiral of maturational processes.

Loose parts as transitional phenomena

A related, yet, distinctive link between loose parts, playing and creative living, can be implicitly found in Winnicott's ideas relating to the transitional object and the transitional space. Loose parts become transitional phenomena in playing. Children use them to stand in the place of something else, as symbolic representation, for example sticks become guns, acorns and leaves, the cups and plates of the tea party. The development in playing of the capacity to present and recognize objects as standing in the place of others is at the heart of sophisticated processes such as reading, writing, role-play and the appreciation of dramatic performance. Loose parts naturally occur in playing and not only develop in the individual the capacity to symbolize but, when shared and involving others, create the transitional space, the to-ing and fro-ing of imaginations, through which meanings and relationships are formed. Winnicott's ideas related to living creatively, interestingly, connect with the theory of loose parts.

Loose parts theory and playwork practice

Values and assumptions

Playwork trainers, for example Maureen Palmer (one of the contributors to this book), have been keen to embed 'loose parts theory' into playwork practice. It is clearly relevant to the first assumption of playwork, which requires the provision of a stimulating play environment, and to the second assumption, relating to the playworker's low interventionist role. Palmer sees that for some children the provision of loose parts stimulates an immediate engagement in creative playing. Other children might lack interest or imagination. For such children, it seems appropriate that the playworker introduces activities that the child can try out, and which might facilitate movement into more personal and inventive playing. In the language of the playwork assumptions, the child moves from 'activity' into 'opportunity'.

Self-directed play, within a loose parts environment, can embody both the experience and expression of personal creativity. The playworker, as privileged observer, has little or no need of interpretation, perhaps only an appreciation and understanding of the language of play. Through the use of loose parts, play becomes a communication. The theory of loose parts is also clearly implicated in the playwork values, those that stress child-centredness, empowerment, self-directed play, opportunities for risk and challenge, growth of confidence and self-esteem, individuality, new experiences and cooperation.

Playwork principles

The recently adopted Playwork Principles (PPSG 2005) seek to establish the professional and ethical frame for playwork. They contain an implicit reference to loose parts in Principle 5, in that 'the role of the playworker is to support all children and young people in the creation of a space in which they can play'.

Quality assurance

Quality assurance is a mechanism that has been used recently to support play service delivery and has included a dissemination of the importance of loose parts in play environments. For example, London Play's Quality in Play scheme states that loose parts are essential ingredients of a warm and welcoming play environment, and that high quality play provision will include the provision of 'all play types and a comprehensive supply of loose parts' (Conway and Farley 2001).

Summary

While the use of loose parts in play settings can be seen to be part of the play process, to facilitate many play types, provide compound flexibility constitutive of personal development, ensure the quality of play provision, and relate to the uniqueness of the professional role of the playworker, and underpin values, principles and assumptions that are central to the work, the theory of loose parts also implies that environments, and what happens within them, offer children the opportunity of having control of their own creative impulses. Such an illustration is provided by Penny Wilson, former playworker at Chelsea Adventure Playground (and another contributor to this book):

> A wonderfully recalcitrant playworker at one of our sites acted in response to interventionist playwork, by dragging out a spool of rope and leaving it around for the kids to explore. They decided they wanted to span a double length between two trees. He helped them with the knots and placed a couple of crash mats around and the kids spent several days exploring ways to get from one tree to another, without touching the ground. There was lots of mutual encouragement, daring, trying again after failure, working as a group, adaptation of method and support from mates for the less able kids. It was a dream. When they got bored with this, he left out some scaffolding boards, and some house bricks.

For a time, Nicholson explored his theory of loose parts in an art appreciation course for the Open University. He would send his students boxes of loose parts for their assignments. The last box in the course was empty, except for a note that said, 'it's up to you now' – a playful reframing of creativity.

10

SUE PALMER
Work-based learning and reflective practice

Playwork practices offer rich experiences for playworkers to develop reflective practice skills in the work place. The circumstance of each playwork setting provides opportunities for individuals to engage with learning and reflection in practice. From the typical after-school club or playscheme through to the more unusual settings for playwork in prisons or hospitals, the role of the playworker is concerned with the development and support of play environments that enable children's play (Hughes 2001a; Brown 2003).

Work-based learning for playworkers can range from being 'dropped in at the deep end' through to a carefully developed programme of induction and training designed to provide new playworkers with the opportunity to develop their skills over time. The extent to which each individual makes sense of their practice experiences can be enhanced by offering links to reflective practices within the community of playwork practice (Palmer 2003).

Some long-standing playworkers will claim to have learned by experience with little or no formal training and support. There is a tendency to refer to stories illustrating instances of good or exemplary practice set in the context of past times when Health and Safety or Ofsted may not have held the same prominence over practice. These stories are valuable in setting out the parameters of the range of playwork practice. However, the social and political climate needs to be borne in mind when applying models from the past to contemporary practice in playwork.

In the present day, playworkers operate within a context of Criminal Record Bureau checks, compliance with national initiatives and an emergent children's workforce agenda which will impact on all professionals working with children. Now, more than ever it is essential that playworkers have a real sense of the contribution they make to children's lives, and the scope and role of playwork practices.

Three broad methods for playworkers to develop their skills in the workplace discussed in this chapter are: training, mentoring and modelling. All overlap to some extent and all are underpinned by personal exploration.

Training

Training is particularly useful where the situation does not change substantially over time or where the training relates to procedures that can be learned and then followed. For example undertaking a risk assessment for an outing or checking play equipment. Training prepares the playworker for a number of fairly standard and uncomplicated situations. However, much of playwork practice is about dealing with complex situations arising from the interactions between children at play and in some of these cases simple training models can be inadequate.

Mentoring

For mentoring in the workplace, the practitioner is teamed up with another playworker who offers support. This can take the form of supervision sessions reviewing recent practice or as co-mentoring where a pair of supportive colleagues meet to reflect and to support each other in developing their playwork practice and repertoire.

Modelling

This is usually provided by an experienced playworker who will demonstrate methods of working and reflection which are discussed and reviewed at a later date. The value of this approach to both parties is that it engages the more experienced playworker in a re-evaluation of practice and can aid the investigation of the relationship between espoused theory and theory-in-use (Moon 1999).

Personal exploration

For many playworkers, the most effective approach for development is through personal exploration, using reflective practice as the means for examining and reviewing their own practice and that of others. This requires an active approach to learning and reflection, taking the opportunities that arise in the workplace to investigate methods of working and to develop a personal history and repertoires of playwork approaches with a framework for action as a playworker.

Methods for developing reflective practice through personal exploration are fairly well documented in the literature, from diary writing through to personality analysis and individual counselling techniques.

An area where there is scope for investigation is in the relationship of intuition to practice. There are times when someone may ask, 'What would you do in this situation?' and the answer may be, 'I don't think I would get to here'. Using reflection tools to investigate your own intuitive practice needs care but can be rewarding in the long run.

Each playworker operates within the specific circumstances of the playwork setting and needs to take this into account when employing approaches to playwork. Playwork practices have evolved from the beliefs held by playwork practitioners about the nature of play for the child and the benefits of playing to human children and for human societies and culture. These circumstances and beliefs interact with the underpinning values for playwork practices. The dynamic relationship between values, circumstances and beliefs make it essential that playworkers engage with a reflective approach to their practice to respond to the subtle changes which affect their work.

Issues affecting learning in the workplace

If you ask any group of playworkers to itemize the key factors affecting opportunities for learning in the workplace, the first item on the list will almost certainly be the lack of time to engage seriously with reflective practices. This suggests that reflection is a practice taking place apart from the workplace. It is essential that we move away from a model of theory and practice that requires theory to be considered as separate from practice. Theory and practice, or practice and theory, for playworkers should be entwined so that we cannot engage with practice without an experience of theories to support and that we cannot conceive of theory without a consideration of the playwork practice relative to it.

The quality of playwork practice in the workplace is a recurrent issue for work-based learners. There is little point in learning a series of poor approaches or misapplied theories from disinterested playworkers. It is also recognized that the quality of practice in any playwork setting requires an actively engaged team of playworkers who support and learn from each other. For these reasons it is essential that rather than depend on the work base to provide all aspects of the learning for new playworkers, some consideration must be given to the establishment of criteria for good practice and reflection that the playworker can use as a tool kit to develop their own practice within the workplace and learn even in the context of less-than-perfect practice. It also provides a framework for breaking out of bad habits and establishing quality playwork.

New playworkers and student playworkers all complain at the 'pointless' exercise of writing out their daily diary or log book. Yet after reflection, many will confess that the diary is one of the most useful techniques learned to support and enable reflection on daily practice. The very process of committing your day to a diary offers engagement with reflection, and many experienced playworkers will find ways to use the diary exercise to support and develop their work. Some use the diary at difficult times or to focus on specific elements or puzzles in practice. The decision on how, when and why any diary may be of use depends on the circumstances of the practice and the particular needs of the playworker.

Learning from mistakes: is it important to always get it right?

Kolb's (1984) learning cycle, and Action Research methods (McNiff 1988 and Whitehead 2005) provide useful models for describing learning through practice. By following repeated passes through the 'plan, do, review' cycle it is possible to engage with successes and failures at all levels of our practice.

Possibly the biggest mistake in learning is to learn only how to avoid mistakes. Developing an approach to mistakes that involves inquiry and investigation means it is not only possible to review failures but also to use the failure constructively as a learning and reflection tool. Failures provide opportunities to respond creatively by considering how this could be approached in a different time and space.

Challenges for playworkers

The means for engaging with the development of quality playwork practice is in our own hands as playworkers. We can begin by actively seeking opportunities to reflect on and challenge our practices in the workplace, not just when taking part in a playwork course, but as an established approach to being a playworker.

See how many of these you can build into your practice. Share with others and add to this list:

- write a reflection on your practice every day;
- take time to observe children at play and ask yourself whether your involvement is necessary;
- look for opportunities to challenge your beliefs about children's play;
- talk to someone about the nature of your playwork practices;
- offer to be a mentor;
- model your practices to someone else and listen to their feedback;
- tell the stories about your practice through any media you are happy with, use written forms, video, pictures;
- be intuitive and watch yourself to understand how intuition works for you.

Read your reflections six months later and re-reflect.

Part 2

The play environment

11

STUART LESTER
Play and the play stage

This chapter explores considerations for developing effective play spaces for children. The ideas presented here are something of a challenge to much of the prevailing orthodoxy of planning for play that focuses on the actions of the playworker in designing and delivering structured activities for children and representing this through a rigid plan that predicts these activities over a period of time. The following is an attempt to introduce a planning process in tune with a playwork perspective.

Open and closed spaces

A starting point to this brief exploration is Sibley's (1995) analysis of open and closed spaces. According to Sibley, a 'closed (or purified) space' represents a strongly defined space where there are clear boundaries and internal homogeneity, where there are prevailing norms and values, and an expectation that everyone aspires to and fits in with these. A failure to do so is a signal of deviancy. Within this space, the rituals and rules reveal and celebrate hierarchy and dominance, determined and maintained by prohibitions and directions. The use of the space becomes highly ordained and defined, perhaps typified by the naming of areas in play spaces (e.g. the quiet corner or the arts and crafts table). Smith and Barker's study of play in after-school provision found that most play activities on offer were planned by adult staff and represented 'an example of the inequitable distribution of power between children and adults inherent to the vast majority of clubs taking part in the research' (2000: 248).

Sibley (1995) contrasts this with '*open space*', where spaces are weakly defined with fuzzy and movable boundaries characterized by social mixing and diversity. This is a fluid space where difference and diversity in culture, identity and activity are accepted and understood as the natural order. Such spaces are 'open' by being sites where space and things have not been named and determined, but provide a site of possibilities and ambiguity.

An open space represents a place for 'provocation and confrontation, dissensus and indocility, complexity and diversity, uncertainty and ambivalence' (Moss and Petrie 2002: 110).

Children's play as performance

In extending this, it is useful at this stage to introduce the idea of children's play as 'performance' (Schechner 2003). Guss (2005) sees children's play as the sensory, sensual, mind–body connection that goes into imagining, forming and enacting roles and dramatic situations; a collaborative reflective process. Schechner (1988: 16) observes, 'Playing is a mood, an attitude, a force ... It may persist for a fairly long time – as specific games, rites, and artistic performances do – or it comes and goes suddenly – a wisecrack, an ironic glimpse of things, a bend or crack in behaviour'. Schechner's analysis portrays play as transformational, often irrational and protean in character, the player can 'pretend almost anything and connect almost anything with anything else' (Sutton-Smith 1997: 61).

In developing their play dramas, children must become co-playwrights, co-directors, co-actors, narrator, choreographer/dancer, composer/musician, sound designer, and props person within their play performances. The creation of make-believe plots proceeds on an invent-as-you-go principle held together by a mix of negotiations and actions (Bretherton 1989; Guss 2005).

The play setting as a stage

Appreciating children's play as performance, an adult-organized play space represents a stage or theatrical space for acting out. We should recognize that this is always going to be structured. Just as a theatre will have a stage and props, there is always an element of artificiality within the confines of the play space. Guss (2005) comments on the apparent weak position of children and their play culture within adult cultural hegemony. Thus, for many play settings, the stage becomes a *closed space* in which the children's performances are subservient to adult values – a form of theatre that is highly stylized and managed; in which lines and actions are learned and rehearsed according to the given script, where actors are directed and movements are prescribed, even though this still requires considerable 'artistry' on behalf of the actor, and a set time pattern is imposed (Schechner 2003).

This contrasts with an *open space* in which individual actors develop their own characters according to their inner feelings and ideas and in response to the cues from other actors and the physical props. Here the play is emergent and improvized, although there will be a containment of the dramatic improvizations through agreed conventions as the play develops, what Sutton-Smith (1997: 195) refers to as the 'language of play ... its framings, its rituals and its stylisation in speech and gesture as well as in action'. This is a liminal space (Turner 1982), an 'in-between' space that is open to all kinds of possibilities and by means of performing could become anywhere. Here time becomes symbolic, the events of the drama take as long as they need to unfold and shift.

Developing this theme, and drawing on the work of Boal (1995), we may find this liminal play space is not simply a physical stage but an aesthetic space that is subjectively created by the players. Open play space provides a stage for acting out, becoming a highly complex and detailed microcosm for children's histories, emotions and desires. On stage, gestures become larger than life, the language becomes more dramatic and objects take on greater significance. Children's play fantasies do not simply replicate the real world, nor just act as therapeutic escape, but build another virtual world that exists alongside mundane reality and carries on its own kind of life, a life much more emotionally vivid (Sutton-Smith 1997).

As in all theatrical productions, we should recognize that children's play will inherently contain dramatic tension. Boal (1995) invites us to imagine going to watch a play in which all the characters are nice to each other, compliant, good-looking and well mannered, and everybody lives happily ever after – not much of a plot and a boring spectacle!

The role of the playworker

Playworkers are directors and performers on the play stage; people who are conscious of using the language, passions, and behaviours associated with children's play to support the emergence of playful dramas and to this end are better equipped to act on an open play stage. Just as children manage multiple artistic functions in producing their play, we find the playworker engaged in adopting dramatic positions to enhance children's playful improvizations.

Planning, in this sense, becomes making preparations for the play and preparing ourselves for the supporting role – the *spectactor*[1] (Boal 1995) on the play stage. The central character of the playworker is developed through a reflective role that may incorporate:

- **Rehearsals** – a recapturing of our spirit of playfulness as an essential part of our character in supporting children's play that clearly acknowledges the nature and purpose of our work; a warming-up to the task at hand and celebration of the value of our role.
- **Using memory and imagination** – using our own memories of playing, both as children and as adults in the play space, not as the basis for replication but as an empathetic process identifying with the landscape and the characters that act upon this stage.
- **Prologues** – the opportunity for playworkers to talk to each other prior to the start of play. The focus for such preparatory conversations is to establish the current overall feel of the space; what themes are children currently engaged with in their play; what are the prevailing emotions on display?
- **Scene setters** – our understanding of play and the nature of attractive play spaces lead us to consider what elements/props are available to support the play and how these might be arranged. We should acknowledge that the playworker themselves may, at times, become a resource within the stage, and they can be a subtle signpost to possibilities and 'permissions' to extend the play.

- **Observation** – taking an observer\spectator role and using these to make impressions of the play; snapshots and patterns of movement and feelings at any given time.
- **Prompts and provocations** – there may be times when lines are forgotten, or improvizations become stuck in an increasingly destructive cycle. Our appreciation of this will arise from a combination of the above actions – an awareness of subtle shifts in the prevailing feel and dialogue with others to express our feelings about such shifts. Our intention at this point may be to intervene to shift the focus of the drama and to redirect the play.
- **Epilogues and postscripts** – examining our thoughts and feelings about children's play following a play session; examining our actions and how they impact on the players; replaying significant events and recapturing some of the existential dilemmas encountered in the play space.

Summary

An *open* play stage offers children 'space and liberty to take control: to question, to speak for themselves, to represent, transform and define themselves, and to choose and to reach the aesthetic effect that satisfies their imaginations and complex wishes' (Guss 2005: 240). We need to be mindful of our responsibility to encourage and support such playful expressions through the development of our playwork character and associated performance within this space.

Note

[1] Boal uses this hybrid word to describe the simultaneous role of observer and actor.

12

TIM GILL

If you go down to the woods today: why nature and adventure matter to children and young people

Take a few seconds to remember your favourite place to play as a child. Where was that special place? What did it look like? How did it smell?

The chances are, it was out of doors. It was away from adults, and it was a 'wild' place – not truly wild perhaps, but unkempt, dirty, and quite possibly a little bit dangerous. Even the UK's current breed of allegedly battery-reared, celebrity-fed techno-kids would, given the chance, rather be outside meeting their mates and mucking about than stuck indoors surfing the Net (CPC 2006). Parents too say they want their children to spend more time out of doors (NFPI 2003). Yet children are disappearing from the outdoors at a rate that would make them top of any conservationist's list of endangered species, if they were any other member of the animal kingdom (Hillman et al. 1990).

What's more, evidence is growing that the outdoor 'play-deprived' child is likely to grow up (1) physically, (2) mentally, (3) emotionally stunted, and (4) ill prepared for the adult world.

Starting with health, everyone agrees: playing out keeps children thinner. Even the government's own 2004 public health White Paper accepts that the lack of outdoor play is one of the main causes of childhood obesity (DoH 2004). One leading US Government expert claims that play may be the 'magic bullet' for obesity, saying in a *British Medical Journal* editorial that 'opportunities for spontaneous play may be the only requirement that young children need to increase their physical activity' (Dietz 2001: 313–14).

The physical benefits of outdoor play should come as no surprise. What's more remarkable is the growing evidence of the benefits of outdoor and natural settings to children's mental health and emotional well-being. For instance, studies on children with Attention Deficit Hyperactivity Disorder have shown that green outdoor spaces not only foster creative play and improve interactions with adults but they also relieve the symptoms of the disorder (Taylor et al. 2001).

In 1999 the Mental Health Foundation warned of the dangers of overprotecting children and stopping them from developing their own coping mechanisms (Mental Health Foundation 1999). Researchers have found a link between children who become victims of bullying and the protectiveness of their parents (Champion et al. 2003). It is suggested that 'battery-reared' children lack confidence as they grow up and become more vulnerable to bullying.

Natural places cannot be made entirely safe. They are unpredictable, ever changing, and prone to the randomness of nature and the vagaries of the weather. But far from being a problem, the uncertainty and variation inherent in natural settings is part of what attracts us to them in the first place. Indeed in evolutionary terms, it is the unsurpassed ability of *homo sapiens* to adjust to changes in our habitat that has, for better or worse, led us to be the dominant species on the planet, which means that a bit of danger and uncertainty is actually good for you. Bringing it back to children's play, the Danish landscape architect Helle Nebelong – creator of some wonderful natural public spaces in Copenhagen – puts it like this:

> I am convinced that 'risk-free', standardised playgrounds are dangerous ...
> When the distance between all the rungs on the climbing net or the ladder is
> exactly the same, the child has no need to concentrate on where he puts his feet
> ... This does not prepare him for all the knobby and asymmetrical forms he is
> likely to be confronted with outside the playground and throughout life.
>
> (2004: 30)

But there's more to outdoor play than learning and health. American writer and parenting expert Richard Louv (2005) argues in a recent book that it is the immediacy, depth and unboundedness of unstructured outdoor play that gives the nature–child encounter most meaning.

Just why is the decline in children's outdoor experiences happening? The root causes lie in changes to the very fabric of their lives over the last 30 years or so. An exponential growth in road traffic, alongside poor town planning and shifts in the make-up and daily rhythms of families and communities, have left children with fewer outdoor places to go and fewer friendly faces looking out for them. These changes coincided with – some would say fed into – the growth of what sociologist Frank Furedi (2002) calls a 'culture of fear', that is, a generalized anxiety that has found fertile ground in turn-of-the-millennium families, even though children are statistically more safe from harm now than at any point in human history.

Successive governments must bear some of the blame, through planning policies that relentlessly favour cars over communities and profit over people: in racetrack streets, in estates devoid of attractive parks and green spaces, and in town plans that wed families to their cars forever. There is no doubt that traffic danger, unlike stranger danger, is a real threat to children and a legitimate worry for parents. Around 100 child pedestrians are killed every year, a figure that puts the UK near the bottom of Europe's child road safety league (DfT 2002). It is no surprise that government figures show a steady fall in children walking or cycling over the last 20 years or more, to the extent that while over 90 per cent of children own a bike, just 2 per cent cycle to school (Gill 2005).

In a textbook demonstration of the mechanisms of the market, these physical, economic and social changes and fears have been exploited by the leisure and entertainment industries, manufacturers and advertisers, whose services, products and messages both reinforce the logic of keeping children virtual prisoners, and compel us to compensate them in the only way our cash-rich, time-poor society seems to know: by spending money on them.

Time is surely running out for those who want to re-engage children with the outdoors. Official government figures say that 1 in 3 children aged 8 to 10 never play out without an adult watching over them (Farmer 2005). Research by Mayer Hillman and colleagues (1990) suggests that, in a single generation, the 'home habitat' of a typical 8-year old (the area in which children are able to travel on their own) has shrunk to one-ninth of its former size. We face the prospect that a generation of children will grow up at best indifferent to, at worst terrified of, the world outside their homes, and will then as adults pass on their fear of the outdoors to their own children – the phenomenon known as *environmental generational amnesia* (Kahn 2002), discussed in greater detail by Natalie Baxter in Chapter 13.

How can this dismal future be avoided? We need to take steps to loosen children's cages and extend their territory. My action plan for outdoor play would start with the spaces and places children find themselves in every day: playgrounds, parks, and streets. We need to put our efforts into creating neighbourhood spaces where children can get down and dirty in natural outdoor settings, free of charge and on a daily basis. That's exactly what the authorities are doing in the German city of Freiburg, where the parks department has stopped installing sterile playgrounds full of tubular steel, primary coloured plastic and expensive rubber surfacing, and has instead been creating 'nature playgrounds' that are a bit more, well, earthy: diverse spaces with mounds, ditches, logs, fallen trees, boulders, bushes, wild flowers and dirt.

The UK is light-years behind Freiburg and for that matter much of Northern Europe. But even here, a 'movement for real play' is spreading. In Newcastle, local residents organized a 'den day' in one park to introduce children to the joys of shelter building. In Scotland, Stirling Council is creating natural play spaces across the authority. In the South West of England 'Wild About Play', an environmental play project, is supporting hundreds of playworkers and environmental educators by sharing playful ideas for outdoor activities. In Cambridge, Bath, Haringey and elsewhere that near-extinct species, the park keeper, is appearing in a new guise, whereby specially trained 'play rangers' run playful activities at set times, helping to build up usage, familiarity and ultimately ownership of these spaces.

Exciting outdoor environments are all very well, but children have to be able to get to them. Streets are (or were) the starting point for so many of children's independent outdoor adventures, and with traffic rising every year, the prospects for reclaiming them may look bleak. But green shoots of hope are springing up amidst the gloom. Some communities have worked with local councils to create 'home zones': people-friendly streets based on continental designs, where the streetspace is transformed from a car corridor to a shared social space. Having been part of the original campaign to introduce home zones to the UK a decade ago, I recently surveyed around 40 schemes to find out their impact. Over half reported more children walking, cycling and playing in the street (Gill 2006).

Giving children more freedoms also means facing up to our fears and chipping away at the free-floating anxiety that can so easily beset us. For instance, in the UK we have become completely paranoid about the threat to children from strangers. Fewer than one child in a million is killed by a stranger each year. Over ten times as many children are killed by cars, and around five times as many by their own parents or relatives (Thomas and Hocking 2003). Yet on the mercifully rare occasions when the worst does happen, the headline that greets us is 'No Child Is Safe'. It's time we rose up en masse and showed this fear for what it is: scaremongering.

Too many children spend far too much time stuck in front of TV screens, not so much couch potatoes as couch prisoners. Too many of the streets where children live have become the sole domain of the car. For too long children's outdoor play has been haunted by the spectre of the predatory paedophile and the fast-moving car. All this is a disaster for anyone who wants to bring freedom, adventure and nature back into the daily rhythms of children's lives. Surely it's about time we all recognized the value of allowing children truly to get to grips with the natural world. Just as we all did when we were young.

13

NATALIE BAXTER
Playwork and the environment

When reflecting on my childhood, my most positive memories of play took place in the outdoor environment. I can vividly recall wading in the stream, picking berries, rolling in the leaves, building dens in the undergrowth, collecting snails and drawing on the pavement with stones. Despite the modern child still desiring outdoor play and contact with nature (Playday 2006), there has been an increasing amount of literature written alluding to a dramatic decrease in children's access to these opportunities in comparison to generations past (e.g. Rivkin 1995; Hillman 1999; Ouvry 2000; Gill 2004; Playday 2006). But why are outdoor play and contact with nature important to children and the environment and how will restrictions affect them?

Positive benefits of outdoor play and contact with nature

The outdoor environment as a playspace can have numerous benefits for children with regard to development. Often when describing play in natural habitats, geographical forms such as hills, banks and rocks form part of the play frame. This variety of materials can be incorporated into the child's play and provide opportunities to climb, run, jump and throw, which aid physical skills and coordination (Fjortoft 2001), and also offer opportunities for risk and challenge. The environment is also variable with regards to seasons, vegetation, terrains and weather. This makes the outdoors a flexible environment (Naylor 1986). Wilson (1995) asserts that these varied opportunities can be a catalyst for development in all areas of the child. Play in 'wild' places is ideal for exploratory play, with earth, water, leaves, twigs and stones being used as play artefacts. Through play with these loose parts (Nicholson 1971), creativity, inventiveness and the potentiality of discovery can be explored.

Although children may play in the outdoor environment alone, more frequently it will take the form of social play with friends and siblings. As the outdoors is larger than that of the indoor environment, more people can be involved, making it a socially engaging experience (Naylor 1986), which allows children to test power relationships, social rules and customs through cooperation (Yeatman and Reifel 1992). Children learn about their surroundings through active engagement with their environment. The skills of mental mapping can be developed as children walk and play in their neighbourhood, using alternate routes, discovering shortcuts and identifying landmarks. Trimble (1994) and Christensen (2003) suggest that through the process of mental mapping in conjunction with independent mobility, children are able to construct a deep understanding of their environment, its shapes, textures and structures.

Having outlined some of the benefits of outdoor play and contact with nature it is essential to explore how restrictions in this domain might affect children and the environment.

Erosion of outdoor play and its effects on children and the environment

There are a number of factors that have contributed to the decline in children's outdoor play and contact with the natural environment. These include parental fears with regard to strangers, traffic and personal injury, society's negative view of children's visibility in the public arena, diminishing play spaces, advances in technology, the demographics of family life and media influence. So what are the implications of this for children, their play and the natural environment?

It is arguable that modern society tends to prefer 'battery children' (Huttenmoser and Degan-Zimmermann 1995) or 'indoor, invisible children' (Hill and Tisdall 1997). Gill (2004) argues that this phenomenon could have a negative impact on children's emotional, social, physical and cognitive abilities. If children are constantly confined to an indoor environment then this may also lead to 'play bias'. Hughes (2003: 68) describes play bias as 'a loading of play in one area of experience or another' which can have a profound effect on brain development in children. He further suggests that if children have limited or unchallenging play experiences they may suffer from negative brain plasticity and thus the brain will fail to reach its optimum size and this can result in violent and aggressive behaviour by the child.

It could also be argued that limiting children's opportunities to engage with their environment may lead to a negative cycle in the process of compound flexibility (Figure 13.1). Brown (2003b) describes the consequences of a negative cycle as potentially damaging to individual and species development.

There are a number of theorists who have postulated how the environment might be affected by restricting children's access to the natural environment. Sebba (1991) and Wilson (2002) both suggest that engulfing children in indoor surroundings will result in a psychological and physical detachment from the environment, with children developing a fault-finding and analytical attitude in place of an appreciative and accommodating one. Thomas and Thompson (2004) discovered that children are suffering the loss of their bond with the natural environment and that future environmental problems will not be addressed as a result of the diminishing access of free play for children within their local habitats.

Figure 13.1 Compound flexibility: a negative cycle

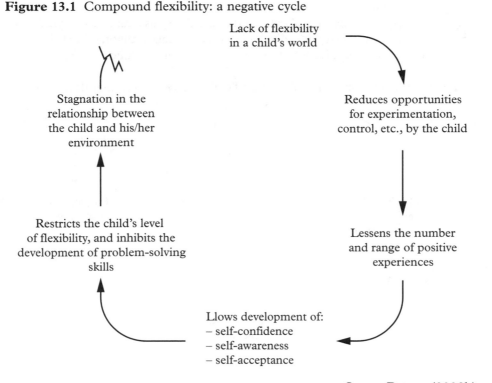

Lack of flexibility
in a child's world

Reduces opportunities
for experimentation,
control, etc., by the child

Stagnation in the
relationship between
the child and his/her
environment

Lessens the number
and range of positive
experiences

Restricts the child's level
of flexibility, and inhibits the
development of problem-solving
skills

Llows development of:
– self-confidence
– self-awareness
– self-acceptance

Source: Brown (2003b).

Wilson (1984) claims that a lack of contact with the natural environment will result in 'biophilia' being replaced by 'biophobia', that is to say that rather than having an affiliation with nature, children will express an aversion to natural things and instead seek out man-made environments, structures and play materials. Orr (1994) further suggests that 'biophobia' will result in a deficiency of the brain in the critical dimension of creativity and comprehension.

Kahn (2002) suggests that society is suffering from 'environmental generational amnesia'. He explains how during childhood we construct an idea of the norm of our natural environment. This construct is then used as a measurement for 'environmental degradation' in the future. As we move through the generations, the amount of 'environmental degradation' increases and the new generation takes this new state as the norm. He suggests that this acceptance of environmental destruction will result in long-term physical and psychological harm to society.

Pyle (1993, 2002) proposes the theory of 'extinction of experience'. The hypothesis assumes that regular association with a combination of experiences will lead to a high regard for a rich setting. Subsequently if there is a reduction in variety in everyday environments replaced by banality, we may become complacent and ignorant with regards to the diversity of the world. Pyle purports that this has a knock-on effect leading to less variety and more destitute environments, thus producing a cycle whereby impoverishment generates greater impoverishment. This theory has some resonance with Brown's theory of Compound Flexibility (1989). If we reverse Brown's theoretical cycle and apply Pyle's assumptions of the extinction of experience to society in general, then we can suggest that the inflexible environment will have a negative effect on the flexibility of the child (see Figure 13.2)

Figure 13.2 Child's attempt to use an inflexible environment in a flexible way

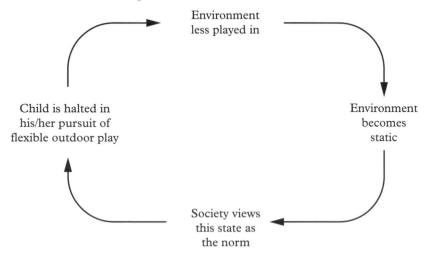

The role of playwork

While we can highlight the potential effects on children and the environment, it is important to identify ways in which playwork can redress the balance. At the heart of playwork is the adventure playground movement. Originally described as junk playgrounds by Sorensen in 1931, their very design and ethos facilitate positive experience in the outdoor environment. Many provide opportunities to create and adapt structures and provide access to play with natural elements and tools, including building fires, climbing trees, water play, digging earth and creating weapons thus facilitating the drive for recapitulative play (Hughes 2001a).

Recently there has been an emergence of exciting projects focusing on children's play in 'wild spaces' (Wild About Play 2004). The aim of these projects is to promote the learning and development of children through their play while exploring and playing freely in the natural environment. Other playwork initiatives have included the introduction of mobile and street play projects, each seeking to provide positive play experiences for children in their local neighbourhoods and creating social interaction between adults and children thus portraying a more positive image of children on the street. We are also beginning to see changes with regards to the designs of fixed-equipment playgrounds with the emergence of more natural materials such as wood, water and planting being used in place of large brightly coloured metal and concrete structures.

Following the 2004 'Getting Serious About Play' review commissioned by the Department of Culture Media and Sport, local authorities throughout the UK are currently developing a more focused approach to play through the development of play strategies. These strategies include audits of all current play provision and opportunity, and will highlight informal outdoor play spaces such as woodlands, green spaces and derelict areas. Guidance also stresses the importance of involving planning, parks, transport, housing departments, the voluntary sector and children, all of which can contribute to the improvement of and access to outdoor play spaces.

Conclusion

By constraining children in their pursuit of outdoor play and contact with nature, we are looking at the prospect of creating a generation of children who are limited in flexible experiences and apathetic with regards to the environment in which they live. The evidence suggests that if we continue to restrict children's pursuit of outdoor play, the environment in which they live will become more destitute and deprived, resulting in psychological harm to society. As playworkers concerned with children's general well-being, we must challenge the current beliefs and actions and enable children to claim their right to outdoor space. If we fail to do this, future generations of children and the environment may suffer.

14

MARK GLADWIN
The concept of risk in play and playwork

The way that playworkers think and behave about risk is one of the things that make playwork a distinct style of adult interaction with children. Playworkers challenge the dominant view that adults' primary responsibility to children is to ensure their physical safety. Playworkers argue that our desire to protect children from harm must be balanced against children's need to play freely and to experiment with risk; that it is indeed possible for children to be 'too safe for their own good' (Lindon 2003).

Although 'risk' is sometimes used as a synonym for 'hazard', the two terms have quite different meanings. A hazard is any feature of the physical or social environment that is capable of causing physical or emotional harm. It can be objectively described. Risk, on the other hand, has been defined as the product of the probability and the utility of a possible future event (Adams 1996). Thus an assessment of risk contains two separate judgements: how likely is it that something will happen, and what are the likely consequences if it does? While these consequences might theoretically be good or bad, in everyday talk, 'risk' usually has a negative connotation. One of the paradoxes of play, to which we will return, is that in play, risk can become a good to be pursued for its own sake. But whether risk has negative or positive connotations, both parts of the risk assessment are subjective: people differ, both in their estimation of the likelihood of a future event, and in their evaluation of its consequences.

In the dominant paradigm where risk is a 'bad' to be avoided, three historical stages of risk management may be distinguished. In the first, pre-modern stage, the causes of many risks remain obscure and they are therefore ascribed to fate or some supernatural cause. All humans can do is to carry out whatever propitiatory rituals are decreed by their belief systems. Avoiding risk is down to luck or divine favour.

In the second, modern stage, risk is objectified. The causes of many risks are scientifically identified and societal strategies of risk reduction are adopted. The fact that some people show poor risk management skills does not invalidate this approach. Cognitive scientists like Richards and Rowe (1999) have investigated the psychological and social factors affecting the way that different people estimate risks.

In the third, post-modern stage, the notion of risk as an objective phenomenon weakens. Authors like Douglas (1992) see risk as a social construct, developed to maintain cultural purity by policing the boundaries between acceptable and unacceptable behaviour. The selection of some contingencies, and not others, as risky, thus varies between cultures. Adult attitudes to pre-schoolers' tool use in the UK and Denmark provide an example of this phenomenon. During a recent study visit by Bradford playwork and early years professionals to an early years setting in Denmark, 4-year-old children were observed using saws and small axes to chop wood to add to the communal fire. The Danish early years workers saw nothing exceptional in this, whereas the English early years workers were amazed.

'Risk society' theorists like Giddens (1991) and Beck (1992) do not entirely de-objectify risk, but see risk management as intimately related to aspects of late-modern social structure. Risk is globalized, but its management is privatized. People focus less on the achievement of 'goods', which are taken for granted, than on the avoidance of 'bads', which are ill defined but ever present.

No matter how risks come to be selected as objects of social concern, within the dominant paradigm of risk avoidance, people still face the daily psychic task of risk management. Douglas and Wildavsky (1982) propose a typology of risk management styles around the dimensions of personal autonomy and group identification, yielding four ideal types as shown in Table 14.1.

Table 14.1: Risk management styles

Personal Autonomy	Group identification	
	High	Low
High	Egalitarians	Individualists
Low	Hierarchists	Fatalists

Source: adapted from Douglas and Wildarsky (1982).

Douglas and Wildavsky suggest that hierarchists seek to manage risks by adhering to official rules, while egalitarians prefer to seek group support in a democratic pooling of risks. Individualists take responsibility and make personal decisions about risk, but fatalists, in contrast, see themselves as powerless and accept whatever comes. Examples of all these risk management styles may be found among children in play settings.

Play, however, is one of the arenas where the dominant paradigm of risk avoidance sometimes gives way to an alternative paradigm of voluntary risk taking – a phenomenon confirmed daily in the media and many people's personal experience, as well as by authors such as Lupton (1998), who argues that over-regulation of individual behaviour causes stress that can be alleviated through the excitement of risk taking. Elsewhere Lupton (1999) suggests that risk taking contributes to self-actualization, and that people try to reach their own personal 'risk equilibrium' between excesses of uncertainty and predictability.

The equilibrium concept of risk taking has close affinities with the neural arousal theory of play adopted by authors such as Ellis (1973), who sees play as the result of a drive state caused by sub-optimal arousal levels. This arousal model of play is implicit in Sutton-Smith and Kelly-Byrne's (1984) development of the concept of play cues, subsequently built on by Sturrock and Else (1998) in their elaboration of the play cycle.

Hughes (2001a) sees the significance of playful risk taking in somewhat different terms. His concept of 'deep play' – one of a number of 'play types' or sub-drives within the general play drive – involves the deliberate and conscious exercise of risky behaviour as children's psycho-dynamic means of coming to terms with growing consciousness of their own mortality and cosmic insignificance.

Both Ellis (1973) and Hughes (2001a) argue further that the arousal drive, of which play and risk taking are manifestations, has had evolutionary consequences for humans, enabling them to evolve as a genotype favouring novel and flexible behaviour. Such behaviour leads to the acquisition of information and skills that are useful in coping with novel circumstances, and thus contribute to natural selection. The genetic predisposition is fine-tuned in playful individuals through the reinforcement of effective responses and the extinction of ineffective ones.

Given this theoretical interest, empirical studies of children's playful risk taking are surprisingly rare, perhaps because of the difficulty of identifying what constitutes risk for individual players. Green (1997) examined children's perceptions of risk in non-play contexts, while Gordon (1999) invited adult subjects to recollect experiences of playful childhood risk taking. My own small study at one adventure playground found evidence to support the Douglas and Wildavsky (1982) typology of risk-management styles (Gladwin 2005). I also suggested that playful risk taking can be classified and scored on four dimensions of content, context, motive and affect as shown in Table 14.2.

Two ideal types emerge from this matrix. 'Reluctant' risk takers score mostly 1s: they take the risks they must, in order to maintain status within the group, but derive no great pleasure from doing so. 'Enthusiastic' risk takers score mostly 5s: they are strongly drawn to risk taking and gain emotional reinforcement from it. Observation at the playground also suggested other varieties of playful risk taking such as

- maintenance of group solidarity through shared enactment of risk taking in an atmosphere of mutual support;
- simulated risk taking within a play frame that largely removes actual risk;
- and skilful, instrumental management of risk in relation to adult sanctions or peer disapproval.

Table 14.2: Risk profiling matrix

Dimension	Score	1	2	3	4	5	
CONTENT	Social						Physical
CONTEXT	Convivial						Solitary
MOTIVE	Instrumental						Autonomous
AFFECT	Reluctant						Enthusiastic

Source: Gladwin (2005).

In summary, there are three reasons why children need to experience playful risk taking. The first is that children need to practise risk management skills if they are not to be practically and emotionally disadvantaged. The second reason, advanced by Hughes (2001a) is that children risk psychological damage if they do not experience risk and thereby confront their own mortality and cosmic insignificance. The third reason is my own suggestion that risk taking is an important element in making and maintaining children's social relationships (Gladwin 2005).

It is now widely accepted that risk taking is an essential part of play, and that attempts to overprotect children are harmful to their physical and emotional adjustment. Best Play (NPFA 2000), Lindon (2003), the Play Safety Forum (2004) and the National Occupational Standards for Playwork (SkillsActive 2005a) all exemplify this standpoint, which has also become commonplace in media comment.

Play providers must therefore approach risk management differently from, say, highways engineers, whose aim is to reduce risk of injury as closely as possible to zero (although the achievement of this aim in practice is subject to a cost benefit analysis weighing the number of additional lives saved against the cost – financial and political – of additional risk reduction measures). Play providers also need to assess the likelihood and severity of possible injury, but against this they must set the play value of the activity, which includes its capacity to satisfy children's arousal drives.

Children can only set their personal risk thermostats by trial and error. Hence the paradox: nobody wants a child to be injured, yet a playground where no accidents ever happen is unlikely to be meeting children's play needs. The aim of risk management in playwork therefore cannot be to reduce risk to the lowest achievable level. Yet play providers' perceptions of risk aversion in wider society have created a fear of litigation that makes a balanced approach to risk management hard to achieve. Happily, there are signs that public attitudes are changing. The view that risk taking is an essential part of life has been publicly espoused by the Royal Society for the Prevention of Accidents (2005) and the Health & Safety Executive (HSE 2006). Playworkers must help to build this new consensus through a confident, professional approach to risk management in play.

15

MICK CONWAY
Quality in play: underpinning thoughts

The first quality assurance system for childcare providers was *Aiming High* (Farley and Williams 1992), which was created to help providers meet the requirements of the Children Act 1989. While a good start, its focus was mainly on management and operational systems, reflecting the priorities of the inspection regime in place at the time.

In 1996, when I was director of Hackney Play Association (HPA), the local authority proposed to move from grant aid and direct funding to a service level agreement model for play services, with quality assurance as part of the monitoring process. It was eventually agreed that we would create a play-specific system because *Aiming High* and other proposed or available systems didn't have a specific focus on children's play.

We ran a series of workshops with playworkers from a variety of provisions to ensure that the play needs of children were met. To avoid reinventing the wheel, we quickly agreed that the system would be based on the UN Convention on the Rights of the Child (UNICEF 1991) and the Playwork Assumptions and Values (SPRITO 1992). It would incorporate the emerging play concepts such as play types, play cues, returns and frames being developed by Bob Hughes, Perry Else, Gordon Sturrock and others, and would focus on how providers could show that their practice was centred on children playing and on what difference this made to their well-being. By putting children at the centre and focusing on outcomes, we were years ahead of the *Every Child Matters* agenda.

Towards the end of our workshops a playworker asked me to explain just what 'quality assurance system' meant. After several weeks of hard thought and head scratching I came up with this:

- *Quality* is providing good play opportunities, and continuously improving what you do by using standards – statements setting out benchmarks for quality.
- *Assurance* is building confidence in users, staff, management and funders by checking your practice – day-to-day operation and longer-term planning.

- *System* is breaking it down into quality areas and indicators ('do-able chunks'), collecting and reviewing *evidence* – written documents and other records showing how your practice meets the standards.

Splitting something so essentially holistic as children's play provision into discrete quality areas in some ways ran counter to everything we believed, but we needed those do-able chunks. We tried to make sure that quality areas and indicators came at similar issues from different angles to encourage providers to think about how the core children's play needs linked to and were impacted on by management and operational issues like health and safety, or training and continual professional development.

For example one provider involved children in reviewing the rules of their play centre, which had an outdoor area, a large hall, a soft play room, a chill-out room, a computer suite and a kitchen. The children questioned why there was one set of rules for the different spaces, and came up with different rules more appropriate for each area – running and making noise and mess was fine outside and in the large hall, but not in the computer suite or chill-out area. Through this simple process, the provider covered elements of six quality areas: personal and physical health and safety; a warm and welcoming environment; choice and range of activities; children's involvement; behavioural boundaries and managing resources.

We wanted the system to be robust but to avoid an over-prescriptive 'if it is not compulsory it is forbidden' approach. We used the concept of 'good enough rather than perfection' with three levels of achievement to ensure that small play projects with few resources weren't set up to fail, and that those demonstrating good practice or excellence would have their achievement recognized.

We also kept in mind the realities of three actual projects. One was a small private sector after-school and holiday play club based in a scout hall. The hall was used in the later evenings by a strict faith group and often hired out for functions, which restricted what they could do. Another was a school-based play centre where there were tensions between what the playworkers and the head teacher (and more importantly, a grumpy school-keeper) thought was appropriate. Putting new play concepts into practice in the school's gym, classroom and sterile tarmac playground was not easy. The third was a voluntary sector open-access adventure playground that was a model of good practice in enabling children to control the content and intent of their play, but struggled with management and sustainable funding.

In those days there wasn't the broad consensus on terminology and concepts that we mostly have today. For example 'free play' seemed to mean something different to just about everyone, so we used 'spontaneous play' instead to describe children's unmediated play to distinguish it from organized play opportunities which we called 'planned activities'. We included a brief introduction to key play concepts such as play types, loose parts, play cues, returns and frames along with a glossary of terms.

Accredited providers at every level have since told us that *Quality in Play* (QiP) has helped them keep children's play as their prime focus during a period of upheaval as the childcare agenda came to dominate funding and Ofsted inspections in some cases threatened their very survival. They said that having the emerging play concepts, a focus on the play needs of children, and the management and operational issues in support of them, brought together in one place, helped to organize their policy and practice around children's play needs, and articulate and defend the play ethos within a compliance regime which had little interest in or knowledge of play.

London Play was set up in 1998, and one of their first projects was to obtain funding to subcontract HPA to pilot *Quality in Play* in a variety of types of provision in nine London boroughs, and revise it for publication. As a result of the pilot we made some minor changes to the quality indicators and levels and added a new area on working with families and the community. We also learned that providers needed help – just giving them the manual and expecting them to get on with it wasn't going to work, but we weren't sure how to deliver the help they needed. There was also growing demand from Early Years Development and Childcare Partnerships (and to our surprise, from play providers) for *Quality in Play* to move from a self-assessment to an external accreditation model.

London Play decided to provide a mentor training programme for development and support workers who could incorporate quality assurance mentoring in their existing roles, and for playworkers, playwork trainers and others who wanted to develop and use their skills to support play projects. It also set up an external assessment and accreditation system, training mentors to become assessors and creating an accreditation panel made up of play and quality assurance experts.

Around this time the government became concerned about the number and variability of quality assurance systems, particularly after one collapsed, and announced Investors in Children (IiC) as a national scheme to benchmark and endorse quality assurance systems against a set of criteria. The intention (which did not become clear until the consultation document on the Childcare Bill was published in 2005) was that only a handful of schemes would succeed, but in the event 48, including *Quality in Play*, were endorsed. The government decided to withdraw direct support for IiC, and funded the National Children's Bureau to develop a sector-led quality assurance endorsement scheme. At the time of writing it is unclear what form this will take, and London Play and Play England are discussing how to develop *Quality in Play* as a national programme, whatever the outcome.

How Quality in Play is delivered in practice

London Play manages the programme, distributes the *Quality in Play* manuals, provides mentor and assessor training and e-groups where they can post questions and answers. It maintains a database of accredited providers, web pages containing a free downloadable provider pack setting out details of the process, frequently asked questions and other information at: www.londonplay.org.uk/quality-in-play.

The process starts with providers using the *Quality in Play* manual and provider pack to self-assess their practice against the standards by building a portfolio of evidence showing how they say what they do (clear aims, good internal and external information, policies and procedures) and do what they say (plan, do, review, evaluate and reflect) as an audit trail of how they have gone through the quality process.

We have found that providers who used the portfolio at regular staff, management, or monitoring meetings to work on quality areas as they went along rather than as an extra chore, found that this reduced rather than increased workloads.

Several have successfully used the portfolio as an evidence base for funding applications by identifying gaps or demonstrating their capacity to deliver good services. One small provider used portfolio analysis of the children's involvement, choice and range of activities, managing finance and resources quality areas to obtain funding to develop their kitchen and train staff in food handling and hygiene to provide healthy cooked snacks and develop a soft play area.

Mentors are 'critical friends' who help providers work through the process, but don't do the work for them, and help providers decide which level to aim for, ensuring that those going for Level 2 or 3 show that they meet all the requirements of lower levels. They are not employed or deployed by London Play and make their own arrangements with providers, usually as part of their existing role, or in some cases as freelancers. They work in a variety of ways: one-to-one sessions with the individual provider lead person or staff and management teams; group sessions where providers come together to share ideas; and with play service managers in local authorities or other agencies where management functions are centralized.

We frequently found a disconnection between management systems and practice on the ground. For example, the play environment audit quality area was problematic for many providers. As well as looking at the physical play environment, it required supervision and appraisal to incorporate understandings of the play concepts. There were two problems: an almost complete lack of supervision and appraisal at playworker level and, where it existed, at management level, play understandings just didn't feature. This is a continuing problem, and illustrates the need to look at play provision in the round, not just at service delivery level.

Assessors are mentors who have been further trained and are paid and deployed by London Play to ensure they are independent of and have no personal or other interest in the providers they assess. They assess through a site visit to look at the portfolio of evidence and talk to staff and management, then observe what happens when the children are playing and talk to them and parents. They write an accreditation recommendation report, which may contain some requirements to meet accreditation criteria at the level applied for, or recommend accreditation at a lower level. This is sent to the provider for agreement or otherwise.

The accreditation panel is made up of an independent chair, quality assurance, training and play experts and the QiP manager. The panel makes the final decision based on the accreditation report and a random sample of portfolios, and accreditation lasts for two years. There is an appeals process moderated by the London Centre for Playwork Education and Training.

The next steps for *Quality in Play* are to roll it out as a national programme and revise it by aligning it with the *Every Child Matters* outcomes, the Playwork Principles and the London Play and Play England databases of good practice in quality assurance, The Children's Plan (DCSF 2007), with its forthcoming national play strategy (planned for Summer 2008) and wider play provision.

Part 3

The playing child and the practising playworker

16

PERRY ELSE
Playing: the space between

Synopsis

The playing child exists in a world of their own making. This world is made up of the child's feelings and fantasies, in constant interplay with the physical world of elements and others. It is 'of the moment'; playing children have little sense of past or future, though their play is reflective of both.

Children may play everywhere and by themselves, though they will experience play better in a complex and varied environment. Through play, children are driven to explore both the material and the imaginary; they play with concepts and concrete objects. This play does not exist in a vacuum but is influenced by and influences the world around the child.

Beginning

When children are born, they create a paradox; helpless in all the essential ways, they exist as fields of potentiality, in both their behaviours and conceptions. In animal terms, human infants are born prematurely. Compared to most animals that are able to walk within a few hours of birth, babies are incapable of independent movement, usually for the first year of their lives (Mussen et al. 1974). Similarly babies have not acquired the cognitive understanding of symbols necessary to use language and are rudderless on a sea of emotions and impressions well into their second year of life. While some studies suggest otherwise (Grof 1998), the general assumption is that babies do not have a clear sense of self and their own identify at birth; they gain the necessary understanding and attitudes as they grow. Yet while it is true that they may have no overt physical power, they can exert significant emotional control over parents and close family members in their ability to make simple but vocal demands to be fed and cared for.

Constraints

As children grow, they will increasingly develop in a world of their own making. They will be constrained by the genetic pattern given to them at birth (Edelman 1994) – this will determine their height, potential strength, potential intellect and even their predisposition to be happy or sad. Children will also be constrained by the social and environmental factors in the world around them. These will include the relationships with (or absence) of close family members, the beliefs and attitudes of those people, the diet children receive and the quality of the environment they grow up in. Yet the choices they make in growing up will help shape a world to their needs.

Genetics will limit how high a child may jump but will not control how high they want to jump. Genes may give a child advantages in peer groups but not necessarily the confidence to perform in groups. Likewise children are contradictory in that at times they will choose to behave exactly like their parents and peers and at other times will rebel and act more independently. The aspect of humans that is most different to animals – their brain development – is the very thing that gives them more choices and so more propensity to play.

Children change in many ways as they grow – from being babies to toddlers to teenagers – yet remain social animals. Observe a young baby, you will see that they will follow the faces near to them and will try to make contact and will react to the sounds and movement around them. If an adult sticks out their tongue to a baby as young as six-weeks old, they will mimic the adult and reflect the action back to them. In early play, babies will respond to an adult lead, though this quickly changes as they begin to exert their own independence in exploring the world around them. Think how often young children offer us 'presents' in their play. These may be stones, sticks, left over bits of food, toys and so on. Sometimes the gift is a cue for communication and our response is the required action; often it may be an invitation to join in the game they are playing. Many parents will have played the 'picking up game' – this usually involves a child in a high chair who drops a spoon (or bowl or toy) on to the floor, makes eye contact with the parent and then squeals with delight when the spoon magically reappears on the chair's tray. After a few seconds the spoon is back on the floor. On every occasion, it is the parent who breaks off the game before the toddler.

The play cycle

The elements of these interactions can be simply described in the play cycle (Sturrock and Else 1998) as follows:

- The child has an impulse to play (seen in the 'play cue' the invitation to play) – dropping the spoon.
- The environment in which the play takes place (the 'play frame') – in this example the high chair and the space below.
- The 'play return' (whether from another person or environmental) – the parent passing back the spoon.

- The child's response (which may be active, passive or non-existent) – in this case it is active, dropping the spoon again.

In the 'picking up game' the play cycle is often repeated till exhaustion is reached in the adult (they fail to make an adequate play return and the play stops). What then happens depends on the child and how they feel about the loss of the game. They may simply accept the loss of the spoon and move to another activity, or they may feel 'cheated' and may express frustration by crying or screaming, resulting in responses from adults that range from taking no notice, restarting the game, distraction into a new game (this time adult led) or a telling-off.

Immediacy

In breaking down the play cycle in this manner, we should not assume that children are explicitly conscious of the process; the playing child exists in a world 'of the moment'; they want to see 'what happens if ...'. While this immediacy is perhaps obvious in the example given, it is also apparent in all truly playful activities.

Think of the times when you have seen children 'lost in their play,' whether in the home, the street or the play setting; they are oblivious to all that is going on around them. Children in play can often forego other obligations, rules or needs – they may not get home at the expected time, they may play despite the No Ball Games sign, they might miss a meal. The pleasure, the fun, the satisfaction of the moment is what sustains them. In play, children have little sense of past or future, though their play is reflective of both.

Reality and direct experience

The past informs the play in that the expectations, desires, beliefs, abilities and choices of the child will inform the play actions. Through play, children are driven to explore both material and imaginary worlds; they play with real objects and intangible concepts. When playing, children will determine the limits of the play frame. At early ages this will be limited by the range and abilities of the child. But it very quickly extends to the far reaches of the child's abilities and imagination. In their play children very easily accept the 'non-reality' of key elements; dressing-up clothes are not necessary for them to play at families, children will adopt the roles and mannerisms of family members quite naturally. And while the physical environment or adults may try to constrain children's play, they may easily overcome those limits to play, both by their actions and in their thoughts.

The future is affected by children's play to the extent that the play is exciting, creative or satisfactory (or otherwise). As well as the direct experience of play, there is also a developmental benefit to play in how children learn about relationships, beliefs, and their place in the physical world. These benefits will be experienced both immediately through the senses and reflectively as feelings and thoughts. Through their actions children will be playing with expectations of future outcomes: 'Will this work? How far can I jump? How high can I climb? Will these people like what I do?' Again this will not be overtly conscious – watching children play, we see them cycling through many play roles and activities quite naturally and without any preconception. Because play is a process, the outcome cannot be predicted, so play is also risky – it can go wrong and often does. The advantage of play as Garvey (1977: 32) states is that play behaviours are 'to a considerable extent revocable' – the game can stop, roles can be changed – play is not real, it is pretend; nothing need be lost in play.

Challenge and choice

This is not to say that the play process is always pleasurable – it can be frustrating, risky, uncomfortable, challenging, rule bound (Csikszentmihalyi 1992; Sutton-Smith 1997), yet strangely, it is often when players are most pressed that they feel most alive. This may be seen in the frustration of a three-year old building a block tower, which topples several times before staying up, and in a teenager on a climbing wall, who pushes her body to the limits before reaching the top. Key to both these experiences is the fact that the individual chooses to engage in that activity, at that time, in their own way. The thrill and satisfaction come from knowing that the process may fail – we feel we may not be up to the job, the environment may let us down, yet we overcome the obstacles and make a difference in the world and ourselves. Just as choice starts the play process, choice determines when to stop.

Adults working alongside children in their play can find this frustrating; the child who spends an hour creating a wonderful world with building bricks or sand then knocks it over and walks away; the child who learns to sing a wonderful song in the privacy of her own room but will not perform on stage. Children (and others) play for their own purposes, in their own way and for their own reasons. We can guess at their conscious and unconscious motivations, their methods and their drives, but it would only be a guess.

It is because of this 'unknowingness' that we ought to recognize that children are best placed to lead their play. Just as children are able to push themselves to go further and try harder, they can choose not to take part, not to do what is expected.

Therapeutic benefits

For all that we believe that adults can lead or teach children in their play, it is only when there is an active engagement from the child that the situation becomes playful – anything else is simply instruction. As the child constructs their own world, even at very young ages, they begin to understand the difference between themselves and those around them, between self and 'other' – all that is not them. It is in the exploration of what Winnicott (1971) called the potential space, the physical and psychic space between 'I' and 'You', that the child finds him or herself. Just as we cannot predict what a child's play may be we cannot say with certainty what is good for the child. The play of the child may be for many reasons: physical development, social experience, emotional fun – health and well-being on all levels. The child needs to navigate their own way through the maze of signs, signals and experiences around them if they are truly to make sense of it. This interaction must be at a level and style that meets the child's needs, for they will decide – based on their sensations, emotions and experiences – what is stimulating, what dull and what painful. It is this that leads us to conclude that ultimately play is beneficial, restorative and healing.

However, Hughes (2001a: 135) is right to remind us that experiences may not always be positive; if the environmental stimulation is too extreme or absent the 'impact on the playing child is severe'. It is here that the adult can support the child in their play.

Our role first and foremost should be to create an environment that supports as many play opportunities as possible (Hughes 1996). That environment of itself will be the stimulus for healthy play. Beyond that if we recognize that our role in the play cycle of children is as observers or passive participants, any intervention we make in the child's play should only be to facilitate further play – to do otherwise would be to 'adulterate' or contaminate that play. Where playworkers are invited or feel they have to intervene, the aim should be to withdraw from the play frame quickly, leaving the child to play freely. Children choose the play activities that they best need for their own reasons; their play drive has its own psychological and biological dynamic that, as observers of play, we cannot know and must respect.

Conclusion

Children play in the space between themselves and others, in the space between reality and fantasy, between what is and what could be. They play for reasons that we can speculate on but never really know. So we believe that:

1. All children and young people need to play. The impulse to play is innate. Play is a biological, psychological and social necessity, and is fundamental to the healthy development and well-being of individuals and communities.
2. Play is a process that is freely chosen, personally directed and intrinsically motivated. That is, children and young people determine and control the content and intent of their play, by following their own instincts, ideas and interests, in their own way for their own reasons (PPSG 2005).

17

WENDY RUSSELL
Modelling playwork: Brawgs continuum, dialogue and collaborative reflection

Ludography:

The playwright writes a play:

a symbolic expression of the ecstasies and anguish,

the joy and grief of human life.

The ludographer writes of play:

a symbolic expression of the ecstasies and anguish,

the joy and grief of human (un)consciousness.

Both use language as their symbolic medium.

Perhaps life and play are both a pun,

a play on words, life, (un)consciousness and play.

(personal communication to Hugo Grinmore, September 2006)

Brawgs?

Sounds like an ancient warlord in a Tolkien adventure or an obscure medical disorder. Actually it is a model of playwork, and its name reflects its collaborative evolution. As with most people, my thinking emerges from my experiences, reading, dialogue and reflection. Two key people, Arthur Battram and Gordon Sturrock, have had a particularly direct influence on the development of this model; 'Brawgs' is an anagram of our initials, a little word play indulgence on my part.

Why a model?

I first encountered the idea of models in discussion with a mentor while preparing for my first university teaching job. This was a liberating idea, removing me from the straitjacket of a single 'right' way to do playwork and into a place where different models could be compared and critically examined. Finkelstein suggests models are neither a 'how to' formula nor a theory or a hypothesis. What models can do, however, is 'give us insight into situations which otherwise are difficult to *begin* explaining … They are merely tools for gaining insight into an existing stubborn problem so that the future may be changed' (1996: 1–2, emphasis in original).

Playwork's 'stubborn problems'

What 'stubborn problems' might we find in playwork? There is a contradiction in the way we talk about playwork, which comes about because of our understandings of the nature of play and of our relationship as adults with children at play. As a sector, we espouse the idea that play is 'freely chosen, personally directed and intrinsically motivated' (SkillsActive 2002; PPSG 2005), yet much of our practice involves structuring, directing or constraining play so that it is safe, constructive and acceptable both socially and personally.

Brawgs continuum

Brawgs continuum is an attempt to acknowledge and work with this contradiction, rather than making a claim for a right or wrong way to 'do' playwork. The continuum presents a dynamic range of playwork responses. It focuses on playworkers' relationships directly with children at play, although its principles can also be applied to the playwork environment, policies and procedures and playworkers' advocacy role. In the early stages of the model I suggested two approaches to playwork.

The first is the *didactic* approach, resting on two key beliefs:

1. Children learn and develop through play. For example, physical play encourages gross and fine muscle development and coordination; play with rules encourages cooperation; role-play allows children to practise future roles, or to see things from others' perspective.

2.   Childhood is a time of immaturity, a period of preparation for the 'proper and complete' state of adulthood. As Harris (1998) might have said, in this model, the goal of childhood is to become a successful adult.

Within this approach, the adult's role is to structure and direct children's play towards learning the right kinds of things. It is to protect children from harm, making competent, mature decisions about what is and is not safe on behalf of incompetent, immature children. This approach also incorporates socialization, inculcating values (whose?) and teaching children how to behave towards others.

The second approach is *ludocentric*, or 'play centred', putting playing at the heart of the playworker's task. This approach also rests on two key beliefs:

1.   Any benefit from playing (either immediate or deferred) comes from the process of playing itself, from its intrinsic and personally directed nature, and therefore the role of the playworker is to support the play process rather than lead it towards any adult determined outcome.
2.   Children are competent at being children and they know how they want to play at any given time, even though they probably could not predict or articulate this. As Harris (1998) might have said, in this model, the goal of childhood is to be a successful child.

This perspective allows for play that is goalless and spontaneous, or that uses symbolism and fantasy for purposes other than practising future adult roles. However, it is not without its difficulties. Trusting children to be competent to direct their own playing is not easy. Nor is supporting the kinds of playing that we may find dangerous, distressing, disturbing or downright offensive.

Dualism

Looking at these two approaches, we can see that the contradiction arises because they appear mutually exclusive: you're either one or the other. It is a dualistic model. Dualisms deal in opposites, neatly dividing the world in two. This tends to oversimplify issues, creating oppositions, demanding that people situate themselves in one camp or the other. It does not allow for the complexity of the play setting, or the necessity for playworkers to develop a range of responses to children's playing. Which brings me to Arthur Battram's contribution to the model.

A few years ago I worked with Arthur exploring his thinking on complexity theory and its application to playwork. We took his 'Wave' diagram (Battram 1998), which illustrates dynamical system states and their characteristics, and applied it to playwork environments (Battram and Russell 2002). Drawing on this, I extended the dualistic model and the continuum was born (see Figure 17.1).

Here, the ludocentric approach sits between the two extremes of didactic (directing and teaching) and chaotic (negligent or egocentric). At the extreme, chaotic playwork is unpredictable; the setting may not open regularly, resources are poorly maintained, playworkers respond unpredictably to the children. In contrast, didactic playwork tries to impose order and predictability onto play settings by controlling children's use of time, space and resources.

Figure 17.1 Brawgs continuum

As Arthur Battram points out, the ludocentric principle is about recognizing that both extremes are inadequate as approaches to effective playwork. It is about working consciously to move towards the *middle zone* (in the jargon the *edge of chaos* – which is also *the edge of order* – the *zone of complexity* where possibilities can emerge). This middle zone is where we can find a mode of working that supports children's play rather than serves other adult agendas, either personal or societal (see Chapter 18 for a more in depth exploration of these ideas).

The continuum stayed in this form until recent work (Sturrock et al. 2004). I was musing on how it feels *natural* for us as adults to want to protect and socialize children, and so a truly ludocentric approach may feel *wrong*. The paradigm of developmental psychology is so deeply embedded in the way we understand children that it feels like the natural order of things. Any other relationship with children, for example, one that acknowledges their social and ludic competence, runs so counter to dominant thinking that it feels *un*natural.

Gordon Sturrock's contribution to the model was to suggest that the continuum needed to acknowledge our feelings and emotions rather than just behaviour. A second, internal dimension to the continuum was born (see Figure 17.2).

Figure 17.2 The internal dimension to the continuum

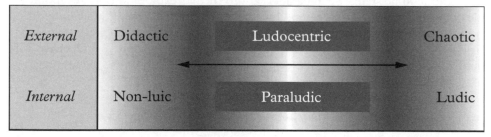

If we see children playing in a way that makes us *feel* that we need to assert our adult authority, then our internal responses will be non-ludic. Our emotions, our gut response and our intent will all be to control, stop or redirect the play in some way. This might be when we feel that the play is unsafe, or unfair, or if we feel the need to teach the children something.

If the children's playing sparks off strong emotions that impel us to join in the playing and direct it towards our own ends, then this is when our internal responses are chaotic. We see this when playworkers join in competitive games and play to win, or when the narratives of the playing touch a memory and they feel the need to control the direction of the narrative, what Sturrock and Else (1998) refer to as 'unplayed out material'.

Intervening at both extremes of the continuum privileges adult needs (either societal at the non-ludic end, or personal at the ludic end) over those of the playing child's. As with external responses, we aim for a position between these two extremes that is paraludic. This is where the playworker supports the children's play, by joining in if invited, but is aware of their own position of power and authority and does not take over. It is what Sturrock and Else (1998) call the 'witness position': joining in but playing alongside, consciously aware of our adult responsibility to support the play and not privilege our own needs.

If our responses to children at play are to be authentic, our emotional responses should be aligned with our behavioural responses. There is the potential here to use the model for personal and professional development: trying consciously to move towards an externally ludocentric response may make us aware that our inner feelings are not aligned. However, with experience, reflective practice and support, we can move towards an internalization of the playwork ethos and so find ourselves responding more frequently towards the centre of the internal continuum. The important thing is to develop an awareness of where we are operating on the continuum, both internally and externally, so that our playwork practice can become conscious and authentically ludocentric.

Since the model's first official outing in 2004 (Sturrock et al. 2004), I have used it in research projects (Russell 2006) and have discussed it with numerous playwork colleagues. As with many concepts, it has dawned on me that in fact it is not an original model for thoughts, feelings and actions. It could be argued, with some validity, that I have merely reproduced Freud's concepts of superego, ego and id; or Berne's transactional analysis ego states of parent, adult and child (Harris 1970), these referring respectively to the didactic/non-ludic, ludocentric/paraludic and chaotic/ludic states. Such parallels afford further explorations, for example the idea of critical or nurturing parent, but this is for another time. Equally interesting is that they also afford a different visual representation of the model other than a straight-line continuum which is becoming increasingly limited and gives little opportunity to explore the three-way trialectic relationship or the dynamic nature of movement between these positions or states.

Conclusion

The evolution of the Brawgs continuum as a model for playwork, through dialogue and reflection, has been a journey of discovery for me, fundamental to my own paraludic development and self-awareness. It has allowed me to think about playwork in a different way, to embrace a range of responses that playworkers can have to children at play and to acknowledge that our inner feelings and emotions are an integral part of who we are both as playworkers and as people. I hope it can serve a similar purpose for readers.

18

ARTHUR BATTRAM
The edge of recalcitrance: playwork in the zone of complexity

(This chapter is a brief introductory extract from a forthcoming paper.)

Here I contend that: play exists only at the edge of chaos – which means that *play exists only in the zone of complexity* – a weird mixture, in *uncertainty* between order and chaos. Because:

- order isn't order – it's predictability and stereotypical behaviour;
- the edge of chaos is present in all complex adaptive systems;
- learning, creativity and adaptation to change – all are initiated and nurtured at the edge of chaos, in **uncertainty**;
- the duty of playwork is to be 'play led' (explained further in Battram 2007).

Recalcitrance: the complexity of ludocentric playwork

Having discovered complexity theory, I spent some time from 1997 onwards sharing and exploring its relevance to playwork, in a number of conference presentations and workshops. Wendy Russell (see Chapter 17) came to share my interests. By 2002, my explorations of the relevance of notions of order and chaos to playwork had developed into a critique of a culture that promotes order and safety as if they are unquestionably good things. I addressed the 'childcare versus free play' debate with Wendy Russell, and developed the notion of a *duty of recalcitrance* as a counterbalance to the prevailing *duty of care*. The playworker's role, I contend, is to support the play-led actions and interactions of the child, *not* to encourage 'free play' (an adult notion), *nor* impose order in order to act out a duty of care. To quote from my own contribution to a joint presentation:

> Avoid dwelling at either end of the continuum – try to exist in the zone of possibility, the Zone of Complexity, somewhere 'between', where patterns can form and change and grow, where there are always possibilities but not too

many – not the extreme of randomness but an exciting, spooky place where the patterns can change and not be fixed for ever in mindless repetition.

(Battram and Russell 2002)

Rubik science: weirdly, it's about the real world ...

Most of what we might call *normal science* is experiments and theories about things like steel balls traveling through a perfect vacuum – explaining things in ideal conditions that never happen in reality. So that makes complexity science *weird science*, because unlike normal science it chooses to study the messy and difficult stuff that happens all the time in the real world. Understanding complexity science is tricky because everything ends up connected to everything else: for example, a flock of birds is a complex adaptive system; it is also an incredible emergent phenomenon generated by just three interacting dynamic rules, at the edge of chaos; and it's also an environment for birds made up of other birds passing through a number of interconnected ecosystems. It's a bit like the 'wave/particle duality' – light is both a wave and a particle, which one it is depends on how you look at it. It's about different perspectives or mindsets or world views; it might be useful to think of a magic Rubik cube with a different idea on each square of one face of the cube, then as you twist the cube, more squares appear as the pattern on the face in front of you breaks up and ...

The 'edge of chaos': where 'order' makes the transition to 'complexity'

So, we need to explain this weird science idea the *edge of chaos*, also known as the *zone of complexity*, while acknowledging that it is also an example of the behaviour of a *complex adaptive system*. Then we can apply it to playwork. Here goes ...

Edge of Chaos is a term describing the point in a complex system when ordered behaviour gives way to *uncertain* behaviour: a *phase transition*, such as the change from ice to water or water to steam. This phase transition is an example of one of four classes of behaviour which occur time and time again in complexity science. Three of them were discovered in research into non-linear dynamical systems; systems which exhibit *chaotic* behaviour. These are:

- Class I – Stasis;
- Class II – Order (then, yes, squeezed in between 2 and 3);
- Class IV – Complexity; (and finally)
- Class III – Chaos.

The fourth state (*the edge of chaos*) was discovered later by several of the founders of complexity theory working independently, including Chris Langton and Stuart Kauffman (Battram 1998). Class IV appears in between II and III. This is because complexity exists on *the edge of chaos*: poised between order and chaos (and they didn't want to renumber them). Langton argues that:

You should look at systems in terms of how they behave, instead of how they're made. When you do, what you find are the two extremes of order and chaos. In between the two extremes, at a kind of abstract phase transition called 'the edge of chaos', you also find complexity: a class of behaviors in which the components of the system never quite lock into place, yet never quite dissolve into turbulence, either. These are the systems that are both stable enough to store information, and yet evanescent enough to transmit. These are the systems that can be organized to perform complex computation, to react to the world, to be spontaneous, adaptive, and alive.

(Battram 1998: 139–40)

The edge of chaos isn't an edge: it's a zone

These four classes can be represented by analogy in the following diagrams. Note that *the edge of chaos* isn't actually an edge: as Langton says, it is a class of behaviours, which share the characteristics of being patterned yet changing. As an orderly system starts to shift, like the wave patterns in the 'Wave System' diagram, the *breakdowns* happen more and more frequently until the system is completely chaotic (see Figure 18.1).

Figure 18.1 The Wave System diagram: the zone of complexity at the end of chaos and order

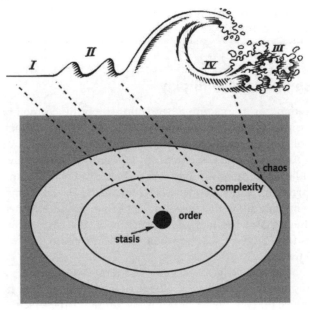

In surfing, the area under the about-to-break wave is known as the *tube*: surfers attempt to ride inside the tube, just ahead of the point where the tube breaks as the wave hits the beach. In this analogy, the tube is the *zone of complexity*. We can also

show the four classes of behaviour in diagram form: this is useful if we want to talk about moving from one zone to another. In Figure 18.1 the lines link the 'Wave System' diagram to the equivalent parts of the 'System Zones' diagram.

Order isn't order, it's predictability and stereotypical behaviour

All living systems operate in the *zone of complexity*. This doesn't mean that it is a comfortable place to be; it's not: the automatic tendency is to avoid the onset of 'chaos' whenever possible. But it's also important to avoid 'order' whenever possible: the place to be is the *zone of complexity*, a.k.a. *the edge of chaos*. Now let's be clear about this term 'order': in this context it doesn't mean a well-oiled machine, smoothly ticking over. Like *the edge of chaos*, it is a technical term. When applied to living systems, it translates as predictability and stereotypical behaviour. Think of a tiger in a zoo, endlessly pacing up and down in its cage, displaying only a narrow subset of its full behavioural repertoire. An ordered organization, in this sense, is one that is not adapting, not responding to change, just 'going through the motions' – repeating a narrow set of patterns of response over and over again, complacent and unresponsive.

The edge of chaos is present in all complex adaptive systems

Ecosystems, brains, the economy, animals and human beings – in groups like hives, swarms or flocks, or societies and organizations. All of these systems display the same emergent patterns of creative, adaptive behaviour, exquisitely tuned to their environment, learning from it, responding to it, changing it in the process and being changed by it.

On the beach: life begins in play

Another way to think of it: imagine a beach on which the council has dumped two piles of pebbles: one black pile and one white pile. Under the action of feet and waves, the pebbles begin to mix. In the middle there is a zone of almost evenly mixed pebbles. At the far ends, the pebbles are almost completely white or black; yet in that middle zone there are patches of black pebbles and patches of white. There is no sharp 'edge': it is a zone. Let's look at the beach from an evolutionary perspective: if you will allow me the pun, the beach is quite littorally, the edge of two systems: the sea and the land. Unsurprisingly, it's where life evolved; at the edge of land and the edge of sea, between order and chaos (from a land-dwelling human perspective).

Sailors will avoid the 'edge of water', 'the dangerous beach', where they may be wrecked, and builders will avoid 'the edge of land', where their houses may sink, but all children love playing on beaches – they know it's the place to be, they know it's the zone of complexity where humans evolved, according to Elaine Morgan (1996). All the edges of any system/s are where the interesting things happen – ideas, change, creativity … and this edge isn't just something big and macho like a surfer in a 'gnarly' wave (an example of the adult *deep* play type), it can also be the edge of the ordered-seeming play of two little girls playing 'my family' with dolls. These are just a few examples of the 'edge'. All examples will share this sense of a boundary, a transition between things. There are many others, though.

The edge of chaos is a 'possibility space': flow, learning and creativity

The 'possibility space', or *zone of complexity*, expands massively at the *edge of chaos*. This space or zone is a metaphor for the place where creative ideas come into being in individuals or groups. Creativity can only happen if individuals are free to operate at their own *edge of chaos*. Mihalyi Csikszentmihalyi has spent more than two decades researching the 'psychology of happiness': his main findings are summed up in his bestseller, *Flow: The Psychology of Happiness* (1992). He describes 'flow' as the feeling that everything is going just right, be it an interesting conversation, a piece of work, a game of tennis or an improvised solo in jazz. We can detect *the edge of chaos* in many 'flow' activities: the mountain biker's perfect downhill, never quite falling off, not daring to control the descent by braking because that will definitely cause a crash; or the surfer surfing inside the tube of a perfect wave just ahead of it breaking onto the beach. Flow happens at work as well; in fact Csikszentmihalyi says that most people tend to experience flow far more at work than in their leisure time when they are likely to be slumped in front of the TV. At work, flow can happen in one of those deep conversations where the insights and the difficulties are mixed together as the talkers learn from each other at the limits of their understanding, or simply working in the sort of office where it always feels like things are going to collapse any minute but they never do.

Play and playwork: ludocentricity at the edge of chaos

Here's a description of play at *the edge of chaos*, observed in a group of children let out to play from school:

> They burst with free energy through the doors, running around, laughing, teasing, squirmishing. The chaos among them increases. Teachers have their hands full trying to prevent anyone getting hurt. Then, suddenly, two or three kids *flock off* to go and play in, say, the sandpit. The teachers smile because 'they know tacitly' that the transition is happening. Within ten minutes the majority of kids will play in the sandpit and the rest in small groups at different other objects. The next day the majority might prefer the climbing frame, or playing house. After an hour in the rooms, another hour on the playground, these kids are hungry and ready to rest for an hour. In primary school children, the swing is either more dampened ('disciplined') or more robust (less 'disciplined'). I think that kindergarten teachers know not to interfere too much in-between the swing from 'order' to 'chaos' and back again, but generally we are perhaps taught that 'order from chaos' is good, while 'chaos from order' is bad. These

kindergarten teachers handle 'order' and 'chaos' best as complementary duals.
(edited slightly from a posting on the now defunct learning-org list, 1996
by At de Lange, Goldfields University, South Africa)

We can imagine this conversation between an Ofsted inspector and a clued-up
playworker:

'Why on earth are you letting the children do that?'
'Because we care!'
'Let us explain, as playworkers we work at *the edge of order*, in the *zone of possibility*, the place where we can all be adaptive, responsive and creative, poised in an ever-shifting dynamic balance. This is not just another 70s playworker's paean to the past; our perspective draws on recent research from neuroscience, evolution and complexity'.

19

BEN TAWIL
Two weeks of adventure play: moving furniture

It would take significantly more words than are permitted in this short chapter to talk in depth about the experience of working on an adventure playground, so I've chosen to focus on one play scenario and address some of the theory and the historical contexts that underpin the practice and provision that supported it. Here's my story.

One day we received a phone call from the local furniture-recycling firm asking whether we wanted some old furniture. It was too good for them to throw away, but too dilapidated to sell on to families in the local community. I accepted the offer unseen, not yet knowing how we could use it. Opportunities like this are just too good to miss – they only come around once a year when factories and businesses spring-clean their warehouses.

The furniture arrived as we were in a staff meeting and too busy to help the men unload. So they left a wagon load of beds, cabinets, chairs, bureaux, cupboards, desks, and assorted bric-a-brac, strewn around the entrance to the playground. As the children arrived for the evening session they took immediate interest in the furniture. A group of about seven children aged 8 to 12, both boys and girls, started to sift through it. At first their search seemed indiscriminate, almost chaotic, with very little communication between them.

The children started describing to one another what they had discovered:

'I've got a writing desk'.
'Look at this book case'.
'Let's take them to the castle'.

The castle is a large building in the middle of the playground – a wooden construction. We decided it was needed when we observed that play within our main brick building was restricted by its dual use for offices and meetings, and 'adult' expectations in terms of mess and noise. The Castle is the 'inside outside' – a dry space, suitable for painting and gluing, dressing up, and watching the football and tennis at those times of year when the children get fanatical about that sort of thing. It is usually empty – left open so the children and young people can take ownership – their play and use of it dictating its function.

Just as well, because that's where the children were heading with the furniture. They naturally cooperated in transferring it 100 yards – under walkways, over paths and sandpits, and into the castle. They were little ants – able to carry far more than their own body weight. Two eight-year-old girls carried a large wooden table, stopping every ten yards to readjust their grip and take breath. A group of boys carried the bureau, banging and dragging it, and remonstrating with each other all the way: 'Lift your end up a bit', 'I'm doing all the bloody carrying', 'Why can't you be the one that has to go backwards?"

I chuckled to myself at their indignation and effort, at how serious this had become to them, at the way organization had been borne out of the apparent chaos of moments earlier. Was an adventure unfolding in their minds – a collective adventure where all the participants had made an unwritten, unspoken agreement to take part and to commit to the process?

The new materials available that evening stimulated an evolving idea that the children controlled – they had complete ownership of their play, and it was evolving naturally without the need for me to intervene or entertain or provide diversion.

The play moved on from the physical challenge of transferring furniture, to positioning furniture. Again there was little talking; the children seemed to have concurrent ideas that stemmed from one person's initial placing down of a piece of furniture. Two leaders emerged – the eldest girl of about 12, and one of the younger boys of about 8. They seemed to be taking on the role of interior designers – telling the rest of the group where to position the furniture. These instructions were followed to the letter with great seriousness. They created a home environment.

Straight away a boy of about 11 sat down at the bureau and exclaimed, 'Can you keep the noise down? I'm trying to write a letter to the council', and without question or hesitation the oldest girl (until this point the chief interior designer) addressed the other children in a sharp authoritarian voice, 'Your Dad's told you to keep the noise down. Now go and play quietly'. Immediately the rest of the group took on roles as brothers and sisters, grandparents, daughter and visiting boyfriend. There was lots of discussion at this point. Roles were decided upon and positions taken around the two rooms. Individual roles started to be acted out.

All I did was observe in fairly close proximity to the action, mostly trying to appear to be looking elsewhere. At times I was asked to help move something, and on those occasions I declined. I knew they could manage by themselves, and I thought the only reason they were trying to include me was because they felt sorry because I was left out.

And then gradually their play changed from dramatic to socio-dramatic play (Hughes 2002a). The children weren't acting out being adults and pretend families anymore, they were acting out their own home life; taking on the roles of their parents, uncles, cousins, brothers, sisters and significant others. Real and significant issues were being played out. This process was relevant and profoundly important to their daily lives, to their childhood; it allowed them to rehearse responses they might need at home, and practise social skills in a safe environment. Later in life these skills and this practice time might facilitate and inform their own parenting style, conflict-negotiation capabilities, and problem-solving skills.

I didn't know precisely what they were learning and working through, but I knew it was of great significance to them. I retreated to a position out of sight to be certain that I didn't interrupt the play and destroy the play cycle (Sturrock and Else 1998).

This play continued throughout the evening – four hours of continuous immersion in a single scenario. New players entered the frame and took on roles and positions of hierarchy within the family. The original players left. Minimal discussion happened at these moments. There was some low-key argument over roles, but the narrative seemed to continue unhindered by the intermittent comings and goings of players.

Indeed it continued for *two weeks* – every evening and for full eight-hour days at the weekend. Different groups of children used the materials and altered the environment and the narrative to suit their needs. Children as old as 16 played together with children as young as 6 – showing compassion, consideration, encouragement, and support – experiencing sympathy and empathy (Brown and Webb 2005), practising skills and behaviours that would support them throughout the trials and tribulations of childhood and inform their adult attitudes and approaches later in life.

Eventually the children's interest waned; perhaps they had played out their need for this type of play for the time being. They had certainly worn out the already dilapidated furniture. The play began to morph once more as the children found uses for panels from the furniture in construction play and the remnants were put to good use fuelling our nightly campfire. But the value of this wagon load of tatty cast-offs was immeasurable – it was a gift horse that had run and run, and we had all learned from the ride, whether we knew it or not.

What I have described is a snapshot of play on the adventure playground. I have purposely chosen a scenario that involved little intervention as intervention styles and modes are detailed in more depth within this book. What I want to explore here is the provision for play and its underpinning philosophy. In the scenario I have described the play opportunities were made available for the children to make use of as they wished. There was a culture of permission in the play setting that enabled children to express their play behaviours and what ensued was a response to that permission and the availability of props and loose parts.

There is a dichotomy that historically divides adventure playground provision. It is the split between playwork practice/provision and theory. It seems to me that in the attempt to elevate the playwork profession from one that operated on the fringes of chaos, to one that has parity with allied professions, the original ethos and mode of practice established by early proponents such as Sorenson, Nicholson, Abernethy and Lady Allen of Hurtwood has been compromised.

They promoted settings where children could create, demolish and recreate their own play environment and opportunities; where the inherent flexibility and array of loose parts and materials and tools at the disposal of children offered the potential for breadth and depth in the children's play experience; where children were in charge of their own play experience; and where they had real ownership of the play environment. The urge to justify and elevate playwork as a profession has led to it becoming one that concentrates on the products, the physical outputs of children's play, presumably in the hope that this will stimulate and provide for the play experience. But such environments have only token ownership by children.

Sometime during those intervening years playworkers saw potential in the children's creations in the play space. They saw something they could do *for* the children – the output of constructions, and so the space began to be controlled by playworkers, and the founding principle of adventure playground work became adulterated. Other factors that compromised the adventure playground ethos were the rise of the health and safety lobby, fear of litigation (the blame culture), and economic constraints. Advances in technology in the construction industry meant limited access to scrap and scrounged building materials.

Now even where adventure playgrounds exist and provide for those basic principles of provision we see them created with a great dollop of funding that means they do not grow organically at the hands of children. They are demolished and rebuilt at a rate that leaves generations of children deprived of the opportunity to experience the adventure and ownership that an adventure playground, indeed any good play provision, should provide.

Drummond Abernethy suggested we should see the adventure as being in the mind of the child. Sadly in much play provision there is so much emotional and financial investment in the equipment that there is a reluctance to see it changed or adapted by the children for whom it is provided. Adventure playgrounds are frequently built to fulfil an adult vision of how they should look, and too often they entirely miss the point: it is the children's space; the children's journey; the children's adventure; and it should be constructed and demolished at their will.

It is critical, therefore, that while striving to become accepted and acknowledged we don't lose sight of their founding principles. Children's participation and inclusion, self-build, loose parts, the opportunity to create, demolish and recreate is the heart of quality provision for children's play. To exclude, ignore, or adulterate it is to accept mediocrity for children and childhood.

20

MAGGIE HARRIS
After-school childcare in adventure playgrounds

In the UK, the demand for secure childcare to meet adults' work needs continues to grow. Government policies to return adults to the workforce have made funding for childcare an important part of public policy and this has led to a huge increase in out-of-school clubs (Smith and Barker 2000). These clubs operate in a variety of settings, most commonly, and rather ironically, *in* schools. This chapter explores my own experience of running an after-school club in an adventure playground setting.

In addition to the employment agenda, real and perceived dangers such as heavy traffic and fear of racism, bullying and 'stranger danger' are cited as reasons for more adult supervision. These views also construct children as incompetent and in need of protection (Mayall and Hood 2001). One effect of this has been a reduction in children's access to spaces for unsupervised play opportunities where they can exercise their intuitive play needs.

The growing theoretical base attempting to identify what play is, compared to what play is not, continues to emphasize the qualities of spontaneity, free choice and intrinsically motivated, first-hand experience in the control of the child (Manwaring and Taylor 2007). Theoretical approaches highlight the importance of the links between the play environment, play context, and play content and suggest regular access to high-quality play experiences is essential to all children's optimum development. Conversely, evidence suggests that lack of access, play deprivation, can result in serious physical, mental and emotional consequences (Hughes 2001a; Brown and Webb 2005).

The expansion of the use of schools into children's leisure time changes the balance of family and school in many children's lives. Impacting on children's social and cultural lives, school now has an even larger influence on children's socialization (Smith and Barker 2000). Out-of-school clubs provide a service for 4- to 12-years olds, often to fellow pupils from the same school.

There are school settings where creative adult playworkers affect and change the environment and ambience to improve play opportunities for children

(Brown 2000). Many children find the opportunity to mix with friends and try different play activities central to their experience of the out-of-school club, and view it as a separate experience to the school day (Smith and Barker 2000).

However, perceptions of what is acceptable behaviour, challenging behaviour and play behaviour are affected by the culture and atmosphere of the setting (Russell 2006). The wider institutional environment of the school with its rules and behaviour guidelines can leave children constrained in their ability to challenge, contest and shape their surroundings. Some children find it difficult to separate the two provisions. This can affect their play behaviour and experience, limiting their play to games enjoyed in the school setting (Smith and Barker 2000). This directly affects the potential for feeling ownership, making the provision not truly theirs (Hughes 1996).

In my own experience the walk from school to the adventure playground with the children who attended our out-of-school provision provided rich examples of the change from schoolchild to 'playchild'. The journey enabled the mental, emotional and physical metamorphosis from an environment where adults hold power to the more autonomous playground environment. The conversations and behaviours exposed the children's understanding of the playworker and the adventure playground setting as more tolerant, supportive and accepting of a wider range of behaviours. The journey could include everything from smutty playground rhymes, practising and building on jokes, tales of events at school delivered in tabloid 'red-top' style, lots of 'shock horror', arguments spilling out from the day, justification of behaviours that offered rich opportunities for moral, philosophical discussions, the rewriting of what happened, thinly veiled secrets ('My dad is going to that place where you have to say whether you did it or not') – all the way through to remarks that caused you to prick up your ears – vivid imaginative play or deeper, coded cause for concern?

To help replace unsupervised play opportunities a provision should involve real risk and need real concentration to develop real skills and real self-confidence (Hughes 1996). Risk here is not just limited to physical activities but includes emotional, cultural and psychic risks (Melville 1999).

In the UK, adventure playgrounds have a long history of compensating for children's lack of access to free play opportunities (Bengtsson 1972; Abernethy 1974). In addition to offering access to challenge and risk, adventure playgrounds provide a different space, within the community, to socialize with a broad age range (usually 5–16 years) and wider social and cultural mix. With access to fire play, water play, sand play, den building, structures and spaces for imaginative play they can offer an *exclusive* play space where play rules and rituals that develop and change over time encourage a sense of ownership (Russell 2006).

'Free of charge' is an important adventure playground mantra – a child should not need to rely on an adult's ability or willingness to pay in order to access the play provision. However, my own experience of an after-school provision within an established adventure playground exposed many variations in adults' perception of what they were buying and children's perception of the difference in the two provisions. In an area of low employment and high deprivation fees had to be low and the service flexible. Sustainability relied on attention to good funding, a budget linked to playwork training on site, and sharing resources with the adventure playground.

Childcare at the adventure playground included collection from school, a snack meal, and the requirement to stay on site until collected or taken home.

Adults chose the paid provision for a variety of reasons, which included:

- Childcare to meet work commitments.
- The service of collection from school and delivery home: for respite, to access leisure activities, inability to accompany children to the adventure playground.
- The child's request to the parent for that service – some children switched between after-school and open-access provision depending on friends, relationships with playworkers in particular teams, and security (if they felt at risk or threatened by children in either provision).
- The journey on the mini bus, which could be very entertaining!
- Fears of perceived risks travelling to and from, and attendance at, the open-access provision (traffic, strangers, bullying).

The 'open-access' philosophy is a unique and important aspect of the provision at adventure playgrounds leaving children free to come and go during opening hours. As a policy it reflects the ethos that the child's most important need is a flexible environment where they can self-direct their play, deciding when to come, what to do, who to play with and how long to stay (Hughes 1996). When children organize themselves their play is much freer and more flexible. This type of freedom is very important as a different way of learning because it is firsthand, experiential and more risky (Opie and Opie 1959). In practice there is no doubt that many play decisions are also tied in to family routines and values, peer relationships and culture, age and gender issues (playtrain 2000), but this policy gives important decision-making powers to the child resulting in more control over their play experience.

Ofsted concerns regarding 'after-school' children walking out of an open-access site were addressed through the daily open-access register. It included a list of the names of all the children attending the after-school provision, so all staff were aware of which child was with which group.

The adventure playground was the only staffed play provision in the community. Some parents chose to pay for childcare to ensure their children could not leave the site without their knowledge. This was sometimes just a formal version of existing practice. Parents can use adventure playgrounds as free childcare by telling their children not to leave until they collect them. The risk is if the child disobeys the request or is sent off site by playworkers. The playworkers were usually aware of these situations, or made aware – 'my mum says I can't leave here'.

Childcare opened the adventure playground space to some children who wished to attend, but were excluded by either the open-access policy or parental perceptions of the level of care in a free provision.

Low fees meant that irregular attendance at the after-school provision did not have huge financial implications. Good relations with families and children meant that if on a particular day, a child expressed a wish not to attend the after-school session, the playworker could support the child's choice as the parent was not tied to financial obligations. This helped return the choice of attendance back to children on several occasions. Childcare requirements could scupper this, but as already stated childcare was not always the overriding reason for seeking after-school provision at the adventure playground.

Some children were also able to take opportunities to come and go as they pleased. A request to call a parent/carer when an older sibling or friend was leaving could allow an 'after-school' child the same freedom to leave as an 'open-access' child.

In this setting the 'open-access' staff were employed by the local authority and the 'after-school' staff by the local voluntary management committee who owned the adventure playground. Negotiations were usually at senior-worker level, but when required, final decisions were taken at the management committee meetings. Both staff teams adopted a playwork approach across the setting, working with all the children who were free to access all the resources and spaces of both provisions including opportunities to take risks.

Responses to unacceptable behaviour required discussion between both teams. Sending children off site was one response available to open-access staff that was clearly not applicable to after-school children. The staff teams agreed that unacceptable behaviour would be addressed by the provision the child was attending.

One difference, the snack meal, initially involved the after-school group moving to a separate space to eat. Children involved in team games, or engrossed in a particular activity could opt to eat 'on the hoof'. While eating offers good opportunities for socialization, the separation was never a satisfactory approach from a playwork point of view. Eventually, funding provided a café, set up in a communal space, offering good cheap food for all.

The benefits of the integration of childcare into the adventure playground included:

- extra resources from extra funding;
- wider social mix (the adventure playground age range and the five schools attending after-school provision);
- the playground was busier, making its future more secure;
- children often outgrew the after-school and moved into the open-access;
- evidence of changes in attitude – childcare parents learned more about how the playground works and came to recognize its positive benefits;
- some took their interest further, taking up opportunities for playwork training on site;
- in the school holidays the after-school staff ran an outreach open-access playscheme widening opportunities for open-access adventure play;
- training courses organized were usually open to both staff teams.

How would this example translate to other adventure playgrounds? Each adventure playground has its own character and ambience, reflecting its own diverse community, which affects the play provision (Hughes 1996). Local variances, for example funding opportunities, the cost of and reasons for childcare, need consideration when attempting to translate practice from one playground to another. The measure of success of this integration was neither group's play provision being depleted or watered down as a result of the integration.

The growth of out-of-school clubs represents a solution to childcare for the economic and social convenience of adults, but the practice in some shows an understanding and awareness of the importance of play for children. This could be enhanced if the clubs took place in more flexible and supportive play settings like adventure playgrounds. Integration of childcare provision could also ease funding problems for some adventure playgrounds.

Recently, six years after the after-school started at the adventure playground, the local Early Years Extended Schools Team consulted families and local schools regarding after-school childcare provision. The request that it be provided at the adventure playground and not the local schools was unanimous.

21

KIRSTY WARD
Play in hospitals

Every year tens of thousands of children are admitted to hospital as a result of injury or illness. This admission to hospital and subsequent medical intervention can be an extremely stressful and anxiety-provoking experience for children and their parents. Research, as well as personal experience, indicates that adverse effects such as behavioural regression, anxiety, fear, aggression and apathy depend on several factors including age at admission, length of hospitalization, the type of illness or surgery, previous level of psychological functioning and therapeutic contact during treatment (Adams et al. 1991; Glasper et al. 1992).

Stress in hospital may show itself in very obvious ways, and staff regularly have to cope with children doing things that no one wants them to do. Common examples are kicking the doctor, or locking themselves in a bathroom and refusing to come out unless their parents take them home. However, when children cope well with a hospital admission they are not the only ones to gain. Family members, as well as members of the multi-disciplinary team, will also reap the benefits, as the child will eventually become more positive and cooperative, and generally happier with their stay.

Children's services were among the earliest health and welfare provisions in England and were widespread before the National Health Service was established in 1948. These health and welfare services are an integral part of human societies and cultures and as such health and welfare professions and services both shape and are shaped by revisioning theories and understandings of children as they emerge. There is no doubt that in the current climate children in developed countries have more autonomy regarding their care as a direct result of psychological research which has been reflected and protected in and by governmental charters worldwide (Foley et al. 2000).

By any standard hospitals are extreme environments (Harvey 1980), and are often unable to incorporate the tacit theories offered by general playwork theorists. For example, Hughes's (2001a) view of playwork is that there should be little intervention encouraging a high response. This is not a theory that sits comfortably within the hospital environment, as the children are hugely affected by the play frame that is this unusual environment, and may require the active curative play intervention suggested by Sturrock and Else (1998). In Winnicot's view, cited by Gopnik et al. (1999), areas within hospitals can be designed to encourage play. Such an approach may also be responsive to Vygotsky's notion that children require interaction with others to enable them to enter the *zone of proximal development*. However, due to their physical and emotional distress children are often unlikely to make use of these areas independently. Nevertheless, there is one thing that the majority of theorists do seem to have in common, that being the fact that the potential variability of children's functioning can be affected by play in any setting, including hospitals.

Play in hospitals is generally facilitated by a qualified hospital play specialist (HPS) who will have undergone specific training in meeting the play needs of this specific group. There are many ways in which the HPS can support the child and family through this stressful time, varying from straightforward facilitation to the more in-depth therapeutic techniques. The specific techniques chosen by the play specialist will be dependent on a range of influencing factors that may or may not be present. It has to be remembered that all children have differing levels of development and cognitive ability, and these can be altered as a result of injury and illness.

Illness and injury may slow, regress or even stop the development of skills. In these circumstances, play intervention in hospitals has relevance to both aspects of the nature–nurture divide. A sensitive hospital play specialist can enable children just to be themselves and give full expression to their nature, but also good quality play intervention can help to nurture the most fundamental aspects of human development (SCY of BC 2007).

Middleton (2001) suggests that in order to observe and assess the effects of play on personality and development it is important for the playworker to build up a rapport with the parents and child. It has been proffered that the optimal basic treatment unit is the family even when the child is seen individually. There is though some difference of opinion about how parental factors affect children's responses. Saylor (1993) cites Ziv and Israel's (1973) opinion that parental anxiety is an important factor in the development of symptoms including problem behaviour in children. In contrast, Saylor's citing of Sugar (1989) suggests that children experience post-traumatic symptoms irrespective of their parent's responses.

Non-directive play therapy can be useful as it gives children a chance to experience growth under the most favourable conditions. Since play is a natural medium for self-expression and an inherent biological drive, the child is given the opportunity to play out their accumulated feelings of tension, frustration, insecurity, aggression, fear, bewilderment and confusion. This can be observed, in order to ascertain specific worries or anxieties that may require a more psychotherapeutic approach, also using play (Axline 1989; Smith 1995).

There are many techniques available to assist children to cope with invasive and painful procedures by means of play preparation and/or diversional therapy or distraction. Part of the HPS role is to assist children to become more autonomous. That does not mean they are allowed to do whatever they want, but rather it's about letting them have the 'emotional space' to be able to reflect upon their actions, and to anticipate how these might influence both themselves and others. Play preparation allows children to act out fears and anxieties, testing out scenarios and changing the end to those scenarios. Role play in any form is valuable to the child's holistic development and is a particularly useful method to aid the child's health, allowing them to develop resilience. Distraction is not only proven to divert interest away from the procedure but also reduce the amount of pain felt (Bancroft and Carr 1995; Meggit et al. 2000).

It is clear that explanation, understanding and preparation for what treatment is to be undertaken are important; indeed many hospitals run pre-admission programmes in order for this to happen. However, in practice I have been faced by upset parents who truly believe it is better for their child to know nothing of the procedures before they happen, in case it frightens them. Although well meaning, in reality they are arguing that sending their child into a room full of alarming equipment surrounded by strangers wearing masks and gowns that hold them down until they are gassed unconscious is preferable to them having some anticipation, understanding and control of what, how and why things will happen. For playworkers this can often mean a constant battle not just to change the behaviours of the child, using play preparation techniques, but also to change the feelings of parents and other professionals whose support is required to aid success.

Children are often brought into hospital with the additional diagnosis of having a phobia: the most common being needle phobia, in other words an excessive fear of needles. It is regarded as normal for children to show fear, and behaviour can only be judged abnormal if the fear is excessive or conversely if it never appears. The question that needs to be asked in these circumstances is to what extent is the child's behaviour a problem for the child and to what extent is it a product of other people's perceptions, or their own difficulties, or biased judgments of behaviours? Only a small percentage of those children labelled with this additional problem actually are needle phobic (Bancroft and Carr 1995).

During recovery periods when play begins again, it has been suggested that children's feelings, attitudes and thoughts emerge and they begin to understand themselves a little better through their play. Freudian theory suggests that deep instinctive urges direct much of our behaviour. Although Jungian theorists also acknowledge that unconscious processes are extremely important, they concentrate far more on human instinct, including power and self-realization, and believe that we are influenced by our own goals and plans for the future, as well as prior causes, and have a desire to discover and fulfil our own innate potential (Ewen 1998). For Maslow this was the search of self-actualization. These theories have helped to shape how play can be used as a resource when working with troubled children, as play has been recognized as a useful tool since it can be considered an examination and re-examination of the self in order to achieve insight on how to gain self-actualization (Axline 1989). Play can assist and encourage rehabilitation as well as channel the feelings of anger and frustration that may arise during admission. Pummelling clay and tiring physical play can channel aggression which, as Freud suggested, may otherwise lead to personality problems (Davenport 1994).

It is always a useful tool for the playworker not only to have sympathy for the child but also to be able to demonstrate a degree of empathy in order to support and prepare the child fully. This can often be difficult, especially when children become distrustful and uncommunicative due to the experiences they have already had. It is always assumed that changes in a child's behaviour are as a result of learning, but it must be noted that they may not always be. They may just be as a result of a child's willingness to cooperate. The reality of gaining cooperation in play rather than any other medium is more realistic as it is something the child feels comfortable with and gains enjoyment from, but it also encourages holistic development (Davenport 1994).

For this reason play in early recovery needs to be simple, and games with rules introduced over a period of time. There is no point in playing a game in which they are going to be criticized by others for not taking turns properly or doing it all wrong. If this happens it will have a serious effect on the child's self-esteem and they will no longer wish to participate in something that they should find enjoyable. This highlights the need for the playworker to encourage these feelings of self-worth by facilitating and planning a play environment a child can succeed in.

Play in hospital has changed over the years. It is clear that play should not be created by adults for children, but is a behaviour that children initiate themselves. Wherever possible play should be spontaneous, self-motivated and controlled by the child, including the choice of playmates. As discussed, hospitals can be environments where play can happen naturally but also where play can be encouraged to support the growth and development of each individual child. It is of great importance to recognize the needs of a variety of client groups, or specific individuals within a group, in order to offer a positive and enjoyable experience, and also to remember, as Ylvisaker (1998) commented, that play can be therapeutic but it should also be fun.

22

JANINE HART and AMY CLUTTERBROOK
Playwork in the prison environment: working with children separated by incarceration

(For all the children who visited the play centre at New Hall.)

New Hall Women's Prison Play Facility

> Time!!! The word echoes around the prison visits room and cascades into the play facility. A wide eyed little girl, aged around four, runs to her inmate mother and wraps every part of her little body around her. Her screams of, 'No, I want my mummy with me!' are only audible through heavy sobs.
>
> (Reflective Diary, November 2004)

Unfortunately this little girl is one of a growing number of children affected by the trauma of separation from a parent through imprisonment. At the time of writing, New Hall Women's Prison on the outskirts of Wakefield, Yorkshire, like many other women's prisons, is becoming increasingly overcrowded; with the women's estate showing dramatic increase in both young and more mature women detainees. The loss of a mother through imprisonment usually brings even greater upheaval in the family, and can be particularly traumatic. The children are likely to experience a whole range of emotions: pain, shame, guilt, anger and hostility. Children may also be confused and frightened by their emotions. They may blame themselves for their mothers' imprisonment, or they may block out their feelings and internalize their emotions.

So far there has been very little research into the needs and rights of children visiting HM prison establishments. Save the Children Fund has produced a resource pack, *Working with Children of Prisoners* (SCF 1998), and while this focuses on the child as an individual in its own right, it is primarily concerned with the child's right to education, as enshrined in Articles 28 and 29 of the *UN Convention on the Rights of the Child* (UNICEF 1991). There is obviously a need in this area for research which places the child at the forefront, rather than adult incentives for providing access to children.

When the play facility within New Hall Women's Prison was piloted in February 2001, the decision to adopt a playwork approach rather than a 'childcare' approach, had already been discussed in some depth. The child's play needs were our first priority, and that is what makes the provision relatively unique and so successful. This is the approach pioneered so successfully by Barbara Tamminem (2000) at the Wakefield Prison Visits Children's Play Facility.

When the children arrive they have often had long, tiring journeys, sometimes for a relatively short visit with their mum in a somewhat restrictive setting, and although the child has usually had no choice about whether they wanted to come to the prison, it is always their choice whether or not they want to use the play facility. Once in the play facility, it is always our practice that the children have the freedom to decide what it is they want to do, and whether they want to stay.

Case Study 1

Katie (2½ yrs) visited mum with her elder sister (7 yrs), Dad and Grandma. Katie presented herself as a traumatized little girl, displaying some of the changes which often manifest in a child when separated from their primary carer through imprisonment. Her behaviour towards her Dad was very aggressive initially, while her attachment to her eldest sister was very strong, with this young 7-year old displaying maternal responsibilities towards her younger sibling. Katie visited Mum with either Dad or Grandma every visiting session; this being possible as Mum was on remand awaiting trial or release. If Mum had been sentenced, visits might well have been restricted to two per month. Each time Katie visited, security checks would be the same: sniffer dogs, metal detectors and prison officers, all looking very official and scary to a small child.

Katie's initial visits were extremely distressing. She was very anxious and avoided any eye contact. The relationship with her Dad was fraught, with both finding this new situation hard to accept. Mum was unable to provide comfort as Katie avoided the formal seating arrangement, and inmates are not permitted to leave their seats throughout visits. Katie had only limited communication with any adult, but it was clear she was a very unhappy and distressed little girl.

It was around Katie's fifth visit that the opportunity afforded by a play environment in such alien surroundings brought change to this little girl. With trained and experienced staff, Katie was free to be whoever or whatever she wanted to be while in the play facility. There were no expectations, and upon an invitation to interact by means of a play cue (Sturrock and Else 1998), Katie was able to begin the healing process of separation, using play as her vehicle. The play cue was extremely subtle, merely involving sitting and touching a toy kitchen. Katie at this point never spoke, only stroked the oven door. A member of the playwork team acted upon this invitation to join Katie in her role play, naming each familiar object the little girl gave her. Katie's older sister made staff aware that Katie hadn't talked since 'mummy went'.

Gradually over a period of weeks Katie began to develop confidence and familiarity with her play surroundings. Her language development had temporarily been put on hold. However, the medium of role play served its function of helping to reduce the fear, mistrust and trauma this little girl had felt. Play provided Katie with an escape from reality (Moyles 1989), and by having the appropriate adult support to encourage and facilitate, pretend play had a very positive effect.

Case study 2

There is no doubting the devastating affects incarceration can have on the family unit, especially the children. The work at New Hall is primarily focused on relieving the stress levels during visiting for everyone involved, with the focus on the child and the child's needs. We have witnessed countless examples of children benefiting from the play facility. However, there are also occasions when the facility can be counter-productive.

Jamie was around 2 years old when she first came to visit. She displayed a very positive attachment to Mum initially, and would sob her heart out at the end of every visit. This was extremely distressing for everyone involved. After a few weeks she built up a relationship with playworkers and began to spend more and more time in the facility. Jamie went from spending 5 minutes in the playroom, to spending the entire session in there – spending no time with Mum.

Although this clearly eased the stress for Jamie, we were left with the feeling that the presence of the play facility had a damaging effect on her attachment to her mother.

Reflection

Prior to the development of the play facility at New Hall Women's Prison, visits were noisy and not fulfilling the needs of children who had been separated from their mothers. Indeed, there were doubts as to whether child-related social policies were being implemented, as required by the *UN Convention on the Rights of the Child* (UNICEF 1991). The children had limited interaction with their carers, and quite often became distressed.

After its pilot period of 12 weeks, the play facility 'New Hall Kidz' was granted funding, and is now an independent charity working in this multi-disciplinary setting. The facility strives to maintain and even develop family bonds disrupted by imprisonment. It continues to provide good quality play opportunities for all children visiting their loved ones, taking the philosophy and practice of playwork as its underpinning ethos into an apparently inappropriate environment. What the success of this facility shows is that the playwork approach has something powerful to offer children, no matter what the environment.

An alternative approach

Our final case study concerns the work of the Family Connections Centre, which is situated inside the Lakes Region Correctional Facility, Laconia, USA, and aims to offer prisoners opportunities to build upon and maintain positive family ties. This is attempted through special 2-hour long, one-on-one visits, between father and child, as well as weekly support groups and parenting classes.

In Case Study 2 we expressed our concern that the impact of the play facility may sometimes be slightly negative. Had Jamie and her mother had access to special visits, such as those often available in America, their attachment might have been maintained and possibly improved. On the basis of personal experience, this appeared to be true of the prisoners who made use of the Family Connections Centre. All those who were connected to the FCC were male, and for the most part did not regard themselves as the child's primary carer. However, there is no reason to suppose the outcomes would be any different if the participants were female.

The underpinning ethos of the FCC is that the family, especially the children, are the most effective tool in reducing reoffending. This raises doubts about some aspects of our work with New Hall Kidz. Was what we were doing enough? Were we failing the children by not doing more to reduce the risk of reoffending? Could we be in fact damaging the relationship between the parent and child, not improving it? What more could be done?

In slight contrast to the playwork ethos, the Family Connections Centre focuses on improving parenting skills. However, by combining those two approaches (playwork and parenting) it was possible to make a positive impact on the families we worked with in America. An example of this can be seen in Case study 3.

Case Study 3

Father S was a single parent to his 3-year-old son Kenny. When he first started receiving visits Father S found it very hard to be consistent with Kenny and would control his play. Father S would also wind Kenny up to the point that he would become distressed. After two months of talks with our staff team, Father S started to show vast improvements in his relationship and parental abilities with his son. Father S started to understand that it was better for Kenny to be allowed to choose his own play. He stopped teasing and started laughing *with* him rather than *at* him as before. He also began to follow through with his directions, and became more consistent with the boundaries he set.

This case study is a good example of how combining parenting skills and a playwork approach can help to improve relationships. Through the visits at FCC, Father S developed a much more effective relationship with his son by being reliable, consistent and fun to be with. This approach is supported by Sutton et al., who writes:

> Maintaining the family bond can reduce the risk of re-offending: providing a happy environment to encourage visits by children to prisons, helps to promote contact between prisoners and their families. Such facilities can also help to minimise the effects that the imprisonment of a parent has on a child.
>
> (Sutton et al. 1999)

Reflection

Whether it be Wakefield or Laconia, every day throughout the world, children are visiting their loved ones in prison. It's an experience that is unpleasant at best. Tamminem (2000) suggests for most children the experience is highly disturbing and even traumatic. It would be wrong to say that Katie, Jamie and Kenny are the lucky ones, because no child should have to go through that sort of experience. Nevertheless, including play provision within the walls of a prison means that some children are able to get through the day without screaming in desperate emotional distress when it comes to home time. It may even help to give a little self-worth back to some children for whom life has been a constant struggle. So why aren't there more children's play projects in our prisons?

23

MEYNELL
Thinking about creating a play environment

What is Ben doing? (The narrative)

Ben arrives at work keen, enthusiastic and ready for the afternoon session with the children. He greets the rest of the team and they have a chat and a bit of banter about what they did yesterday evening. Ben asks who's got the planning sheet for today's session, so that he can find out what he is meant to be doing. While taking his coat off and making a cup of tea, they discuss what is going to be happening that day, and who is going to be taking responsibility for what. Ben asks what still needs to be done and asks specifically what the rest of the team want him to do. Sacha is preparing the snack while Gueljentseya is getting together a variety of sports type equipment to be taken outside. Charleen, the supervisor, is sorting out papers and working out which parents are due to receive the invoices. This means that no one is setting up the main room. Ben suggests he does that.

He starts to think about what the children were doing yesterday, and asks Charleen who is in tonight. In his head Ben is pondering, 'What bits and pieces, equipment, material and resources shall I get out and where shall I put them?' The normal practice at club is to set out the room with various areas, one where the children can run around and play active games; another area for chilling and hanging out; and another area where the children can be involved in creative art and craft type activities. Ben recollects that last week a number of the girls who were at club had invented a game using quoits. He gets a couple of crates from the store room and loads up a variety of materials – indoor physical play equipment, foam balls, foam rugby balls, some skipping ropes, throwing discs, quoits and bean bags, some short tennis posts, bats, and small indoor high bounce balls. He takes these crates to the end of the room that is often used for lively games, and puts some benches across the middle of the room to mark a kind of barrier between the physical area and the rest of the hall.

Next, Ben considers what is required for the creative area, he remembers yesterday evening he had conversations with two different groups of children. One group of the older children wanted to make boomerangs, so Ben puts together a crate with saws, hammers, files, glass paper, spoke shaves and wood. He also puts in some thin cotton gloves. The other group had recollected a time when they had been making jewellery out of paper. Ben puts together a resource pack for them including a book with ideas, newspaper, glue, paints, scissors and a whole variety of odds and ends. In the craft area he puts up a couple of tables for the children to work at, and another table on which he lays out all the jewellery-making equipment and resources and materials he has got. Then it is back to the store room again and numerous journeys from the store room to set up the quiet area.

Ben takes out beanbags, the book box, board games, packs of cards and a box with paper, crayons and coloured pencils. He looks around; it seems everything is there. Plenty of different opportunities for the children to choose from, and he has remembered the things the children have asked for from yesterday and last week.

Ben calls over to Sacha to see if she needs any help with the snacks, but she doesn't, so he goes over to Charleen and asks if anyone has done today's health and safety check and risk assessment check. Charleen says no and gives him the checklist. Ben takes the list and starts to check each area of the setting. It is quite a structured list so he doesn't have to think too much, just tick after he has checked things. The toilets are clean, there is plenty of toilet paper, the lights and the locks all work, the front door is secure, the bell works.

Part of the process is looking at the equipment that has been set out. Ben looks at the spoke shaves, they have a sharp blade in them. He is not sure whether they should be there or not. He goes to ask Charleen, who asks what the problem might be. Ben knows the likelihood of someone cutting themselves with the spoke shaves isn't great, but that if the children mess about with them, they could cut themselves. The blades are quite sharp and need to be angled the right way in order for them to cut. He explains all this to Charleen, who says perhaps Ben ought to keep the spoke shaves with him, and when the children start making the boomerangs, ask them if they want to use them and then give them out. She tells Ben to remember to warn the children they are potentially dangerous pieces of equipment when he hands them over.

Ben continues to fill in the checklists. When they are completed he hands them back to Charleen for storage in the appropriate file. Sacha has finished the snacks and is looking over the room that Ben has set up. Ben asks her if everything is okay, and is there anything else that the children asked for yesterday or last week. The doorbell goes; the children are arriving.

Why is Ben doing this? (The annotation)

What does all this mean? What was behind the way Ben was today? Well to start with, he got himself in the right frame of mind before he went to work. There is no point in turning up for work if you can't be bothered to be there. Okay, sometimes you may be distracted, have other things on your mind, but your job, as the playworker, is to be there 100 per cent for the children. If you are consistently unable to do that, then you need to speak to your manager to establish a method so that you can go to work in a positive frame of mind. Often the 'not wanting to be there' attitude comes from something not being right in your setting, and you have to take responsibility for trying to work this out.

Time taken at the beginning of the day chatting to other members of staff helps to build positive relationships within your staff team. The development of these positive relationships means it is easier for you to work together. A good working relationship is dependent on mutual respect. Mutual respect comes through an understanding of who you are, what your strengths and weaknesses are, and the better you get on as a team, the better your working relationships are.

You will notice that throughout today's setting-up, Ben was comfortable offering help and asking for help, clarifying what he was meant to be doing and seeking advice when he wasn't sure. There was no ambiguity in Ben's conversations with his colleagues; they clearly understood what he was saying and what he was asking. Ben clearly understood the importance of the need to communicate clearly. If he hadn't communicated clearly, his offers of support might not have been recognized, leading to a deterioration of the good working relationship of the team. His requests for clarification and direction may have been misunderstood, leading to resentment from other members of the team, if they perceived Ben not contributing fully to the work of the team.

We have been looking at Ben today as he went through the process of setting everything up, and creating the environments for the children and young people's play. Ben knows that the environment needs to be stimulating. He knows his job as the playworker is to offer opportunities and help create environments for the children and young people to play in. He knows that if the same resources and equipment are provided every day, then the level of stimulation will be reduced. Ben reflected on which children were going to be there; he sought clarification from his supervisor. He knows that different children come from one day to the next, and that he needs to consider both the children who come everyday, hence reflecting on what the children from last night said, and also the children who just come on this day every week, hence reflecting on the children who came last week.

Ben knows that the play environment belongs to the children, it is their play environment not his. Therefore it is important that what goes into the play environment is what the children want. So Ben used not only his own reflections and memory of discussions with children, but also checked with colleagues. Ben's choices of materials and resources not only responded to what the children requested, but also provide the opportunity for the children to go where they like in terms of the direction they take with the materials and what they decide to do with them.

Within the main room of the play setting Ben has created three different environments where different types of play can take place. He has done this because he understands that different children will want to do different things at different times. The way he has set the main room out means the children have the choice of where in the room they wish to go, and how they will utilize various materials and resources.

Part 4

Playwork values, ethics and professional practice

24

MICK CONWAY
The Playwork Principles

When Play Wales commissioned Bob Hughes, Gordon Sturrock and myself to develop proposals for new Playwork Principles we considered whether we should merely rewrite the Assumptions and Values in the light of current thinking, but decided to start again from first Principles and try to describe the underpinning philosophy of playwork. There was some controversy about the decision not to include explicit statements on issues like equality of opportunity and diversity, health and safety and children's rights, but we took the view that these were properly in the realm of the existing legal and regulatory framework. We wanted the Principles to be a fundamental professional and ethical framework describing the unique playwork perspective, avoiding the need for continual revision and tweaking at the margins as the law and regulation changed.

As a reality check on what we were proposing we analysed around 20 playwork-related job descriptions and person specifications spanning the years 1981 to 2004. In most cases only a quarter of the content was about children's play, while the rest concerned operational and management issues. Looked at in chronological order, this was a history of the introduction of legislation and regulation over the years. I have to confess that one I wrote in the mid-1990s showed exactly the same pattern.

In May 2005 SkillsActive endorsed the Principles, and for the time being the scrutiny group holds them in trust for the sector as there continues to be debate about how they should be contextualized within the playwork occupational standards.

A fuller history of the thinking, processes and the consultation phases can be found on the Play Wales Website.

The Principles, and some issues about what they might mean in practice

Preamble
These Principles establish the professional and ethical framework for playwork and as such must be regarded as a whole. They describe what is unique about

play and playwork, and provide the playwork perspective for working with children and young people. They are based on the recognition that children and young people's capacity for positive development will be enhanced if given access to the broadest range of environments and play opportunities.

(PPSG 2005)

The preamble to the Principles introduces the concept of a professional and ethical playwork perspective that gives primacy to the child at play:

1. All children and young people need to play. The impulse to play is innate. Play is a biological, psychological and social necessity, and is fundamental to the healthy development and well being of individuals and communities.

While this principle is an assertion, it is based on the scientific research literature on play behaviours in children and human physical, mental and social evolution and development. The studies of ontogeny (the development of the individual) and phylogeny (the development of the species) show that there is an innate need to play, which implies a right to play, and 'all children' quite simply means all.

However, this needs a bit of unpicking in the context of playwork. A place to start might be to ask how many children and young people live in the catchment area of the play space and what percentage of them use it regularly. There are well known factors outside the play space, such as traffic, and parental and children's own fears about safety, which deter or prevent children from accessing and using the play space. However, we also need to take an honest and critical look at any factors inside the play space, and at just how welcoming it is for *all* children and young people.

An example of what I mean comes from a Hackney Play Association (HPA) play project in the early 1990s. There were large numbers of Turkish, Kurdish, Somali and Bengali refugee and displaced children living on estates with little or no play provision, and who didn't use what provision there was. HPA set up an estates mobile play project but the children from these communities did not use it. The main reasons were that the playworkers were not from their cultures and didn't speak their languages; and the children stayed indoors because they and their families were subjected to continual harassment, racism and abuse on the estates. HPA tried to recruit playworkers from the communities but couldn't find any with the experience or skills needed, despite lowering the minimum requirements. The answer was to set up a playwork training project for the communities, and the result was a dramatic increase in their children using both the mobile project and other play provision.

2. Play is a process that is freely chosen, personally directed and intrinsically motivated. That is, children and young people determine and control the content and intent of their play, by following their own instincts, ideas and interests, in their own way for their own reasons.

This principle is based on a definition of play developed by Bob Hughes from the research literature and elaborates on a definition in Getting Serious About Play (DCMS 2004) that has since been adopted by the BIG Lottery Children's Play Initiative. The proposition is that play appears to be universal and instinctive, but while many of the play behaviours of children individually or in groups can be observed and described, the internal mental states and intentions that drive or produce them can only be inferred. *Play Types: Speculations and Possibilities* (Hughes 2006) explores 'whether what we think we see when we observe children playing is what is actually going on' and is highly recommended by this author as an essential text.

What it boils down to is that children are the experts in their play, and this is further elaborated in the subsequent Principles:

3. The prime focus and essence of playwork is to support and facilitate the play process and this should inform the development of play policy, strategy, training and education.

This means the child at play is central, and everything else should be in support of their play. This has always been a fundamental concept in playwork theory, but as we discovered in the job description and person specification analysis, management and operational issues and compliance with legislation, regulation and inspection regimes have gradually come to dominate in practice.

It could be argued that there has been a similar pattern in some playwork qualification training, with operational training taking precedence over the more conceptual underpinning knowledge and education, particularly at non-degree levels. The play process has only very recently started to feature in play policy and strategy development, and it was a major battle to get play even mentioned in the *Every Child Matters* agenda and inspection regime.

4. For playworkers, the play process takes precedence and playworkers act as advocates for play when engaging with adult led agendas.

This principle is about the playwork perspective that children's engagement in the play process is an outcome in itself. In the *Every Child Matters* consultation children and young people put more and better places to play and things to do at the top of their agenda, well ahead of educational achievement, but the government combined the two in order to pursue their own education agenda – a perfect example of an adult and political agenda overriding what children and young people said they needed and wanted.

The bottom line is that children have a need to play, which they clearly articulate time and time again. The role of the playworker is to champion the right of the child to play and question adult agendas. This includes their own agendas as playworkers, and this is further elaborated in the next three Principles:

5. The role of the playworker is to support all children and young people in the creation of a space in which they can play.

The emphasis here is on supporting children in the creation of their play space by enabling rather than directing or controlling. Space includes social, emotional and imaginative as well as physical space. A test of how well this principle is put into practice is to look at the percentage of the physical play space that has been created by children and young people, rather than playworkers or other adults, and to what extent children are enabled to control the content and intent of their play.

The playworker's role is to provide an accessible, inclusive and welcoming environment and to enrich the play space with a wide range of props and opportunities:

> 6. The playworker's response to children and young people playing is based on a sound up to date knowledge of the play process, and reflective practice.

The emphasis is on responding to children playing as playworkers, not as play-leaders. Knowledge includes training, education, reading and continuing professional development, while reflective practice includes observation, recalling our own childhood memories, thinking and recording. Until recently, the playwork field has been poor at building and sharing the knowledge base, with the result that we've continually had to reinvent the wheel.

Playworkers should have a good understanding of key concepts such as play types (Hughes 2002a, 2006); play cues, returns and frames (Sturrock and Else 1998), and the theory of loose parts (Nicholson 1971), and be familiar with Best Play (NPFA 2000).

> 7. Playworkers recognize their own impact on the play space and also the impact of children and young people's play on the playworker.

This principle recognizes that there are deep and complex interactions between playworkers, the play space and the children. For example, some play behaviours can be subversive, transgressive, unexpected and just plain weird! Playworkers need to understand that some behaviours, however disturbing, are how children work through difficulties, resolve conflicts and build resilience.

> 8. Playworkers choose an intervention style that enables children and young people to extend their play. All playworker intervention must balance risk with the developmental benefit and well-being of children.

The final principle is about a 'high-response, low-intervention' style in a rich play environment with the widest possible opportunities for exploration, discovery and challenge. For example, as a society we accept that the developmental benefit of learning to ride a bike outweighs the risk of bumps, grazes or worse, and the only way we learn to ride is by falling off enough times until we get it right – the stabilizers have to come off sometime.

25

FRASER BROWN
The Playwork Principles: a critique

A critique is a methodical examination of the thinking that underpins a concept, and an analysis of its possible outcomes and limitations. At the outset, I want to make it clear that I'm not criticizing the idea of having Playwork Principles, nor would I wish to criticize most of the Principles that resulted from an extended consultation process in 2005. Principles 3 to 8 clearly represent some of the main priorities of the playwork profession. What I want to take issue with is the second Principle, and since that provides the definition that underpins the remaining Principles, to suggest that we risk misleading ourselves, society, and most importantly the children with whom we work, if we hold fast to this untenable definition. So first, I'll be offering a critique of that definition, and second a brief summary of the 'principles' that appear to be missing from the Playwork Principles as currently written (PPSG 2005).

Definitions

Garvey (1977) suggests the most effective way to explain play is to identify common threads within the leading theories. This is not simple since some of those theories are directly contradictory. For example, play has been seen as both the consumer of surplus energy (Spencer 1873), and the recreator of lost energy (Lazarus 1883). Theories also cover a wide range of disciplines: behaviourism (Berlyne 1960), cognitive development (Piaget 1951), psychoanalysis (Axline 1969) and so on. Caillois (1961: 9) suggests that there are six essential characteristics of play. It is 'free, separate, uncertain, unproductive, governed by rules, and has make believe'. Given this range of debate, it is not surprising to find Huizinga (1949: 7) concluding that play 'is not susceptible of exact definition either logically, biologically, or aesthetically'. Nevertheless, Garvey (1977) identifies five commonly accepted characteristics of play: positive effect, intrinsic motivation, free choice, active engagement, and non-literality.

Garvey's summary will be familiar to many in the playwork profession, because it is so similar to the definition developed by Hughes (1996), and subsequently used in *Best Play* (NPFA 2000: 6): 'Play is freely chosen, personally directed, intrinsically motivated behaviour that actively engages the child'. This same sentiment reappears in the second Playwork Principle, which defines play thus:

2. Play is a process that is freely chosen, personally directed and intrinsically motivated. That is, children and young people determine and control the content and intent of their play, by following their own instincts, ideas and interests, in their own way for their own reasons.

(PPSG 2005)

In 30 years, from Garvey's summary to Hughes's definition and now to a Playwork Principle, this reflection on play is becoming increasingly embedded into playwork thinking, and therein lies a problem. We now find ourselves working to a definition of play that doesn't stand up to scrutiny, and a number of supportive statements that are also somewhat tenuous. Much of the following exploration is taken from an email debate that took place in the autumn of 2006 on the UKplayworkers Website.

Is play freely chosen, personally directed and intrinsically motivated?

Play takes many forms, and they don't all manifest themselves in the forms of behaviour suggested in the second Playwork Principle (freely chosen, personally directed and intrinsically motivated). That definition is not just idealizing play, it is actually understating the value of play – something playworkers should never do. You only have to stand on a school playground during playtime to appreciate the complexity of play, and the fact that many forms of play are:

- 'chosen', but not 'freely';
- 'directed', but not 'personally';
- 'motivated', but not 'intrinsically'.

The crucial point that is missed by this restrictive definition is that play has developmental value, even when it is not freely chosen, personally directed and intrinsically motivated. For example, children who join in with the large game of football that often dominates school playgrounds are clearly playing, but some are playing because they've been bullied into it. Obviously the quality of their play is substantially different from those children who have freely chosen to join in, but they still gain all sorts of developmental benefit.

Lots of children take part in group activities that they are not personally directing – some children freely choose to be part of the crowd, even if that means being directed by someone else. In role play, the child who is directed to act the part of the baby when they would rather be the mum or dad is clearly not personally directing their play, but they may be gaining enormous social benefits as a result of their compliant behaviour.

The play behaviour of teasing, which is often quite cruel, has clear developmental benefits for both parties involved. However, the person on the receiving end cannot be said to be intrinsically motivated to take part. One of the most important benefits of play is the way in which it teaches us about hierarchies, and helps us find ways of coping with the injustices of everyday life. Those are often harsh lessons, but nonetheless valuable.

That is not to say that playworkers should stand by while children learn lessons the hard way. I am simply stating my view that the definition provided in the second Playwork Principle, and most commonly used by the playwork profession is untenable. There are as many definitions of play as there are play theorists, and most people who have studied the subject in any depth have come to the conclusion that a definition is impossible. In fact, we are seriously underselling the value of play in terms of both individual and species development, if we continue with this restrictive definition.

However, it's not necessary to abandon the idea altogether. In my opinion a more realistic approach would be for the profession to argue that playwork should be seeking to encourage the sort of play that is 'freely chosen, personally directed and intrinsically motivated'. The Play Wales Website uses an interesting phrasing. It says, 'play which is freely chosen, personally directed and intrinsically motivated is vital in a child's development'. I totally agree with that statement – those forms of play are absolutely 'vital', and those are the forms of play that I think it is ethically responsible for the playwork profession to prioritize. So I suppose I'm asking for a careful rephrasing of the statement, so that we can be quite clear about where our priorities lie.

Do children determine and control the content and intent of their play?

Again, rather like the 'freely chosen' definition, the idea that children determine and control the content and intent of their play is too often stated as if it were a fact. Clearly, this is often the case, but in reality there are many instances when children do not determine the content of their play, and yet they still gain great benefit. For example I used to play 'house' with my sister and her friends. She is four years older than me, so I pretty much had to do as I was told. The 'content' of my play was largely dictated to me, but the buzz I got from being able to play with my older sister and her friends was immeasurable.

As for children controlling the 'intent' of their play, in many cases there is no 'intent'. Children are just playing for the hell of it. Once again I want to argue that this slightly dogmatic use of the terminology is unhelpful. It would be so much more accurate to say that children benefit greatly from play when they are in control of the content and the intent. The circumstances where that is possible are rapidly reducing. From a playworker's point of view our aim should be to recreate environments that enable children to claim and retain control of their play experiences.

What's missing?

The preamble to the Playwork Principles states that children's 'capacity for positive development will be enhanced if given access to the broadest range of environments and play opportunities'. This is a recognition that playworkers are in the business of child development. I welcome that, although I know some playwork colleagues have reservations. The preamble also states that the Playwork Principles 'describe what is unique about play and playwork, and provide the playwork perspective for working with children and young people'.

However, the Playwork Principles focus almost entirely on statements about what we do, rather than how we do it. There is reference to supporting and facilitating the play process (PP3); acting as advocates for play (PP4); supporting children in the creation of a play space (PP5); choosing an appropriate intervention style (PP7). These are well meaning statements, with which most of us would agree. However, they are not really what they claim to be. They are not principles.

In the sense in which it is being used in the PPSG document, a Principle is a statement that should guide our conduct. Thus, a Playwork Principle should be a statement that makes it clear how playworkers should conduct themselves. There would be no point in making such statements unless they also make it clear what is unique about the playwork approach. For example we might expect one of these principles to state that playwork is essentially non-judgemental.

If the Principles are going to 'describe what is unique about playwork', then we should be asking the question, what is it that sets us apart from the rest of the 'children's workforce'? The answer lies in our methods, as well as our focus. At present the Playwork Principles tend to concentrate on our focus, to the detriment of our methods; the most significant of these being that playworkers work to the children's agenda. That is far from simple, but no one else does it. All other professions work to an adult agenda. Clearly, this is one of the things that is unique, but it's not mentioned.

Here is a brief summary of some of the other unique playwork methods that are not mentioned in the Playwork Principles:

- Drummond Abernethy said adventure playwork should be viewed as an attitude of mind, rather than a physical framework. The Principles should address the idea that playworkers work holistically.
- Playwork is substantially concerned with enabling children to exercise control over their play by recreating the flexibility that is increasingly absent from children's play environments. The Principles should mention the concept of compound flexibility.
- Each child has his/her individual social, physical, intellectual, creative, emotional and spiritual needs. Working with children where they are in their lives at this moment in time is a fundamental element of playwork, and should be mentioned in the Principles.
- Childhood is essentially a social construct. Playworkers should recognize that, and avoid making too many socially constructed judgements about the children's play behaviour. The idea that play is always freely chosen, personally directed and intrinsically motivated, is one such judgement. Playworkers should therefore adopt a non-judgemental, non-prejudicial, non-directive, and largely reflective approach to their work. These are Principles that most playworkers would espouse, and yet they are not mentioned in the Playwork Principles.

Conclusion

All this may seem to be nothing more than pedantic nit-picking, but it actually goes to the very heart of the two main views of what relating to children via the medium of play is about, and tries to point the way to a middle ground. On one side we have those who espouse an evolutionary view of playwork. I would characterize this as the Darwinian 'survival of the fittest' approach. For example, this group feel that if children are damaged during their play, that is all part of the survival process. On the other side we have the developmentalists who see play as an excellent tool for persuading children to learn the things that adults feel they should learn. This is the view embraced enthusiastically by many nursery teachers. In the centre are those of us who see the play process as essentially developmental, but not in the traditional sense that children are adults in waiting. Rather, we would characterize the play process as follows: children learn and develop both while playing and through play – in other words they are both learning how to cope with the immediate world around them, and at the same time acquiring skills that will serve them well in the future. Opportunities for that to happen are fast diminishing. It is the role of the playworker to create environments that enable children to benefit fully from the play process. (see Chapter 1 for a fuller exploration of what this might mean in practice).

26

CHRIS TAYLOR
Some reflections on the history of playwork in the adventure playground tradition

This chapter explores the ideas and events that characterized the early days of adventure playgrounds in Denmark and England. It takes a personal view of playing and working on playgrounds in Manchester during the 1970s, and from both folk histories suggests some key features of the adventure playground tradition. The conclusion briefly identifies more recent contributions and invites the reader to use these resources to inform a sense of their own tradition of contemporary adventure playwork.

Early days

The idea of the first adventure playground was outlined by Prof. C.Th. Sorenson (1931), a Danish landscape architect, and was based on his observations of children playing outdoors. The first junk or building playground was opened at Emdrup on the outskirts of Copenhagen, through his work and that of the local Workers Cooperative Housing Association. The design of the playground was influenced by a perceived need to address the negative impacts of urbanization by providing an outdoor environment that afforded the play opportunities of the countryside, and included junk and scrap materials to be used freely and creatively by the children. The playground was seen to be a child-centred place, where children were free to build, destroy and change their environment.

The first playworker was John Bertelsen, an ex-seaman and nursery worker; from the outset, he kept a diary of his work – the first reflective practitioner! Through his observations, experiences and reflections he came to describe the qualities of playwork and the role of the playworker. This meant having 'a positive attitude towards the whole concept of play'; and children feeling physically and emotionally safe on the playground – what he called a 'pro physical' and 'pro play' environment. (Bertelsen, cited in Bengtsson 1972: 16). The key task of the playworker was to facilitate creativity, play and building work to provide a child-centred environment. During the first two years of the playground Bertelsen witnessed Emdrup become 'the children's community within the adult society' (Bengtsson 1972: 21).

Lady Allen of Hurtwood visited Emdrup and, impressed by what she saw, introduced the idea of the adventure playground to a wider audience in the Picture Post in 1946. Her aim was 'to give children in towns the same chance for creative play as those in the country' (Allen 1968: 1). Her campaigning and enthusiasm led to the introduction and development of adventure playgrounds in England. She was on the management committee of one of the first adventure playgrounds, at Clydesdale, Kensington and also established the Handicapped Adventure Playground Association.

During the 1950s adventure playgrounds were opened in Crawley, Grimsby, Liverpool and London. There were 17 by 1960. Drummond Abernethy, head of children's play department (1956–77), at the National Playing Fields Association, played a central role in promoting the idea of adventure playgrounds, and by the 1970s their expansion was such that regional officers were appointed to support their development and further growth.

Most adventure playgrounds emerged during a time when there was a belief that collective action could affect social change. For example, this was the period that saw the growth of feminism and the women's movement, and the emergence of civil rights campaigns for racial equality. The adventure playground movement was seen to provide an alternative play setting for children and new form of organization for communities, and fitted comfortably into the socio-political context of the period. Many came to see it as an institutional form that exemplified libertarianism. Ward (1961, p. 193) described the adventure playground as 'an arresting example of ... living anarchy, one which is valuable both in itself and as an experimental verification of a whole social approach'.

Not everyone was as enamoured with the adventure playground as its early proponents. They were sometimes described as messy, unruly and unwelcoming places. Abernethy (1968: 2) reported fears that they were seen by some as a 'threat to family life' – the playworker, being perceived as an alternative and potentially disruptive influence in the life of the child. 'Over my dead body' was the alleged reply of the Director of Parks and Recreation to initial requests to develop adventure playgrounds in Manchester. He survived their eventual appearance, funded from other sources, but such anecdotes capture the sometimes rebellious, controversial nature of adventure playgrounds and those that work on them. From their origins to the present day they can be seen to be tinged with recalcitrance.

Personal reflections

I began working on adventure playgrounds in Manchester during the 1970s. Politically, I felt drawn to the work. I enjoyed being outdoors, experiencing the elements, having a job that involved being paid to play, meeting and being with lots of children and young people – the kids – who accepted me on their own terms and shared a part of themselves and their lives. I enjoyed the freedom and spontaneity of being a playworker; the 'let's-make-some-soup-tonight' approach. I felt reassured by the Jack-of-all-trades, Jill-of-none nature of the work: of being able to introduce ideas and experiment, without having to be an expert. Debriefs on the working day were often held in the local pub. The Manchester Adventure Playground Association, a federation of playgrounds met monthly to promote playwork across the city. There was a feeling of belonging and doing something that was innovative and important. This is my own sense of the tradition. If the truth be told, there was much of my own desire to play, embedded within it.

Bridget Murphy, now an adult, regularly played on the adventure playground, and recently emailed me her recollections.

Memories

Always having a fire to sit 'round.

- Eating potatoes cooked in the fire that were 'burnt to a cinder' but tasted great – especially if it was freezing outside.
- Being trusted to sell the penny sweets in the hut and how great this made me feel.
- Being able to talk to Playground Workers about anything and everything and never feeling as though I were being judged.
- Going on trips to the seaside and countryside – thinking they were hundreds of miles away.
- Eating the best stew in the world which was cooked in a massive pan on the fire, had everything chucked into it (including dirt), and was thickened up with lots of rice.
- Doing a sponsored swim to raise money for an exchange trip to Germany, we camped on their playground, and even learnt to sing 'Blowing in the Wind' in German. The return visit was great because it was like meeting up with long-lost friends – we all camped in Formby and the guitar came out 'round the fire'.
- Going to Anzio Army Training Camp and the snow being about 3ft deep.
- Feeling like I had friends (Playground Workers) who were adults.

These are personal recollections of a tradition in the making. Some themes of continuity can be seen to continue to characterize the ever evolving tradition of adventure playwork one that includes:

- the idea of the playground as a compensation for urban living and for addressing material and emotional deprivation;
- the importance of working outdoors, and with the elements, earth, water, wind and fire;
- the provision of an environment that provides for and allows manipulation, construction, destruction and change;
- a place that contains junk, and loose parts, elements that can be found, and manipulated to create life anew;

- the scrounging ethic as part of the play process, discovering and using what comes along or can be foraged, rather than a consumption of what is provided for and given;[1]
- the provision of an environment that allows for play – coming at life unconventionally;
- a place for personal physical and psychical risk taking;
- a holistic way of working and being with children – the whole person present in play and relatedly, the absence of age segregation, the earliest playgrounds were for children from 2½ to 20 years (Abernethy 1977);
- a spontaneous organic form of relating that includes the provision of materials and activities, but entertains the possibilities of anything else that comes up;
- an appreciation of alternative, a somewhat recalcitrant approach and a commitment to advocating for children and their right to play environments for playing in;
- the importance of local involvement and management of the playground;
- the importance of fire, food, trust, relationships, new experiences, opportunities and friendships – and fun.

Conclusion

The tradition has developed considerably since its early days, gaining many resources of relevance to present-day practitioners. Cranwell (2003, 2007) continues to document the history of the adventure playground and does much to formalize and bring coherence to the origins of the work. Brown (2007) has recently published an in-depth case study of the history of one of the most long-running adventure playgrounds, *The Venture* in Wrexham. The British experience has seen the emergence of distinctive traditions of practice, inspired by the individuals or groups who worked on the playgrounds, for example, the evolutionary reflective analytic practice of Hughes (2001a), and the ludocentric approach developed by Sturrock and Else (2007). The various playwork theories outlined throughout this book add further to the evolution of the adventure playwork tradition. There has also been a refinement of the tools and methodologies of playwork research, for example through reflective practice (see Chapter 10) and story telling (see Chapter 54). Such resources will hopefully be used by practitioners reflecting upon contemporary experiences, ideas, and beliefs that are important for and belong to the evolution of both an individual and shared playwork tradition attuned to the context of adventure playgrounds in the 21st century.

Note

[1] These key ingredients of the tradition, featured in the early names of the playground, initially conceived in Denmark as junk playgrounds (*Skrammellegeplads*) and building playgrounds (*Byggelegeplads*), imported to England as the former, but quickly renamed Adventure Playgrounds.

27

MAUREEN PALMER
'The place we are meant to be':[1] play, playwork and the natural rhythms of communities

This chapter draws on my experience of working on Cornwallis Adventure Playground in the London Borough of Islington during the 1980s. It makes extensive use of conversations that took place during the production of a DVD about the life of the playground. I have tried to think what was important about those years of my work and what key themes emerge: the children allude to these when they speak of their 'sense of belonging', or 'feeling part of something', and refer to the idea of community and of personal identity, one developing in conjunction with the other; the sense that they were free to try and do anything, nothing was off the list; their sense of control over the space, how it changed and developed, and how they were able to be the catalyst for this; their sense that in all this they were solidly held, respected, valued and cared for; that they felt they had aware, thoughtful and committed playworkers who would go the extra mile.

The adventure playground acted as the hub of the community. The dialectical relationship, which grew between the outside adult space and the play space, developed a living community culture, originating from and transforming the wider adult-controlled community. How was this able to happen? How were these children able to do this? My proposition is that it was possible because of the nature of the adventure playground, the playwork practised there, and the way it worked with the natural rhythms of the community within which it operated.

It is this important organic process that is increasingly missing from children's play spaces: potentially, it is only within adventure playgrounds that this organic process can emerge and develop. The very ethos within the craft of playwork enables it to happen. If we fail to understand and respect this, we will continue to see more 'new ideas' moving in trying to fill the void – elements called regeneration, and citizenship for example; concepts, rather than processes, imposed from outside communities, and having little short-term impact, and even less long-term effect.

My contention is that an adventure playground is a children's space, where children can change and grow in their own way, and by osmosis develop a community culture of which they are the key and the catalyst. Some evidence for these assertions can be found in Reflections on Adventure Play (Palmer 2002), a DVD presenting some of the data from a longitudinal study of children, young people and their families on an adventure playground, derived from video recordings, oral tapes, daybooks and numerous discussions.

Excerpts from *Reflections on Adventure Play*, and discussions with the children of Cornwallis

Leggy talks about his 'feeling that you felt you were part of something'. He lets us know that one of the reasons he and his friends felt they could be there was that though 'it wasn't the street, it still felt like you were part of the street'. He says, 'it felt like someone cared about you'. He describes the games of volleyball played there as an 'exotic sport'. I think he does so because those games were played in rhythm with those who participated. So you would have Lorraine, aged 6 in her wellies, 14-year-old Dempsey, Chuck at six foot would be overpowering when he wasn't distracted, our Joanne who was a key character on the playground, and many more. This incredible group of mixed ages, sizes and abilities would play this game in which luckily, no one really ever knew what the rules were – well, get it over the net: and playworkers who understood it really didn't matter. This wasn't sport, it was play and what flexible play!

Vicky talks of the level of love she felt, and Leggy bravely talks of feeling unloved as a child. Both found a place they felt safe, in their 'venture', both had challenging relationships with their playworkers; as Leggy describes it, he had an 'explosive' one with me! Ryan says, it was somewhere that was 'community based, and I was allowed to go to'. Ryan is also clear that parts of their lives as children were played out on the venture, where they felt held, and therefore crucial events were mostly 'a drama and not a trauma'.

It could be hard on the workers, keeping pace with the children and their changes. There was acute observation of what was going on individually and between the different groups. Planned and spontaneous change and modification had to happen all the while. As Sammy Collier says, 'I went every day because there was always something new happening'.

We worked late: 8.00pm was the official closing time, but by the time the ropes were in, the clearing-up done, finding where children had hidden ... it wasn't 8.00pm anymore. When the whole playground was involved in getting ready for the Notting Hill Carnival and our three-day stay-over, you might not get out till midnight. When Diane decided to paint the hut red inside and we all suddenly realized we had to have it finished by the end of the session (!), I can't remember what time everyone stayed until.

One winter we realized that hardly anyone was coming in for the Saturday morning sessions and that the few children who did come wanted more. We discussed options and the idea of doing a trip and not opening till after lunch emerged. This was a big decision, but one the children wanted. Following much grilling by our play officer, we tried it. In two weeks we had over 30 on the outing, and had two winter months of fantastic fun, all going to the swimming pool together on Saturday mornings.

I recall heated debates with parents about what the children should be doing, and debates between the children and young people. I can see Lori, 6-years old telling Yinka, 17-years old, to get out of her space as she had been working there. I remember the discussion about her right to assert herself. The older ones didn't always find this easy!

I remember Leggy saying how he had managed to get through the day at school, and how he did it by focusing on knowing he would be able to get to the playground later. He told me he couldn't describe his emotions when on one occasion he got to the gate and read the notice saying we couldn't open because of staff shortage.

Agi talks about preferring to be at Cornwallis and how he hated school and was bullied all the time. Beverly says, 'I felt I could try anything, and the venture helped me hold on to my childhood longer'.

Vicky says, 'Cornwallis was my favourite thing, it was our place'. She also talks about feeling 'everything and anything was open to talk about'. Vicky says, 'she [the playworker] always seemed to know what was going on for us'.

Our focus was on providing a child's play space within which they could grow and change themselves and the playspace, and one which supported them in dealing with their issues. As Leggy puts it, 'the playground was the only place I was praised for my anger. They simply wanted you to think about how you might do things another way'. Yes, we did want him to gain some control over that anger, but at the same time we wanted to validate his right to be angry about his life.

Validating the evidence

In the summer of 2006 I carried out a small piece of research at one of the borough's adventure playgrounds to test some of the key learning points that had emerged from Cornwallis decades earlier. I negotiated with the playworkers to open the playground two nights a week over the summer till 9.00pm, so children could play from 10.00am to 9.00pm at night. Several key playwork people were asked to come and carry out observations and interview children and parents on site towards the end of the summer and I maintained detailed reflective diaries.

Early outcomes indicated that this later opening showed a marked change in the way the parents and the children saw their playground and their workers. The playground began to feel far more a part of the community, and the community felt they had been made an offer and it was one they responded to.

Some externally observed and recorded snapshots

Mums came to cook for the whole playground in the evening; several different mums and they had not been asked to, it just happened. Food was provided this way nearly every late session. Parents spoke to me about how their days operated and how the late opening allowed them to get all their tasks done, and still get their young children to site and have a good few hours to play. They also got something out of being able to meet other parents and children. They made the point that the 5.30pm closure meant it was hardly worth them bringing the children over.

A 9-year old said, 'it's much better that it's open later, it's easier to check in with the playworkers, and is somewhere to get away from TV and family'. An 8-year old said, 'I like the late nights when its quieter, and you can go on the swings and I like to play with my friends and we sit up there [she points to a platform on one of the structures] and watch the sunset. It goes down over there, and we watch it till it disappears'. Several children mentioned this. A 10-year old, and his friend, 12 years old, say, 'we get to stay out late. We wouldn't be allowed to play out this late if the playground closed earlier. During term time it would be good to close at 7.00pm'.

A parent said, 'I have noticed new children, but most of the time it's the same children as during the day. My son has really enjoyed late opening and likes to be the last one to leave, when it's open till 9.00pm. It's much better. He doesn't get bored and it gives you a break'. Another mother with a daughter and a son, 10 years old said; 'my daughter gets really tired. She loves it and she sleeps really well ... I haven't been well (recent operation) so the children being able to be out here late, has helped me recover'.

This playground was beginning to lay the foundations to work with the natural rhythms of its community.

The implications for playwork of retuning to community rhythms

Times and opening patterns

To be part of a community and enable the growth of a community culture you have to be around enough to be so! Opening hours are so important! I worked in an era when you didn't shut till 8.00pm and you didn't touch a shutter or take a rope in till then. Today, I see and hear about playgrounds closing at 6.30–7.00pm. This is not enough for building solid relationships; it's not enough for those who don't have idyllic home situations; it's not enough to provide safe spaces in hostile environments or for children who have a bad time at school and need a place to be loved and valued in their day.

Communities of Children

We need to operate across the age range, being together to grow and learn and build identity and community, no false separation of ages. The Cornwallis experience shows that ages and stages find their own space where aware playworkers operate to give away power but are trusted to hold the overall process securely.

Power and control

Playworkers need to be planned and focused upon giving away power to enable the children's own culture to grow, for them to feel their own sense of self, and feel they are powerful people in our communities. Children need to experience having control, and this requires playworkers who are confident enough to let them do so. Playworkers must not be scared of conflict. Change comes from conflict; growth comes from conflict; and we can build more meaningful relationships through conflict.

Freedom

- By establishing an environment that says anything is possible, all things are up for discussion, nothing is taboo and an attitude and approach that shouts loudly, 'give it a go and see, explore it, test it, and its okay to do it here'.
- By enabling children to discover there is no one way of doing things or of thinking. Children need to feel they can fly! They need to feel held, supported and valued for who they are, to be able to do so.

Keeping it real, having an impact

- Consistency and continuity are essential – no fly by nights wanted or welcome here!
- No skating on the surface – giving real commitment and always being willing to go the extra mile.

Responding to and meeting needs

- Being aware and forward thinking, knowing where the child might move to within a month, three months, and being ready to be there, ahead of the game, able to respond in the time and way the child needs.
- Enabling children to take control, take real risks and break the chains of learned helplessness.
- Finally, love – our children need to feel loved.

It's not rocket science. On the DVD, and through the interviews, you can hear the voices of the children who experienced it. They speak for themselves. There is nothing more important for them!

Note

1 Vicky Loki when reflecting back on her feelings about the adventure playground described it as 'the place we are meant to be'.

Part 5

Special feature

28

BRIAN SUTTON-SMITH
Beyond ambiguity

My book, *The Ambiguity of Play* (1997), indicates that current attempts at play theorizing are limited by their authors' unwillingness to take into account all the varied types of play that exist. After an analysis of their varied rhetorics, however, I came to the conclusion that they were perhaps all a distant facsimilization of the Darwinian 'struggle for survival' (1997: 231). It is generally accepted that in lower creatures the struggle for survival is largely a matter of access to food, territory and reproduction. But in human cases these three basics do not sufficiently express the multiplicity of social conflicts with which humans are engaged from birth to death. Thus we struggle about control over others of all kinds because of our differences in politics, religion, social and racial status, as well as our innumerable social habits and psychological dispositions. However, if we look at the major classes of games that have engaged human beings for thousands of years, their conflicts as represented in the games, give us a much simpler variety of struggles. Thus:

- *teasing-hazing* is about difficult initiations into social memberships;
- *games of chance* are about taking risks and being judged successful by fate;
- *contests* are about being competitively successful in physical and mental games of multiplicitous kinds;
- *festivals* are about celebrating our cultural identities;
- *imaginative play* is a celebration of our personal originality;
- *flow experiences* celebrate our own special feelings of successful play prowess of all kinds (from achieving goals to imaginative musings); and finally
- *nonsense* allows us to deviate from orthodoxies of all kinds.

While my earlier *Ambiguity* book was about these play types describing them largely as historical and philosophical rhetorics (progress, fate, power, identity, imaginary, self, and frivolity), my current study deals with the same categories but in more biological and psychological terms. I began with the bias that play was a kind of dialectical experience, a position I had taken in my book *Die Dialektik des Spiels* (1978). My general rather simplistic thesis there, based on two years of elementary school playground observations in New Zealand, described in my *A History of Children's Play* (1981), was that play was always both a form of order and of disorder and the variety of these were what we had to discover. But in the years that followed, my pursuit of the theoretical dualities that might underline any such dialectic did not seem particularly fruitful. Thus the first great play theorist, Schiller, made a distinction between aesthetic play – 'the human is only wholly a man when he plays' – and the 'mere' play of the streets (1965: 80). Possessed as I was of a painting of Breughel's (16th century) 'Children's Games in Flanders', I was not too impressed with Schiller's derogation of such street play. But it was to get worse. In 1800 Kant praised the playful imagination as the source for all scientific hypotheses but then wrote that an excessive play fancifulness could degenerate into a deadly poison.

Groos (1901), the first great advocate of play as a preparation for life, also suggested that play could become an indulgence of the violent and unruly. Herbert Spencer (1873) contrasted cooperative civilizing play with the agonistic play of the lower faculties. Freud (1922/1974) said that play was a form of pleasure seeking (the life instinct) but could also become regressive and a repetition compulsion (the death instinct). Erikson (1977) distinguished between true play and pseudo play (as with Barbie dolls). Piaget (1951) said play was a form of cognitive assimilation but that it could also become a self-centred distortion of reality. Carse (1986) suggested that some play was infinitely creative, but there was other play, such as all games, which were quite repetitious and finite.

However, the greatest modern obstacle to thinking of play as in some way a struggle for survival is the modern notion that children are too innocent to be so engaged. This again puts Freud and Piaget in the same category of insisting that children begin with their playful irrationalities and in due course slough these off and replace them with rational egos and logical competencies. This view has led unfortunately to giving priority to curriculum-based play (to enhance language, numbers, etc.), but also to attempts to curtail playground play during recess and so on.

Against this trend is the clear evidence that the recreations of children, like those of adults, deal endlessly with the mimicry and mockery of the perils and disasters of everyday life. For support of this view read the psychologist Steven Pinker's book, *The Blank Slate: The Modern Denial of Human Nature* (2002), and historian Gary Cross's *The Cute and the Cool* (2004), both of which critique the false distinctions we make between the role of play in the hands of children and those of adults. Obviously adults are more complex, but like children they also constantly rehearse the same seven play forms above in their struggles to represent and to understand for survival.

With this background then I began my inquiry into the motivations for play. Almost immediately I came across the work of Antonio Damasio who, in his book *Descartes Error* (1994), divides emotions into those that are primary (shock, fear, anger, sadness, happiness and disgust) and those that are secondary (embarrassment, shame, guilt, envy, empathy and pride). I found that this was a duality I could apply to some of the play forms that I had studied in my *Ambiguity* book.

I got my first cue from the contents in *The Lore and Language of School Children* by Iona and Peter Opie (1959) in which most of the games they described fitted these six emotions. Thus shock could be said to dominate the games of teasing and hazing; fear is the key in risk taking; anger dominates all forms of contest; loneliness accounts for festivals of all shapes and sizes; happiness is the best label for our modern consumer play subjectivities known as peak experiences; and disgust fits all forms of nonsense and profanity. Now these are the six most impassioned forms of emotions and they determine the main performance directions of all the plays in which they are represented.

Damasio's secondary emotions have more to do with the way the play is conducted than with the character of the actions themselves; thus one gets embarrassed when found cheating or alternatively and most typically is proud of one's own performances and so on. The secondary emotional concern here is definitely with the governance of the play forms which emerges also as the regulation by rules and referees.

Given these materials it was possible to describe all of these six play dialectics as having to do with *affect expression and regulation*. But further than that, within the performances themselves there is always also a duality. Thus hazing involves harassment which is rebutted by player resilience; risks involve dangers rebutted by courage; contests involve attacks rebutted by vigilance; festivals involve loneliness rebutted by inebriation; flow experiences describe narcissisms rebutted by fame; and finally profanities involve deviance rebutted by wit.

Still, this immediately suggests that if these are indeed facsimilizations of the struggles for survival they are also a brave player commentary on distinctive appropriate cultural contexts. Thus I suggest that: the shocks of teasing and hazing mimic and mock initiation procedures; the fears of risk taking mimic chances with physical and economic fate; the angers of contests mimic combat, wars and predation; the loneliness underlying the inebriation of festivals mimics the absence of membership identity; the happiness of peak experience mimics the central role of individualistic consumer subjectivity in modern life; and the disgust of nonsense and profanity mimics rebellious iconclasm. In all of these then there is both the mimicry and the mockery of these institutions which otherwise dominate the lives of the participants. In play, like sex, the pleasure of these parodic play-forms engages the participants' commitment without great concern for the adaptive consequences, which in the sex case is a reproductive outcome, and in the ludic case is outcomes having to do with the political civilizing of the participants.

But as it is necessary to assume that these struggles are a part of the ancient struggles for social survival, we need further support in order to find parallels in neurology and evolutionary history. Current research on the relationship between the amygdala located emotions in the ancient limbic region and the anterior cingulate located in the frontal lobes, has found that these are very much like the expressive-regulative duality already mentioned (see recent articles in the *Journals of Cognitive Neuroscience and Emotion*). This is an integration of the ancient, quickly firing off primary emotions, and the modern more cognitively defined secondary emotions. It is also a parallel to be found between the major adaptive behaviour of reptiles which are dominantly reflexive and the adaptive behaviour of mammals which include as well reflective behaviours. Gordon Burghardt, the leading contemporary animal researcher, in *The Genesis of Animal Play* (2005), has shown that mammals (which includes animals and humans) have larger brains, greater amounts of energy, prenatal early care and a higher need for stimulation. But most importantly they play extensively, and reptiles by and large do not. This makes it possible to hypothesize that the play has to do with the mammal need for protection and for stimulation (which is Burghardt's theory of play's origins). But another possibility that arises is that because the mammals have both reflexive and reflective adaptive systems, they might often have to deal with a conflict between these two systems which could be a life or death matter. Given that there are conflict-reducing genes (see Allman 1999), it is possible in this situation that play emerged in the first place as a mutant gene alternative to the conflict between these two types of adaptation. My interpretation of this situation would be that play has become the mutant gene which allows for the mutual integration of both the reflexive and reflective aspects of the brain. As such play, with all of its six major reflexive and reflective adaptational variants, is a preliminary form of civilization reflecting the cultural survival struggle problematics of initiations, fates, wars, fame, identities and deviances.

All of which might be taken to mean that the good/bad dualities of the earlier play theorists were not entirely false. They were right about play as dialectics, but mistook the relevant antitheses.

Part 6

Play links, relating and communicating

29

CHRIS TAYLOR and PENNY WILSON
Mother and baby: the first playground

This chapter seeks to introduce Winnicott, his life and work; to consider his theory of playing in relation to the parent–infant relationship, and to put it in the context of playwork. This can be read in conjunction with the subsequent chapter written by Val Richards.

Winnicott: the man and his work

Donald Woods Winnicott (1896–1971) enjoyed a comfortable childhood in Plymouth, Devon. He attended boarding school and went on to study medicine at Jesus College, Cambridge, where he specialized in paediatrics. In 1919 he read Freud's *Interpretation of Dreams* (1900/1974), and this inspired his desire to become a psychoanalyst. He entered training for the profession, including undergoing psychoanalysis himself, qualifying in 1939 and effectively becoming Britain's first child psychiatrist.

Winnicott worked at the Paddington Green (NHS) Clinic treating children and their parents for over 40 years. He also worked with patients of all ages, in private practice. He wrote voluminously, developing theory from this experience and from his observations of patients. He worked from practice to theory, seeking to discover new knowledge and effective treatment methods. The reflective analytic practice of playworkers, which seeks to improve practice through theory, based on observation and reflection, has a similar methodology.

In terms of his early theoretical formulations, Winnicott was working and writing within a psychoanalytic context characterized by division. Following the death of Freud, two groups had emerged, the Kleinians and Freudians. Winnicott refused to subscribe to the dogma of either; he sat uncomfortably between them expressing his independent thoughts and ideas. In 1940, when children were being evacuated to the countryside to avoid their feared death and injury by wartime bombings, Winnicott was appointed Psychiatric Consultant to the Government Evacuation Scheme in the County of Oxford. His recommendations drew attention to the possible effects – in some cases detrimental – of the separation of young children from their families.

Between 1939 and 1962 Winnicott made around 50 public radio broadcasts. Kahr, in his biography, suggests that Winnicott's motivation was to help parents to 'understand that their babies and toddlers could be interesting people in their own right, not mere bundles of nuisance languishing in their cots' (1996: xxviii) – perhaps a necessary message, given the prevailing view of that time, that children should be seen and not heard. It's interesting that many playworkers today continue the tradition of advocacy for children, through campaigning for the promotion and provision of increased play opportunities.

Winnicott, the person, was slight in build with a largish head and was frequently described in terms of his reputedly elf-like qualities, looking something like a garden gnome. Charles Rycroft, a renowned contemporary, describes Winnicott's 'odd posturology', referring to his tendency to twist his limbs in various distracted and pretzel-like shapes (Kahr 1996: 104).

Winnicott enjoyed singing and playing the piano. He is remembered as a warm, zestful personality, interested and interesting. As a child-expert and analyst, paediatrician, lecturer, writer, and broadcaster, Winnicott's contributions to psychoanalysis are arguably second only to Freud's.

Winnicott used games in his therapeutic consultations. Through observing the process by which a baby or toddler reached out, grasped the spatula from his desk, and played with it, Winnicott was able to reach an understanding of the patient's psychological health or disturbance. Similarly, he used the Squiggle Game in his initial consultations with older children: a shared turn-taking doodle evoking the communication of inner meanings. In such contexts, Winnicott sees playing as an indicator of psychological health.

Playing and the theory of the parent–infant relationship

Winnicott frequently uses the term 'holding environment' to describe the conditions that the mother creates for her infant. Before the child is born, she typically will prepare a sleeping space and an attractive area set aside for the use of the child. She will provide clothing, bedding, toys, nappies and baths. She will have formed her preferred parenting style, knowing that for healthy psychological development, the child needs to have the right environment. At this stage, physical care is psychological care. The mother does this for the child, who cannot yet know and meet his or her own needs. The holding environment adapts to meet the changing needs of the child. Winnicott calls this the phase of absolute dependence. It's interesting that, within playwork, the effective play setting is seen to be one that is constantly adaptive to the growing needs of the children who attend.

At this point, the mother is in a state of what Winnicott (1956/1958) calls *primary maternal preoccupation* – a sort of healthy madness – a time when the mother is empathetically attuned to the needs of her baby. The spontaneous, hungry cry of the baby brings forth the feed from the mother. All being well, this is a period of idyllic union between mother and baby, aided by the baby's illusion of being omnipotent, the centre of the universe. Winnicott sees this as the baby creating what is waiting to be found.

Such a period, when all continues to go well, is nevertheless short lived. The baby moves from illusion to disillusion, from absolute to relative dependence. The baby is gradually let down by the mother, and external reality introduced. A growing sense of separateness emerges. The mother cannot be perfect: nonetheless, in spite of delays and some failures to meet the needs of the child, the good-enough mother provides a facilitating environment that allows the child to develop a sense of the world as a place to be trusted, and a sense of personal continuity of being.

A sign of this growing sense of separateness can be found in one of the earliest interactions between mother and child. This is something along the lines of the mirror game: mother and child copy and stick out their tongues at each other. Mother is showing the child that s/he is there to be seen – and the child through playing continues to develop a sense of self and other.

In the play setting, the child should be free to explore the environment and those in it, to discover a sense of self and others, rather than to have this imposed through heavily regulated programmes of activity and behavioural rules. The often-heard tenet that the playworker should be high on response and low on intervention (Hughes 1996) seems appropriate here.

The prototype of early playing has its relevance to settings for older children. Conway (2004) provides an example of this in one of his recollections of working at Bermondsey Adventure Playground in South London. He recalls that the playworkers were very proud of their newly built very sophisticated structures: a sandpit with cranes and chutes and mechanical diggers, and a splash pool with a hose and water slides. One night, when the playground was closed, the children returned and changed the play equipment, mixing sand and water, creating a moving beach. This became the play area of preference for the summer!

Conway and his team proved good enough to welcome the improvements to the environment they had provided, being impressed and humbled by the amount of invention, coordination, and engineering on the side of the children. This example illustrates the precarious nature of the important to-ing and fro-ing of playing and of playworkers getting it right, and children being free both individually, and in this case collectively, to express their true selves through play.

Winnicott's (1971) most famous and original contribution lies in his 'discovery' of transitional objects, the child's first favoured possession, typically the comfort blanket or teddy bear. His contribution is to consider these creatively, theorizing their relevance to healthy emotional development. The transitional object is the first 'me/not me' object, standing in the place of the mother, and representing her at one and the same time. It is never challenged. The transitional object is the first symbol used by the child and opens up all other manner of imaginative possibilities; for example in later childhood, loose parts can become transitional objects within a play space – sticks become guns, shoot-outs are played out, and the guns are eventually abandoned, to become sticks, once more – such playing being a developmental achievement with links to the first transitional (symbolic) object – of the proverbial teddy bear – or whatever was chosen by the infant.

Winnicott (1964: 146) described the playground as 'a potential space between mother and baby, or joining mother and baby'. It is part of the process of developing a sense of self through playing at both being separate and merged. He was fascinated by the relationship between inner and outer worlds. The play setting can be seen as a place where this transitional space is held for many children, all mingling their worlds. An observation by one of the authors illustrates this:

> Billy is on the adventure playground with his mate, they are playing together – they are digging in a puddle and very quickly they daub mud on each other, washing their faces meticulously with it, all the time engrossed. Mum and sister walk along the top of the park. They call over laughing. The mobile phone comes out.
>
> 'Here you two – smile'; the boys stand up, arms around each other's shoulders, and grin into the camera. The photo is taken, playing resumes.
>
> Mum and daughter compare photos – a new transitional object – part of the unfolding drama of creative living.

Living creatively, for Winnicott, meant living each moment anew, savouring each experience, fully engaging with and constantly recreating each experience. Within playwork, Hughes (2001a) has borrowed Morris's (1964) term *neophilia* to describe this. A playworker from Chelsea Adventure Playground recollects:

> A child with autism plays with a puddle of mud and paint and water. He is absorbed and excited by this play. The playworker sits a few feet away, mirroring and validating his playing, understanding something of it through sharing it. A child with ADHD comes and finds a still moment to lean against the playworker and watch the absolute engagement of the playing child and the shadowy attempts of the adult to share this. He waits. When the play is ended by the child with autism, the other whispers to the playworker: 'I am so envious of him. The most ordinary things are so exciting in his world'.

For Winnicott (1960), the individual true self results from the child being able to reach out and act within the world, and to receive a response that both validates the sense and experience of self, and involves the presence of others. A false self results from a failure in this area. The child's gesture goes unnoticed, or is forced to comply with the requirements of the environmental provision, for example with the depressed or dictatorial mother/parental carers. Again, a belief in the role of the playworker, as live, responsive to, and respectful of the originality and integrity of the developing child, has resonance here.

Hopefully, this chapter has introduced some key theoretical concepts expressed in Winnicott's very distinctive words and phraseologies. Winnicott would probably have approved of his ideas being disseminated within the world of playwork, but would have warned against them being used prescriptively. As he famously proclaimed, 'Come at the world creatively, create the world. It is only what you create that has meaning for you. For most people the ultimate compliment is to be found and used' (Winnicott 1968/2007).

30

VAL RICHARDS
Playing and relating: the contribution of Winnicott

> On the basis of playing is built man's whole experiential existence.
>
> (Winnicott 1971: 64)

In this chapter, I focus on the interconnection between playing, symbolic mastery and the development of a sense of self as portrayed in the work of Winnicott. From vast experience as both a paediatrician and a psychotherapist with children and adults, Winnicott evolved his distinctive theory of early development and needs. The consequences of deprivation or damage to the process of self-integration and relating to others are graphically presented in his accounts of work with infants. But beyond infancy, he further demonstrates the frequent primacy of urgent unfulfilled infancy needs in his adult and child patients. His work shows how a holding, tender but tough therapeutic environment, with possible regressive features, can help recovery and growth. Knowledge of his key concepts helps playworkers to foster the links between playing, symbolic capacity and self-integration.

Winnicott declared that those who are initially *unable* to play must be helped to play. For playing is, supremely, reciprocal communication through words and other modes of creative expression. In playing the imagination awakens, assisting the child to interpret the world to him or herself, and to become centred in time and space. Winnicott also stresses that an essential boost to becoming a separate person is the experience of negative feelings – hate and destructiveness. Equally crucial in becoming a whole person is the dimension of dreaming, both daydreaming about the future and dreaming while asleep.

Central to these developments is a positive relationship to another or others evolving from the earliest communication between the baby and mother or other primary caregiver. Invoking the metaphor of 'mirroring' Winnicott asks, 'What does the baby see when it looks at the mother's face?' I am suggesting that, ordinarily, what the baby sees is itself. In other words, the mother is looking at the baby and what she looks like is related to what she sees there (Winnicott 1971: 112). Here is an experience of reciprocal communication, where the mother's feedback nourishes and confirms the baby's sense of itself by allowing it to see its own face reflected in hers. Implicitly, also, the visual interaction is supported by sounds, smells, talk, listening, touch and holding – the basic ingredients of human communication and cultural activities.

But of course infancy is never merely a state of unbroken intimacy. What is the effect on the baby when the mother is out of sight or absent? Winnicott (1963/1965: 75) suggests that at first, the infant has, as it were, 'two mothers': the immediate, present mother is the 'environment mother,' while the child's developing inner version of her is the 'object mother', as she starts to become a being distinct from himself. As long as the length of any separation is manageable, the baby can represent his mother to himself relating to her as an *inner* imagined figure. Because this inner image tends to be generated by an *out-of-the-room* mother – a missing mother – this dawning symbolic capacity is bound up with a kind of loss: the loss of the presence of the object. Such loss is seen as the *gain* of symbolic power, and in Winnicott's account of the process, accompanying storms are eased by the time-honoured teddy bear's key role, which I shall refer to more fully later.

So the inner relationships formed from experience of mother and others in the baby's world get tinted – and   tainted – with the child's own phantasies and pictures of these others. The status of these figures in the young mind is a key to psychic health, for they play a major part in shaping how, consciously and unconsciously, we learn to regard *ourselves*, a decisive factor in psychological and social well-being.

Faulty mirroring and helping those who cannot play

While it is never possible to account fully for anybody's rocky relationship with others or for their own inner insecurity, Winnicott evokes a chilling picture of failed mirroring and its consequences, in stark contrast to the mirroring that promotes playing, symbolic mastery and sustaining inner figures. If the mother is depressed, impassive, cold or swamping, then the child is no longer given back to itself and ceases to see itself (Winnicott 1971: 112). When a child's 'looking', its communication, is thus rebuffed, it reacts with shame. The original, vital spark of personality, sometimes referred to as the 'true self' is dulled or hidden away and a stand-in self takes over, relying on a pseudo-vitality. Cut off from vital inner resources, this stand-in draws almost solely on external supplies for nourishment. Manic over-activity, attention-grabbing, obsession with appearance and consumerism, boredom, grandiosity, schizoid withdrawal: all signal an inner depletion through estrangement from one's fullness of being; the earlier the deprivation, the greater also the risk of psychotic elements forming in the personality.

Further, as implied in Winnicott's chapter title, 'The Mirror Role of Mother *and Family*' (my italics), mirroring extends beyond vertical adult/child interactions to the horizontal 'family'/sibling peer group. Whether undermining or supportive, mirroring by one's peers becomes as formative as the mirroring by adults, and therefore needs to be carefully monitored within groups of young people, for bad mirroring by others can occur at any stage in life.

Therefore people who fall into Winnicott's (1971) category of those who are unable to play and who must be helped to play, far from being seen as largely victims of their bad history, can be helped to acquire a sense of agency and therefore of destiny. As in the original mirroring process, for playworkers this implies that *being with* and communicating with children is no less essential than *doing* things with them. 'Being with' evolves from openness to the child's initiatives, with the kind of feedback that makes the child feel seen, heard and validated.

As well as allowing space for airing current feuds and gripes, it is possible to encourage talk and thought of hitherto unformed future hopes or dreams. Daydreams and, importantly, the sharing of *asleep* dreams, connect the child to hidden or split-off parts of his or her own personality, contributing to fuller integration (Winnicott 1971). Such mutual participation offers the satisfaction of being listened to and simultaneously listening actively to oneself speaking to others. Playworkers have reported the benefits of 'dream-swapping' sessions with children, and also of set-apart dream-sharing meetings for themselves.

The following account of a 4-year-old boy's dream illustrates the benefits of sufficient trust in a person who also facilitates the dream telling, which might otherwise not have happened. The boy, who had enjoyed his first day at 'big school', had assumed this first day also would be his *last* day at school. He was bitterly upset at having to go back tomorrow. During the night, he climbed sobbing into his parents' bed, settling straight back to sleep. Next day, the parents asked their son if he had been woken last night by a bad dream and the boy recalled that a monster had been gobbling up his teacher. Then, instead of resisting his second day at school, he hurried in eagerly, to inform his teacher of the dream (Richards 2005).

Dependence and destructiveness

From the mirroring, communication and playing with playworkers and peers, growing trust, attachment and dependence may be accompanied by regressive tendencies. Rightly understood, these are potentially therapeutic; enabling the child to accept what may be a vital experience of recognition and validation.

Also common are expressions of destructiveness and hostility, distressing to all concerned (Winnicott 1971). But Winnicott regards destructive behaviour as a necessary component to personal integration; to achieving one's own separate relationship with others and with the outside world. Destructiveness and even hate are painful but welcome signs that the child perceives others as real and significant people who must be put to the test. 'Can you survive my destructiveness and continue to hold on to me?' might be the implicit plea (Winnicott 1971: 90). So playworkers, by conveying that they will withstand but not tolerate extremes of behaviour, provide the necessary containment for children to feel secure, while the more withdrawn or anxious may begin to relax and play. This containment is greatly helped by the appointed, set-apart-space of the play setting and the regular times of sessions. Challenging behaviour may well arouse perfectly natural feelings of hate in their playworker, which are best contained by including regular opportunities for offloading to colleagues (Winnicott 1949/1965).

In the words of Winnicott's close colleague, Barbara Dockar-Drysdale, at the Cotswold Community, for fragmented children who cannot yet play:

> We have to supply the functioning ego ourselves, and contain and *hold the violence and the child together*. Unintegrated ones cannot contain violent feelings … By helping them to communicate, by *listening* and responding in an appropriate way, we may enable them to contain their feelings by transposing them into the symbols we call words.
>
> (Dockar-Drysdale 1991: 132)

Like Winnicott's mirroring metaphor, this assertion points out the necessity of two-way mirroring for forging or reforging the vital link between a centred self and symbolic mastery. Only through such holding and communication can the child's feelings be represented by thoughts, words and other symbolic forms instead of by inner fragmentation and acting out.

As affirmed by Winnicott (1971), a boost to symbolic mastery and self-integration is the infant's relationship to its 'transitional object' – the teddy bear or equivalent. Acting as a bridge between an out-of-the-room mother and the mother within the baby's mind, the bear as part of external reality *stands for* that mother and is also felt as an extension of the child's own self. To the child the bear may at times even be preferred or mean more than the mother. The comfort and presence of the bear makes the seeming loss of the 'gone-away' mother more bearable and extends the necessary space between mother and baby, in which an image, a thought can be born (Winnicott 1971).

Barbara Dockar-Drysdale (1991) reports that reversion to or variations of the transitional object may fruitfully occur with children of all ages and, for playworkers, may be valuable as aids in the progress towards integration and playing. She describes a group of teenage boys who could not speak in a group situation. But their teddy bears could, in distinctive high-pitched voices, and the initially nonplussed worker learned to communicate satisfactorily with the bears, thereby getting through to their owners.

This helping to find one's voice and voices via another medium is one key to the 'doing' aspect of playwork and the activities facilitated by playworkers. For the self, however, well integrated, rather than singular is manifold. Every one person has many voices needing to be coaxed out, often revealing quite submerged parts of the personality. These voices arise through creative activities in contained and specific times and places for playing – theatre, play centre, classroom *et alia*.

Especially, in drama, role-playing, work with puppets, and dressing-up, there is the potential for reaching a greater balance within the personality. A boy with a bad stammer in everyday life plays another character and his stammer vanishes. Another boy raids the dressing-up store and, in perfect naturalness, dressed as a girl, marches around, leading a tribe of his mates – no jeers or humiliation. Long unvoiced rage, protected by the player's chosen role may safely get a voice and therefore become transformed 'into the symbols we call words' within a firm structure and in the presence of an attentive adult.

The more withdrawn and disturbed child may avoid the playing that involves such freedom of expression and may blossom in the tighter security of 'games' with fixed rules and prescribed outcomes. One 14-year old girl, always silent and unapproachable, would only engage in silent card-games until one day consenting to a game of snakes and ladders with the playworker. Whenever, to her annoyance, the dice forced her counter down a snake, her own tongue was loosened and she became able to express, in most juicy terms, her pain and fury towards her mother.

Whether release of free expression and communication comes through reflective talk, creative activities or tightly rule-driven games, Winnicott's vast contribution to the concept of playing is nicely epitomized in his use of the Squiggle Game where he and his young patient would communicate, make meaning, together not only through words but also by drawing and building on each others' doodles in their highlighted 'time and place for playing'.

31

ANNIE DAVY
Exploring rhythm in playwork

The cosmos is not a blind and stupid rage ... but a friend, our element and matrix, the beginning and the end, the gentle rocking of a great cosmic womb, a friendly flux from which we take our origin and to which we return like the steady beat of ten thousand waves in the sea. Then the love of God means to learn how to dance or swim, to learn how to join in the cosmic play, to move with its rhythms and to understand that we are each of us of no special import other than to play our part in the cosmic ballet.

(Caputo 2001: 139–40)

From writings in cosmology through psychology, to biology and musicology, rhythm and play provide the patterns that bridge between order and chaos and that contribute to probably all creative and artistic processes. Play has a well documented relationship to many aspects of healthy human development. Rhythm is a natural part of the development of all living organisms. Rhythms run throughout our human interactions with the environment and with each other – in breathing, eating, sleeping, exchange and connection through conversation, movement, and creative enterprise of any kind. Exploring play through its various rhythms can provide a window of discovery for all of us who are interested in play and playwork.

Rhythm, movement, structure and time are organizational principles which humans are biologically programmed to recognize and use to order human experience (Scheflen and Ashcraft 1976). Babies are 'pre-designed' for perceiving rhythmic patterns that provide a structure for organizing experiences in human interactive events. Research demonstrates that musical qualities such as rhythm and tempo are significant components in very early brain development. The capacity to interact through mimicry and rhythmic patterns is essential also in developing parent–infant relationships (Trevarthen et al. 1999).

As we grow up, pattern and rhythm continue to influence our healthy development. Music and dance give us access to artistic forms of rhythm and enable us to develop as human beings and be playful in our interactions with others, deal with our own emotions, and respond to the environment.

Disrupting rhythms of eating, sleeping, breathing and communication can quickly lead to breakdown in psychological and physical health, and these are forms of human torture. Children who experience lack of rhythm in their lives and relationships (albeit less extreme than in circumstances of torture) can find the world a confusing place – a hard place in which to make attachments, build relationships, understand themselves and others or explore and learn about the world around them.

Environments and practitioners that give children opportunities (time and space) to play freely can help them to find or re-establish rhythm that makes sense in their lives. Playworkers are particularly well-placed to support this process. Rhythm should not be confused with structure in any rigid sense. Rhythm, like breathing, is infinitely flexible and responsive to external and internal stimulus, to individual variation and subtlety.

There are various ways in which rhythm can be observed in children's play and developed in playwork. I will briefly explore two of them in relation to children at play: schemas and play cycles, and then suggest that the context of the playwork setting also contains rhythm, and that this can be used by playworkers to support their work.

Schemas

Taken from the work of Chris Athey (2001), building on earlier work by Piaget (1959), a schema is a pattern of repeatable behaviour. Children exhibit these when they are playing and trying to find out about the world. The concept of schema has thus far mainly been applied in early education and to the development of patterns of thinking, but it may have merit in being explored as an observable phenomena in children's play for its own sake – patterns that are connected to affective behaviour as well as cognition; feeling as well as thinking: patterns of play that have meaning primarily to the player.

Common observable schemas in early childhood include: *trajectories, connecting, rotational, transporting, enveloping* and *containing*. There is currently little research on the schemas observable in children's play as they grow older or even in the kind of hobbies and recreational activities chosen by adults. However, children's play with 'loose parts' in an adventure playground – or even in an imaginative school playground – quickly shows individual children's preferences for trajectory, rotational or transportation patterns of play with each other and with objects and the environment. For example, the child who is constantly building 'roads' with lines and lines of bricks, guttering, rope, whatever is available, or the child who lines up chess pieces, dolls, coins, into elaborate linear formation – these are examples of children using trajectory schema. On the other hand, the child who is constantly wrapping up presents, packing bags or covering things in cloths, paper or with other objects is using an enveloping schema.

Most children use many different schemas but some can spend weeks or months exploring just one. These are the more noticeable schema which can well be supported by a skilful playworker though the kinds of resources provided. What all schemas have in common is a repeated pattern, a rhythm which can be explored in a variety of different ways through play. This is an area that could be meaningfully developed in more depth in playwork practice and research.

The play cycle

Developed in the context of playwork by Gordon Sturrock and Perry Else (1998), 'the play cycle' describes the process whereby all play begins inside the child – as a thought or idea or contemplation – which may be stimulated by external factors within the environment or other human beings. This is followed by a 'play cue', a signal made to a person or an object or even to something in the child's imagination. The response to this cue (if there is one) they called the 'play return'. A play return comes from outside the child – another person or something in the environment that responds to the cue. This may develop into prolonged interactions where the play gets into 'flow'. Any observable play cycle might be itself framed by rhythm. The following example is taken from personal experience of playwork practice:

> Paul enters the play setting – barely making eye contact as he wanders nonchalantly around looking at what is there to excite his interest that day. He pokes at the box of bricks, flicks the paintbrushes at the easel, reads a notice on the board and then looks at a pile of large cardboard boxes in a corner. He picks up a long square one and crawls through the centre of it. Martin has been watching him until that moment when he runs to the other end and crawls in from that end to meet Paul. Much giggling and wriggling ensues before a more elaborate and collaborative construction process begins, with the two boys using a whole lot of boxes to build an elaborate internal maze.

The play with boxes can itself be seen as rhythmic play cycling from the first 'cue' through to the end of the game, and incorporating a range of play types (Hughes 2002a). Paul's play starts slowly, solitary, exploratory, he sends his first involved 'cue' to the cardboard box, but possibly inadvertently, also cues Martin. The play then picks up energy and speed as it gets into 'flow', and reaches its crescendo when the maze is ultimately destroyed. The play then winds down with Paul and Martin sitting in the heap of cardboard chatting about what went on – and ultimately clearing away the debris.

The context of the play setting

Gabrielle Roth (Roth and London 1998) has developed a method of movement called '5 rhythms' which she connects to feelings, life cycles, archetypes and levels of consciousness: *flowing*, *staccato*, *chaos*, *lyrical* and *still*. Playworkers may be able to observe these rhythms as a familiar sequence framing children's play within the play setting. The following example from personal playwork practice serves to illustrate this process:

It begins from the time the children arrive and begin to 'flow' into their play – finding their own space moving around the space entering into their own imaginative worlds. It moves seamlessly through the rapid 'staccato' exchanges of words, jokes, bat and ball, rough and tumble. It peaks in the 'chaos' of full on imaginative adventure game, a ride on a water slide, or deep and risky play such as balancing on high beam. It begins to subside in the 'lyrical' rhythm of chat and stories, shared food and hand-clapping games or songs and settles into the 'stillness' of daydreaming, rest and reflection.

Beginnings and endings are important. Each child will enter the play setting in a different way, establish his or her own rhythm and warm up in his/her own way. The physical environment can help or hinder rhythm in play. If children get 'stuck into' the flow of their play they may need support in bringing their play to a conclusion and to 'wind down' at the end of the session. Play that satisfies will have a creative 'buzz' or 'flow' where children are 'wallowing', a term coined by Tina Bruce (2001), in the creative chaos of their play. Usually this is observable by playworkers, but sometimes such play may be internalized such as in creative daydreaming.

I began by stating that we know that biological rhythms are essential in enabling us to function as human beings – breathing, beating of our hearts, eating, sleeping. Humans have a biological predisposition to use rhythm and pattern as an organizational principle, which also enables us to develop interactions with others. Play is essentially a creative process. Artistic forms which incorporate rhythm such as music and dance may enable us to attune these principles and gain ever increasing layers of understanding about ourselves, our interactions with others and the environments we find ourselves in. Like play, these artistic forms may be used in therapy to help disturbed physical or psychological functioning to become more attuned to individual natural patterns, and to the patterns in the environment and in those around us.

Through schemas, play cycles and an understanding of rhythm alongside a deep understanding of individual temperament and development, we can observe patterns in children's play – through the way they organize play, respond to others in their play, and interact with the environment. As playworkers we can use this essential element in our lives in the way we plan for our work with children in play settings. We can use it to understand our observations of children and support their play in our planning of physical play space and resources. We can pay attention to the rhythm in play over time during each session the children are with us, and we can use it to help us respond to the temperament, needs and inclinations of each individual child we meet.

32

STEVE CHAN
Community-based play projects: somewhere to play, somewhere to grow

Introduction

When adults are asked to recall their childhood play experiences, almost certainly this will evoke memories of playing out with their friends on the street, den-building, riding on bikes, finding secret play places away from the gaze of adults and having the freedom to play with few restrictions (Hughes 2001a; Cole-Hamilton and Gill 2002b). Play spaces with an element of risk, full of loose parts, wood, leaves, sand, clay, water, stones, vegetation, trees to climb on and an abundance of slush, stimulate creativity to explore and learn (Nicholson 1971; Moore 1990). These positive recollections reflect parents' instinctive desire for their children to have similar opportunities to express their natural propensity to play.

This chapter will investigate the role of parents as 'play activists', advocating good play opportunities for their children, and how and when parents support the development of socially inclusive, community-based play projects, which encourage children's participation, and help revitalize communities. It will also examine adult perceptions of children's outdoor play and the notion of children playing independently in the street.

Restrictions on children's play and adult perception: a culture of fear and safety?

Before examining the role of parents in children's play projects, it is worth considering what restricts children from accessing play, and parents' perception of children and young people on the street.

Increasingly, children and young people have become polarized in the public domain. A combination of parental anxiety about child safety, due to highly publicized abduction cases and increased volumes of traffic, has considerably limited children's access to the outdoor play environment. The abandoned pieces of wasteland, unwanted nooks and crannies adopted and cultivated by children as play places in the past have been surrendered for housing development and parking schemes. The government's policy to reclaim and develop brownfield sites has isolated children in stifling mono-cultural environments of concrete and pavements. This has progressively moved 'the street' from a public place to a private domain, controlled by adults, and one to which children, as protected citizens, have minimal access (James et al. 1998).

The Jamie Bulger case was captured on CCTV and very publicly broadcast to the nation (Thompson 1998). It served as a warning to parents who allow their children to roam freely, having a profound effect on children's independence in public space, triggering parental anxieties, heightened by the intensive media frenzy surrounding the case.

Likewise, an increase in road traffic has had a similar impact. Car ownership in the UK has increased, resulting in an escalation in child-related road traffic accidents, with a reported 15,000 children injured in 2002 (National Statistics 2002). Mayer Hillman's study of Children's Independent Mobility revealed that in 1971, 80 per cent of 7 to 11 year olds travelled to school unaccompanied. By comparison in 1990 only 9 per cent of children were making the same journey (Hillman et al. 1990). With more than four times as many children being driven to school compared with 20 years earlier, ironically, this has only served to increase road traffic and compound the problem anxious parents are most concerned about.

Adult attitudes and low tolerance levels of noisy social street games often lead to labelling children and young people as 'youths causing annoyance', where more often than not, they just want to 'hang around' with friends in groups for safety and want to 'see and be seen', utilizing shops, street corners and bus shelters for their social gatherings (Wheway and Millward 1997). This increasing trend of intolerance towards children and young people has led to the Antisocial Behaviour Act 2003, which gives powers to police officers to disperse groups of two or more people. Adults who feel intimidated by large groups of children and young people want authorities to control their movement and behaviour. Although these same adults may advocate the need for better play and youth facilities, it is nearly always under the proviso 'not in my backyard'.

So where can children play in modern society? The perception of children and young people on the street is that they are out of control, not welcome, and that adults are in need of protection (James et al. 1998).

Recently, at a local public meeting to discuss the antisocial behaviour of a group of young people within the community, the residents were outraged at the young people's behaviour. However, they also complained about the dog fouling, litter, poor street lighting, graffiti, state of the roads, and the general environment in which they lived. Eventually, the discussion returned to the original reason why they had gathered. It was then recognized that maybe it was a minority of young people causing the disturbances, and anyway, there weren't many places where children could play. Even if the wider community is sometimes not tolerant of children and young people in public places, they do recognize children's need to play and socialize with each other. Parents can very often be the initial catalyst: They can act as powerful advocates for children and can be vocal in the debate for justification of local children's play facilities.

Community development: engaging with communities

Part of the current government agenda is to work in partnership with children and communities, to assess local needs through a consultative framework. This current trend signifies the government's intent to establish a culture of participation which will encourage community regeneration and allocate resources to improve the quality of community life (Tucker 2001; Douglas 2003). For many parents, a safe place where their children can play is the barometer by which they measure an improving community. This is evident in the assessment of local needs through community consultations, where it is common for recreational provision for children and young people to be given a high priority. For example, creating safe havens for play can be the impetus for parents to lobby proactively for their children's right to play. Here are some case studies, illustrating the involvement of local parents in the inception and delivery of community play projects.

Less talk, more action

Case study 1

The Beaconsfield Play and Youth Project is located in Tranmere, an area consisting of distinct territorial enclaves, dissected by a number of major thoroughfares, which feed Birkenhead town centre. Once the site of a major ship-building industry, the area has suffered high levels of deprivation and severe social exclusion, culminating in educational under-achievement, unemployment, crime, youth disorder and poor health. A high conglomeration of children and and young people, nearly 30 per cent of the total ward population, have limited access to supervised play facilities. The motivation for local parents was simply to provide somewhere for their children and young people to engage in safe play activities. The parents lobbied local politicians, highlighting the need for doorstep play provision, eventually securing the use of a building and some regeneration funding.

Here, local parents were the instigators of the community play project and through the formation of a steering committee found themselves managing the delivery of the service. At this stage, it is important for the statutory and voluntary play sector to pool resources to work together for the benefit of the project. For example, a Play Development Officer can offer pragmatic advice on sources of funding, building capacity, training opportunities and guidance on the legislative framework in which they will be expected to operate. So, a working partnership with all stakeholders is a key component in the success and sustainability of community-based projects.

Case study 2

Leasowe is an outer lying council housing estate on the Wirral. It is here that a group of parents, passionate about their belief in the provision of play facilities, started a playscheme for local children, involving an element of adventure play.

The formation of Leasowe Playscheme Group became the focus of operations. It had only been open for a few weeks when local residents on the fringe of the site objected to the scheme and the local authority moved to close it down. Threatened with closure, the group began to lobby local councillors. Then followed an incident enshrined in local folklore. On 17 March 1975 a deputation armed with a black wreath with the legend 'Leasowe Playground, born 22 July 1974, died 17 March 1975' emblazoned upon it was presented to a full council meeting, along with a 1600-signed petition (LPYCA 1987). Playscheme members held the doors shut to prevent the deputation being ejected. This may seem almost anarchistic behaviour, but the point was made and the ensuing publicity and subsequent meetings with councillors ensured the continued existence of the Leasowe Playground.

Eventually, a new site was granted, and with financial support from Leisure Services. However, it was local parents acting as a local volunteer labour force who helped erect perimeter fencing, telegraph poles for basic playground structures and a temporary hut. The influence and motivation of parents was paramount, along with locally based playworkers; eventually they would build a new purpose-built centre and regularly take 150 children every year to the infamous 'Addy' summer camps. This was a much needed outlet for local children and families who fundraised throughout the year to visit places in Yorkshire and South Wales.

So, this initial group of parents and friends, the archetypal 'Play Activists', felt empowered to act for themselves and to champion something they believed in. What had been an unwanted piece of land with poor drainage had been turned from a swampland to a children's adventure playground. Here, their children could socialize and experience a flexible, noisy and messy play environment, with freedom of choice, challenge and acceptable risk (Else and Sturrock 1998; Hughes 2001a; Brown 2003a). The inspiration for the project had been the parents and people of Leasowe. However, an embryonic concept of joint management with the Local Authority would eventually deliver and manage the project, which would become a template for others to emulate throughout the Wirral.

Today, the Leasowe Adventure Playground affectionately known as the 'Addy' is going through another refurbishment programme, and there will be new celebrations as it opens its doors to another generation of local children.

Conclusion

The role of parents in the development of children's play provision can be that of advocate, fundraiser and/or facilitator. Whatever their role, parents want to improve the lives of their children. When they remember how they played, and what it meant to them, it means they now have a better understanding of the benefits of those play experiences, so they feel resolute in support of opportunities for their children to play, where they can join in and be with other children.

Overall, the visual presence of children at play is a sign of a healthy vibrant community, something to aspire to, where families can grow up, establish roots, and where children have somewhere to play.

Part 7

Working with professional diversity

33

PAUL BONEL
Common core number 7: the missing link?

By the time you read this I hope that myself, members of my team at the SkillsActive Playwork Unit and a number of colleagues in the field will have got our campaign under way. The purpose of our campaign is not new for the Playwork Sector; indeed it is a perennial one. We wish to raise the profile of children's play and embed it in the hearts and minds of ... well, everyone actually. It's an ambitious project but an exciting one. We wish to influence all those who come into contact with children from parents and carers to bus drivers and supermarket managers and, of course, play, early years and youth workers. Most importantly those who make and implement the policies that affect children and young peoples' lives: the politicians, planners and government officials at national and local level. We also wish to 'legitimize' playing for adults and promote the notion of play-friendly workspaces. Much has been said about work–life balance but for many people it still feels like a lot of work and not much life and actually there are some big assumptions here. For instance the work–life paradigm is usually based on the concept of less time at work and more time in leisure, which is absolutely fine but it could be interpreted as more fun at work and hence less compulsion to get away from it! However, the focus for this part of our campaign will probably have to wait a little while.

One of the issues that has been exercising us is why, over 50 years since the first adventure playground and around 150 years since the first play centre, and despite the huge advances in the development of children's services in the last ten years, play and playwork continue to be on the periphery? We have considered a number of answers to this. For example,

- ours is not a child-friendly society;
- adults forget what it was like to play as children;
- too much work and not enough play – see above;
- an obsession with formal education;
- a diminishment of the play process;
- and a general lack of understanding of the riches that pertain to playing freely.

We reached no firm conclusion; there may not be one and no doubt all these factors contribute to a greater or lesser degree, but one thing is glaringly obvious. The play sector continues to struggle to win hearts and minds in a meaningful and sustainable way.

However, perhaps we have been using a sledgehammer to crack a nut, perhaps we need to employ more poetry and less polemic, a little less earnest theorizing and a little more joyful sloganeering. So this will be the methodology of our campaign: to promote the importance of play and the provision of play opportunities through accessible, uncomplicated means. A key aim is to devise a slogan that will encapsulate the message and stick in people's minds. A play version of 'A Mars a day helps you work, rest and play' or 'The future is Orange' or even 'Vorsprung durch Technik'. Well perhaps not, as although most people remember the Audi advertising slogan 20 years later few can pronounce it without difficulty and even fewer can say what it actually means! Our campaign will begin with a statement including a slogan on one side of A4 paper, something a politician can read in the lift between meetings, a mum can read before breakfast, a teacher before playtime, a retailer before opening up the shop and a playworker before opening the doors for business, something that will get them thinking and, hopefully, feeling.

In these times of celebrity endorsement we are also going to seek out a high-profile media personality who, with the right credentials, could be our champion for play.

So what's all this got to do with the Common Core? Well, in September 2004 I received Draft 3 of the *Common Core of Skills and Knowledge for the Children's Workforce*. The Playwork Unit at SkillsActive had been actively engaged in the generation of the Common Core and members of the Unit had been able to attend each one of the consultation workshops commissioned by the DfES. The Common Core has been one of the first and most important of the building blocks that the Department of Education and Skills has put into place as part of the reform programme known as *Every Child Matters* (DfES 2005b). This important initiative came about following the circumstances leading to the tragic death of Victoria Climbié in February 2000 and the subsequent report by Lord Laming presented to parliament in January 2003. The overwhelming message in the report by Lord Laming was the failure of the services that came into contact with Victoria to prevent her abuse and eventual death.

The Common Core sets out the skills and knowledge that government sees as essential to relevant, efficient and effective performance by staff and volunteers in their work with children and young people. It must be seen in the broader context of the Children Act (2004) and its five outcomes for children and young people. These are:

- staying safe;
- being healthy;
- enjoying and achieving;
- making a positive contribution;
- achieving economic well-being.

Every Child Matters: Change for Children

In our involvement in the DfES workshops we sought to embed the importance of play within the Common Core as much as possible. In the final version play appears directly in the knowledge section of Common Core area 2: Child and Young Person Development. It states, 'recognise that play and recreation – directed by babies, children and young people, not adults – play a major role in helping them understand themselves and the world around them as well as helping them realise their potential'.

There is nothing wrong with this statement and my colleagues and I were pleased to see play in the final version. Nor is there anything wrong with the rest of the Common Core. All six areas embrace a range of skills and knowledge that are relevant and important to work with children and young people and they do have the ring of the child at the centre. But there's something missing, and that something is the understanding that play inhabits the life of children and young people in a way that is innate, fundamental and entirely necessary to their well-being and development. For this reason, while we were pleased that play had been included and our efforts were not without result, we were also more than a little disappointed too.

Children never stop playing. It may be argued that adults don't either but that's for another time. It's in their being. They do it naturally and without compulsion. They do it from babyhood to adolescence. Wrap it up in other names but playing is what it is. What seems to me crucial in relation to the Common Core is that:

1. You can't stop children playing and it is counter-productive in the short term and positively damaging in the long term to do so.
2. Children, certainly in their younger years, have an innate drive to play wherever they are.
3. Playing is good for them in every sphere of their development.

The children's workforce needs to know and understand this. Play is not just for playworkers. Teachers need to understand that children learn and develop through play in a way that is both meaningful and sustainable. Has anyone ever considered how much of the national curriculum could be delivered through play opportunities in the classroom? Planners and designers need to know that children and young people require access to space for play. We can't keep them cooped up like battery hens and then complain that they are overweight and obsessed with computers.

Similarly police officers need to understand that often the root cause of teenage crime and vandalism is lack of play opportunities. If children are allowed to play out when there is no provision for them, then is it any wonder that some may stray into what adults term 'antisocial behaviour'. Health workers need to know that play is the most natural and, evidence is showing, one of the most successful in keeping children physically fit. Play is enormously therapeutic too in helping children work though trauma and stress. Retailers need to know that when children touch their products uninvited it is usually not because they are being naughty but because they are being playful. I could go on.

It's because so many of us in the playwork sector believe in this innate drive and importance of play that we are passionate about including it more fully within the culture of children's services. I think the Common Core, as good at it is – and at SkillsActive we are mapping where it is and could be in our underpinning standards – would benefit children greatly if it included more play.

Of course a seventh Common Core on play is fanciful and, in current circumstances unrealistic. However, I am optimistic that we can and will reach a greater understanding of the importance of children's play, which will, in turn, lead to both more, and improved play opportunities and a more appropriate place for children and young people in society. The recent announcement of The Children's Plan (DCSF 2007) includes the promotion of play spaces, opportunities and services for children, and the expansion of the qualified playwork sector. This certainly suggests that the message has been heard! The future promises to be a time when the importance of play is more fully appreciated and realized across the UK.

34

MIKE WRAGG
Guerilla playwork

Introduction

This chapter will explore the factors that lead to playworkers compromising their principles (consciously or otherwise), and whether those compromises can be managed to give a positive play outcome for children. Constant reference throughout this article will be made to the Playwork Principles (PPSG 2005).

It could be suggested that compromising one's principles is an occupational norm for many playworkers. For example, the majority of qualified, practising playworkers in England are employed in private out-of-school childcare provision. Whereas it may be perfectly possible to create rich, stimulating play environments in these settings, the ultimate agenda of such provision lies with the generation of income and meeting the needs of the parent. Therefore the assertion could be made that the prime essence and focus of such provision is not to facilitate the play process, but to satisfy the childcare requirements of working adults.

The adventure playground manager, who bans children from using the I.T. room because an adult training class has been arranged for the following day, is similarly compromising his principles. Rather than supporting the children in the creation of a space in which they can play, s/he is adulterating the play space as a consequence of the prioritization of an adult agenda.

Arguably the point at which playworkers compromise their principles is generally arrived when external, adult agendas take precedence over the prime focus of supporting and facilitating the play process. Almost invariably the main factor in these agendas becoming dominant is financial.

Yet this chapter is being written at a time when play and playwork have never featured so prominently on the government's agenda, and at a time when more money than ever before is being made available in England, specifically for the development of children's play provision. However, questions are already being asked of how all this newly developed play provision will be maintained.

One obvious option will be to revert to the time-honoured fund-raising approach of diversifying provision in order to appeal to as wide a variety of funding opportunities as possible. A recent raft of government initiatives has created myriad funding opportunities for playworkers. However, the focus of such initiatives is seldom concerned solely and directly with children's play. Rather, they may be concerned with agendas such as health promotion, reducing antisocial behaviour, increasing access to education and training, extending school services or creating safer communities. These are certainly areas in which play and playwork can have an impact, but the main concern of these initiatives lies with an adult agenda.

Therefore diversifying provision in order to become eligible to access these sources of funding can be a risky survival strategy. Meeting the funders' requirements can often necessitate compromising the very principles that the funding was intended to maintain. This approach to accessing funding by diversification creates an extra dimension to the playworkers' role, which, for the purpose of this chapter will be referred to as *guerrilla playwork*.

The guerrilla playworker

> Guerrilla: n. a member of an irregular force engaging ... in the harassment of the establishment, operating in small bands, and often politically motivated.
> (*Chambers Dictionary* 1998)

It is probably fair to describe the playwork profession as a small and irregular band, whose political manifesto is the Playwork Principles. If the various funding bodies and external agencies in all their guises could be described as the establishment, then the amount of campaigning and stealth tactics that have been used by play-workers to access funding to support their practice could certainly be regarded as harassment.

The successful guerrilla playworker can, not only use the funding to support and facilitate the play process, but also introduce further aspects of the manifesto by infiltrating newly established contacts and networks to inform the development of policy and strategy. However, the funders' stipulations must also be met, and the trap of compromising one's principles, and/or, worse, adulterating the play environment must be avoided. The following reflections will seek to illustrate the difficulties faced, and approaches used by the guerrilla playworker seeking to secure funding, advocate for play, satisfy funders, uphold principles and ultimately improve the play experience of children.

Reflection 1

The management committee of a successful, but cash-starved adventure playground saw the opportunity to replace their dilapidated building, increase capacity and update their I.T. equipment by applying for funding to deliver adult training courses. The application was successful and additional members of staff were appointed. The building was replaced by one with improved facilities and a dedicated IT room. The new building allowed more space for the children to play inside and provided them with the use of computers.

So far so good: however, it became apparent over a period of time that in order to meet the funders' requirements the training element of the adventure playground had to take priority.   Training courses had to be delivered at times when children were playing, which meant that they no longer had access to the computers. It was decided by committee that now that the playground was also a training centre the site needed to look professional.

Children were no longer allowed to paint and chalk on the walls, anything scruffy such as self-built structures had to be removed, loose parts tidied away and more playworker time spent supporting training delivery. Although the children had a large, modern, well-equipped space, it was no longer *their* play place. The play process ceased to take precedence; playworkers ceased to recognize their own impact on the play space; and they failed to support children in the creation of a space in which they could play.

In this instance the pursuit of funding for projects that didn't sit comfortably with the fundamental ethos of the adventure playground, and the mismanagement of the process of guerrilla playwork led to the compromising of playwork principles, adulteration of the play space and ultimately the closure of the playground.

Reflection 2

While working as a play development officer, I observed a group of children in a storage yard attached to the premises in which I was working. As I discreetly watched the children having great fun playing with pallets, supermarket-trolleys, timber, tyres, wheels, pipe, bricks, cargo nets, rope and all sorts of other things they'd found dumped in the yard, I found myself thinking about the original junk playgrounds, and by contrast, the lack of opportunities for children to play with loose parts and manipulate their environments in the play settings that I was responsible for supporting.

Consequently I had the idea of developing a service that would source large items of commercial waste such as those that the children were playing with in the yard, and distribute them to local out-of-school clubs. On investigation, funding for such a play project did not prove to be forthcoming, until that is, I began to think about alternative ways of selling the project to prospective funders. Rather than describing the play benefits to children of such a project, I gave it an educational and environmental spin, and began to talk about the learning and health benefits and how it could teach children about recycling and environmental awareness.

Ostensibly the agenda had been skewed, and arguably, principles compromised. However, the funding materialized and the targets were met as a by-product of facilitating the play process and supporting children in the creation of a space in which they could play. As the project became established and successful it became possible to publicize and promote the original aim and concept of the project and thereby begin to convince outside agencies of the value of play.

Reflection 3

Part of the quest to seek funding for the project mentioned in the previous reflection involved delivering a promotional workshop to a delegation of senior managers working for the Local Authority in Children and Young People's Services. A number of local children had also been invited to attend. On discovering that he would be required to play outside with a load of junk, one particularly officious delegate told me that 'this was the most ridiculous and unprofessional thing he's been asked to do in 25 years of working for the council' and asked, "how dare I expect him to piss about with a load of crap and a bunch of kids?" '

After an hour of building, dismantling, inventing, creating, experimenting and exploring, the same person told me that this was 'the most fun and interesting day he'd spent in 25 years working for the council' and that he 'didn't realize he – never mind the kids – had so much imagination'. The following day he came to my office and told me that the workshop had inspired him so much that he'd gone out that evening and helped a group of children build a tree house on the local recreation ground. I concluded that the play process had ultimately taken precedence and advocacy for play had been achieved.

Conclusion

Although brief, when examined closely, these reflections reveal a lot about the tactics of guerrilla playwork and how they can succeed and fail. Reflections 1 and 2 both show that the children's play experience need not necessarily take precedence in respect of the funding application for it to be successful. In both these instances funding was granted because of, rather than despite, the absence of any reference to children's play in the bid.

It's probably fair to say that the child's right to play was at the heart of the motives to diversify in both Reflections 1 and 2. However, it was obvious in Reflection 1 that at some point during the delivery of the diversified project, the play process ceased to take precedence. In Reflection 2, although the Playwork Principle was subverted, it was retained throughout the bidding process and delivery of the project. In this instance it's probably fair to say that principles weren't compromised, more disguised in order to protect them from compromise.

At no point in the diversification process did the approach in Reflection 1 advocate for play. Diversification was never more than a means of accessing money. It never sought to promote the value of play to newly established contacts. In both Reflections 2 and 3, play was advocated, and in both instances it was the tangible result of positive play experiences and playwork practice that began to inspire and change attitudes.

In Reflection 1, the playworkers' compromise of their principles inevitably affected their practice. More time was spent concerned with training than playwork. It could be suggested that in this instance, if the playworkers' principles had been retained and practice had remained good, the diversification process could have been managed more effectively. For example the children could have been consulted on the design and use of the new building and staff could have been deployed more effectively.

Reflection 3 illustrated the need for tact and diplomacy when harassing the establishment. It is quite clear from this reflection that the delegate in question felt very uncomfortable at the prospect of engaging in the workshop. His response was to attack the thing that he felt uncomfortable with, the inference being that if this person were asked to read something advocating children's play he would dismiss it out of hand. But having experienced play both as an observer and participant, his attitude was altered dramatically.

Similarly in Reflection 2, once the project had become established it was possible to reveal to funders the true vision behind its success and consequently begin to alter attitudes. Ideally the tactics of past guerrilla playworkers would, by now, have ensured statutory funding for children's play. However, the recently launched dedicated national play fund is only temporary. Therefore it seems inevitable that for the future at least, the guerrilla playworker will have to continue harassing the establishment while remaining true to the principles of playwork.

35

KATHERINE FISHER
Playwork in the early years: working in a parallel profession

A deep understanding of the value of play is essential for anyone working with very young children, as they discover their world through play. I have been working with children at this stage for five years. While studying for my Playwork degree I came across some literature on Montessori education which led me to believe that an understanding of playwork could have a substantial impact in a Montessori setting. I subsequently trained as a Montessori teacher.

Maria Montessori's work began in Italy at the end of the 19th century. Her aim was to make the most of every child's potential. To do this she adopted an innovative child-centred approach. Certain aspects of Montessori's philosophy relate well to playwork theory. For example she says:

- education/development happens naturally if the environment is right;
- do not interfere, but observe carefully;
- integrate the indoor and outdoor environments;
- wherever possible, offer children real-life objects to work with;
- independence is important;
- prepare the classroom so that children can access everything for themselves. This gives children freedom and enables them to take control of their environment;
- most importantly, the child leads the learning. The teacher is part of the environment, not the centre of it!

Despite all this familiar philosophy, the Montessori environment still contains challenges for the playworker. Montessori believed in a 'well-ordered' environment, and wanted to discourage young children from engaging in fantasy and make-believe. Furthermore, many modern-day Montessori teachers are inflexible in the way they use the materials that Montessori designed. However, even though most early years settings are not strictly playwork settings, there are always opportunities to apply playwork principles. Where there are children there is always a potential for play, even though the setting may place limitations and restrictions on this. I would like to suggest three prerequisites for the playworker herself. She should be:

- Pliable
- Perceptive
- Playful.

Principle 1: being pliable – adapting to a setting

In one school where I worked, the children were taught using the traditional, and very specifically designed Montessori equipment. Applying the Montessori Method, teachers typically demonstrated a piece of equipment, and then encouraged children to explore its use in 'appropriate' ways. However, the children often had other ideas.

Observation 1

The 'Long Rods' are ten long red rods of varying length, which children are expected to order from shortest to longest or vice versa, in order to develop the concept of length (Montessori 1912). I observed the following:

> Michelle picks up the longest rod and puts it in between her legs – 'Neigh!!' She trots across the classroom to the other side and puts the horse against the wall. She then walks back to the rods, picks up another 'horse' and again trots across the classroom. She does this with two others, but decides the rest are too small. Finally she goes back to the biggest rod and starts galloping around the classroom.

Observation 2

The 'Solid Insets' are three rectangular blocks of wood, with ten holes of different sizes, each containing solid wooden pieces. These pieces are cylindrical in shape and handled by means of a brass knob fixed to the top. Children are encouraged to fit the cylinders into their corresponding holes to develop visual discrimination (Montessori 1912). I have seen this piece of equipment explored in many different ways. This is one example:

> Caleb takes out the knobbed cylinders and lines them up. He pushes the rectangular block along the table, 'Choo Choo'. He then picks up one of the cylinders, 'I am going to the beach please'. He puts the cylinder (passenger) into the block (train). 'Choo Choo'. He repeats this with all the other cylinders (passengers) until the train is full.

Working within this setting was sometimes difficult, as the teacher's inclination was to encourage the children to use the materials in the precise way in which

Montessori designed them to be used. However, every day I saw how children would make anything playful. As a playworker I encouraged them to take control, and wherever possible use the equipment flexibly and creatively. I felt the children could achieve the objectives in their own way. Perhaps Montessori would have been happy with this.

So for me one of the most important principles for working as a playworker in a non-playwork setting is to be *pliable*.

Principle 2: Being perceptive – observing children at play and being sensitive to play cues

Sensitive observation is at the very heart of the Montessori Method. Montessori (1912) said teachers should teach little and observe much. She had faith in children's ability to learn about the world from their own experience. However, the fear of Ofsted inspection often means nursery schools become over-focused on academic outcomes, which may mean the opportunity to observe children's play cues, and respond appropriately is curtailed. Sutton-Smith and Kelly-Byrne (1984: 317) suggest that 'play requires a display of sufficient cues to keep the distinction between this realm and others in the forefront of awareness ... otherwise the activity will breakdown into anxiety or violence'. Sturrock and Else (1998: 5) call this condition 'dysplay', and suggest this is 'the precise point where neuroses are being formed'. They therefore, exhort playworkers to be sensitive to children's play cues, and to develop an array of appropriate responses.

Observation 3

I have been noticing for the past two weeks that Ben was either being bullied by other children in the school or sitting alone in a corner of the playground. Today I was doing an outside duty and decided it was time to engage with him.

During playtime I saw the red box (a disused water tray) moving. 'Rat? Mouse? Fox?' I wondered, but then I saw a small streak of blonde hair. It was Ben. He had managed to curl himself up into a tiny ball. The temptation was to flip the red box up and shout 'boo' but I held back. I waited until he lifted the box himself. As he lifted the box he caught sight of my leg and threw the box off and looked at me. I smiled at him: 'What a fantastic hiding place!' He jumped up and ran off.

Another teacher saw Ben by himself and shouted across the playground, 'Hey Ben – catch!' She threw the ball and he caught it. He was delighted and threw it back (*play cue*). Together they played catch for about two minutes. Another child fell over and the teacher became distracted. Ben held onto the ball for a while then threw it against the teacher's bottom. He laughed as it hit her (*play cue*), but the teacher didn't turn around. I decided this could be my opportunity to engage with Ben so I called to him and held my hands out (*play cue*). Ben threw the ball straight back and we played catch for a long time until I was called inside!

When I returned, he was throwing a hoop over another child and laughing (*play cue*), but the other child kept walking off (obviously not wanting to play that game). I picked up a hoop and threw it over him. He laughed hysterically and ran off, but this time he kept looking back and smiling (*play cue*); obviously he wanted me to chase him – so our game developed. I was chasing Ben and to catch him I had to throw the hoop over him. Other children watching the game decided it looked like fun so also joined in. The game started to get a bit rougher – the hoops were making the children trip so that then became the game's objective!

My attention was then drawn to another child crying by the shed. As I was comforting her I felt a ball land on my head. It came from over the shed roof! I looked round to see Ben laughing (*play cue*). He was rolling the ball up the roof so that it would fall down the other side. I picked up the ball and copied him. Another game was invented – rolling a ball up the shed for the person on the other side to catch. There was a surprise element to the game, as you never knew when it was coming. The child I was comforting started to join in with the game. Ben heard the other child's voice and peeped around the shed, smiling (*play cue*). After a while I stood back and watched them play for the rest of playtime.

I think it was my playwork training that made me sensitive to the play cues – for me this is one of the most important aspects of working with children. Thus, for me, the second important principle for working as a playworker in a non-playwork setting is to be *perceptive*.

Principle 3: being playful – working creatively

There is some ambiguity in Montessori's writing about creativity. On the one hand she believes that children learn through personal exploration of their environment. On the other hand she says make-believe is an unhealthy interruption to the serious endeavour of learning. Working in an early years' setting with a large number of children can be very stressful at times, but a playful approach can be a helpful coping strategy.

Observation 4

A group of two year olds with whom I was working always wanted to take off their shoes and socks. However, because they had to wear shoes at certain times of the day (lunchtime, etc.), I had somehow to convince them to put their shoes on. I decided to make a puppet that needed to put its shoes on. I made a spider puppet and managed to get hold of some very small dolls' shoes for the spider's feet. The legs of the puppet were the puppeteer's fingers. I introduced the spider, using a song. I then showed the shoes and the children put them on the spider's feet. I then played a game of 'Who can put on their shoes before Arachne the spider?' This worked brilliantly. The children loved trying to beat the spider and the spider sometimes chased the ones who still refused!

So, remembering to be *playful* really worked in turning a stressful situation into something positive and fun.

Conclusion

In this setting I was often labelled as 'The Play Expert' because of my playwork training and was often expected to leap into organizing play activities. There is sometimes a place for being *playful*, but holding back and being *perceptive* about what is happening, and going with the flow of the play (being *pliable*) is far more important in the long run (Bruce 2005). This is perfectly summed up in a term coined by the poet John Keats: 'Negative Capability'. Keats first used the term in one of his letters to explore the creative process. He described it thus: 'when a man is capable of being in uncertainties, mysteries, doubts, without any irritable reaching after fact and reason' (Keats 1817).

This is at the heart of what I understand playwork to be. It describes the paradox, that by sometimes appearing to do nothing, we enable ourselves to do most. By hurriedly reaching to 'solve' situations we limit our capability, but by actively 'being with' a situation, without trying to change it, influence it, explain it or understand it, we keep all options open – anything is possible and nothing is closed off. Negative capability is not passivity; it is not sitting back, spacing out and doing nothing. It is really being aware of the situation without jumping to conclusions and leaping to intervene. Intervention may be necessary sometimes, but a certain 'space' must be allowed. We need to recognize that the play itself will do what it needs to do, but we need to watch the play carefully with this attitude of negative capability so that we really 'know' what is happening. We will then know intuitively when or if an intervention is needed.

36

KEITH RAMTAHAL
Play, learning and education: common core of skills and knowledge for the children's workforce

As an experienced playworker and teacher, the Common Core of Skills and Knowledge for the Children's Workforce opens up opportunities for me to explore some of the ways we can work meaningfully with children, young people and their parents and carers, through play, learning and education. Here are some of the ways in which I have been fortunate to be part of this very complex, and at times difficult but opportunistic relationship:

Loud and clear!

Within schools as anywhere else, play is a powerful vehicle to promote communication and engagement with children, young people and their families. All staff in a school will have to communicate and engage with parents and carers, children and young people at some level at some time. One would hope this would always be in a positive context, but that is not always so as there is a core of parents and carers who have had very negative experiences of schools and fear the same for their children. In order for schools to keep interactions and communication positive, parents and carers need to be respected as the child's first play mates and educators. They also need to be welcomed into the classroom and playground and involved in play activities that promote positive engagement and communication between all three groups of stakeholders. Children and young people need to know 'loud and clear' that they and their parents' and carers' opinions and views are as important and respected within a school as anyone else's and that they are part of an ongoing dialogue which uses play as one of the mediums. The beauty of play is that it has a universal language that can open up and strengthen communication. So let's get talking!

'You're in the big school now'

Young children progress from playgroup or nursery and are about to start life at school. Many policy makers, curriculum developers, educators, parents and carers see this as a time that children should stop playing and focus solely on education which is usually formal and didactic. Although the 'Foundation Stage' Curriculum for nursery and reception children in England and Wales has play at the heart of its core values, this is not nearly so well recognized in the National Curriculum from Year 1 onwards. It is as if play and education are separate entities not two things that can complement and promote each other.

Hofkins (2006) highlighted how Bexley Council in London wanted to put the creativity back into learning and has taken the step of basing its entire primary curriculum from Year 1 to Year 6 on the Foundation Stage's six areas of learning which are: personal, social and emotional development; communication, language and literacy; mathematical development; knowledge and understanding of the world; creative development; and physical development. This has been named the 'creative learning journey'. Bexley's innovation closely resembles the introduction in 2008 of the 'Early Years Foundation Stage' (EYFS) by the government, which will extend the six areas of learning to all children aged 0 to 5. The success of this will hinge largely on planned and unplanned creative play opportunities being seen as the anchoring of roots for learning, not something you 'earn if you learn'. It must be a curriculum that embeds and promotes the five outcomes set out in *Every Child Matters* (DfES 2005a) and acknowledges and builds upon the success of *Birth to Three Matters* (DfES 2002) because in the world of play each and every child matters.

Different scenarios, different decisions

Safeguarding all children in our care and continually promoting their welfare is one of the most important responsibilities for anyone who works with children and young people. Parents and carers are skilled observers of their children and will be the first to notice any changes in them. By building trust and respect, members of a school's community should be able to talk openly and honestly with children, young people and their carers and respond appropriately.

In many scenarios when children and young people feel relaxed, respected and trusted, when engaged in activities in a safe environment which may include art, drama or other creative play, they may sometimes attempt to put right what is wrong in their life, or make a disclosure to someone either directly or indirectly. Staff must adhere to work place policy and procedures at all times. Staff may be put in difficult situations sometimes and will need to make important decisions that may save a child being harmed further and even save their life. It is important that everyone knows that policies and procedures are there not only to safeguard the children and young people they work with, but themselves also.

All change!

Transitions or changes in children and young people's lives come in so many shapes and forms. Some are positive transitions and some are not. That is why the handling and facilitating of them by all persons and agencies is crucial. Two of the biggest transitions that children and young people undertake in life are starting school and the transfer between Key Stages. For some children it is already one of many transitions in their life that have occurred such as coming to the United Kingdom as a refugee or asylum seeker, leaving behind friends and family, coping with loss of loved ones, having to learn a second or third additional language and so on. An example of managing this is by 'buddying' up children and young people in their final term before transition with older pupils. This should include having the opportunities to engage in playing in the unfamiliar places such as the main school playgrounds and other outdoor spaces – places that open up the opportunities to engage alone or with others, in play related educational activities that are braver, bolder, bigger, louder and faster. Bruce (2001: 47) states that 'play helps children dare to learn, even when they are uncertain about what will happen. It creates an attitude of mind which is curious, investigative, risk taking and full of adventure'.

There's no 'I' in team

In order to be part of effective multi-agency working it is crucial to identify and recognize your own role and responsibilities in your job and that of others. You need to know what value and expertise you bring to a team and that of others. Isn't this essential for children and young people and their parents and carers too? As well as people knowing their roles and responsibilities, people need to be able to be team players, communicate effectively, and be organized and assertive.

Play provides the perfect forum for developing all these skills and knowledge. Schools need to organize situations where staff, children and young people and their parents and carers can carry out their roles and responsibilities, play in teams, communicate clearly in a variety of ways, get organized for different purposes and be positively assertive. Examples of this are: organizing and attending a residential journey, hosting an Open or International Day, holding a Play Day, really anything goes! As stated, there is no 'I' in team but there is in 'valuing individuals', 'multi-tasking', 'networking', 'skill sharing' and 'enjoying and achieving'.

It's good to share

Unfortunately we normally hear about the outcomes of when information is not shared, rather than when it is. By building a climate of trust we can gather from parents as much information as possible about themselves and their children. When I was in charge of early year's admissions for a large London primary school, a large percentage of the families admitted had or were seeking refugee or political and/or religious asylum status. Prior to the admission process I provided numerous opportunities for parents and carers and their children to visit the school, meet other parents and carers, and engage in school routines and play activities.

When admission procedures began, any information gathering and handling took place in private, bright, child friendly rooms. Current parents and carers, interpreters and the School Liaison Officer were available to facilitate discussions throughout the entire process. Important personal documents that were needed for admissions such as passports and Home Office documents were promptly photocopied and returned, lists were made of documents that were further needed, and parents and carers informed of where and how to obtain them.

After the admission meeting, parents and carers and their children were welcomed back to the nursery and reception classes for the rest of the day to continue to participate in play, learning and education.

An important key message to all schools: in the words of Ellie Katz (2007), adventure playground designer and 'playologist', 'The world is your playground. Why aren't you playing?'.

37

JULIE GRIFFITH
At sixes and sevens: the transition of play to secondary school

This is an observation of the relevance and importance of play opportunities to Year 6 students as they make the transition to Year 7. The reflections are based on my experience of working in a secondary and local primary school.

Extended schools

> Extended schools provide a range of services and activities often beyond the school day, to help meet the needs of children, their families and the wider community.
>
> (DfES 2005c: 7)

The *Every Child Matters* (DfES 2005a) and *Extended Schools Agenda* (DfES 2005c) has clear outcomes for children and young people and schools are making every effort to ensure these are met. As educators we continually strive for higher levels of achievement, attainment, increased motivation and self-esteem for all our students. Many secondary schools already offer extended activities and some employ extended schools coordinators. The *Extended Schools Agenda* can support whole-school policies, make a very useful contribution to the school's improvement plan and provide an opportunity to develop a whole range of services for students, their families and the local community.

The transition process

Transition in this context is defined as 'the process or period of changing from one state or condition to another' (OED 2006), and the transition from primary to secondary school can often be a mixture of anxiety and excitement for many students.

Staff from primary and secondary schools are committed to ensuring the transition process goes smoothly. It is in everyone's interest that Year 7 students are happy and settle in to their new school. They have a lot to settle into – an earlier start to the day, the journey to school, new uniform (with or without the dreaded tie), a timetable, (which they have to decipher and then follow), new teachers and subjects, finding their way around the school, homework, and generally coping with the hustle and bustle of being 'the little fish in the big pond'.

Schools spend a large amount of preparation time on the transition process – individual interviews, open evenings, small group visits, whole induction day and special first day arrangements. However, nothing about the primary to secondary transition fully prepares children for the sometimes stark reality of the playground at break and lunchtimes.

Playing the game

Many primary schools provide numerous play opportunities for children. They may be able to play in the playground before school starts, some at breakfast club. They can play at break time, at lunchtime, possibly in clubs, and in some schools with equipment provided by the lunchtime supervisors. They may then have the opportunity to 'play' after school in a range of out-of-school hours learning activities. Primary school environments with marked-out playgrounds, benches, giant outdoor games and plants go some way to promoting good play opportunities.

Secondary school playgrounds on the other hand can often deter positive play experiences and unlike their primary school counterparts, the secondary school midday supervisors have a thankless and often difficult task to perform in managing lunchtime play. So what happens to 'play' when children reach secondary school? Well, it practically disappears with little or nothing to replace the void. Everything about going to secondary school implies change and although many schools have extended activities there is often little organized or structured play.

It is hard not to generalize about what constitutes play in a secondary school. Is it large numbers of older boys playing football? Is it younger boys playing patball against a wall, or groups of girls sitting together talking? The reality is, it is all these things. The following definitions used in the play review *Getting Serious About Play* published in 2004 sit well in this context: 'Play means what children and young people do when they follow their own ideas and interests in their own way and for their own reasons' (DCMS 2004: 6) or

> a space, some facilities or equipment or a set of activities intended to give children the opportunity to play as defined above. At its most successful, it offers children and young people as much choice, control and freedom as possible within reasonable boundaries. This is often best achieved with adult support, guidance or supervision. The children and young people may themselves choose play involving certain rules or in some cases, informal sport.
>
> (DCMS 2004: 9)

An example of the experience of one secondary school

Tell us what you really want ...

At Year 6 open evening, children are asked to complete a questionnaire about their hobbies and interests and the sorts of activities they would like to do at lunchtime and after school. Their parents are also asked what they would like their child to do and any training needs they might have. The results are often gender specific, the boys want football, ICT and more football. Girls, on the other hand, want some sport and ICT but more than anything a space to sit, chat and do what they want to do. The biggest response from girls when asked what they want to do at lunchtime is to have a 'chill-out space'.

What's on today miss?

Observation of Year 7 students at lunchtime showed many of them wandering aimlessly, playing the occasional game of football, leaning against walls or sitting on steps talking. After discussion with other staff, it was evident that more lunchtime activities and appropriate spaces were needed for these students. As a result, several lunchtime clubs were set up specifically for Year 7s. These were very successful and are now well attended by all year groups. Lunchtime clubs are a mixture of play, learning and social interaction.

Playing the game!

Lunchtime is 45-minutes long and other schools would say (and I know they do) that this is too short for lunchtime clubs. I would argue that a student who is happy at lunchtime is more likely to settle into lessons and have a productive afternoon. On average 20 to 25 clubs run at lunchtime and after school, everything from ICT to Tai Chi, many as a result of consultation with students. The benefits for students, staff and the welfare of the school in general far outweigh the costs in running these clubs especially those at lunchtime.

Some students make positive decisions about what they want to do at lunchtime and this is an interesting phenomenon in itself. Students who may be feeling vulnerable or less social can often find an activity where they feel safe on their own or with their friends. They gravitate to library and book clubs, to the girls' and boys' clubs, specifically set up for this reason.

However, not all students need help with playing. Take this example – a parent wanted her son to attend some of the lunchtime clubs. She rang the Head and he asked me to speak to the student. I tracked him down in the playground and the conversation went something like this:

'Do you know what's on offer at lunchtime?'
'Yes'
'Would you like to attend any clubs at lunchtime – keyboards, chess, computer, book club ...?'
'No'

'Why not?'
'I just want to play pat-ball with my friends'.

What a wonderful, confident response from a student who did not feel the need to participate in organized activities.

From Warhammer (model club) to chill-out space!

When approached by a learning mentor to start a Warhammer Club (a sort of model club) I struggled with the reason for offering such a club, not withholding the vast expense of the materials (special models, paint and scenery) required to make it a success. This all changed when a Year 7 student she was working with expressed an interest in this activity. I met the student and said I would set up a Warhammer Club if he helped to organize it. He devised a poster for Year 7 tutor rooms and did some internet research but lost interest as the club started.

The Warhammer Club attracted a very mixed group of boys, many of whom were on the Special Educational Needs register. Coincidence? Maybe, but the club became a haven for students who wanted to 'play' in a safe environment. At the end of the summer term the group decided that they would like to develop a boys-only club. This was agreed and they are being supported by the same member of staff and a youth worker.

Playing together

The success of these clubs is also due to the commitment and support of the staff. Clubs are run by teaching staff, cleaners, youth workers, administrative staff, learning mentors, teaching assistants, all of whom have something to offer the students. The lunchtime clubs at this school are part of a wider strategy of developing extended activities for students, parental involvement and links with the local community. None of this work would be possible without working in partnership with the community, youth services and other external agencies providing services for children and young people. The extended school co-ordinator plays an important role in co-ordinating and bringing together some of these services.

There is no doubt that students of all ages enjoy 'playing' in whatever form that may take. In particular, play opportunities can definitely support students in making the sometimes difficult transition from primary to secondary school.

38

CHRIS TAYLOR
Play and youth work: a qualitative case study of integrated practice

This case study is based on interviews with heads of play and youth services in two local authorities that have an established tradition of integrated service delivery. They enjoy a reputation for excellence both locally and nationally, recently confirmed by the Joint Area Review of Children's Services introduced by the Children Act 2004. This chapter explores, through the managers, their work within the context of the *Every Child Matters* agenda (DfES 2005a), particularly with regard to integrated services, transitions, and a rights-based child-centred approach to the delivery of play and youth services. The conclusion summarizes some features of this 'work in progress' that are felt to account for its success.

Both local authorities are characterized by a plethora and diversity of play and youth settings. These include adventure playgrounds, school-based play centres, community-based playschemes and adventure playgrounds for disabled children. Youth centres and clubs provide the core of youth services, complemented by specialist provision, for example in music, water sports, and outreach and detached youth work on many local estates. A strong infrastructure of organizations underpins service delivery, providing training, development, support, and resources across the authorities. Play inclusion officers are also in post to support the integration of children and young people with special needs into mainstream provision, where appropriate. Services provided are for children aged 4–19 years.

The local authorities are urban, ethnically diverse and characterized by areas of economic deprivation that are among the worst in the UK. There is a long-standing tradition of youth and play service provision. In the two authorities that provided the focus of this study, around 500 part- and full-time staff are in post serving in the region of 75,000 children. Many identify distinctively as play or youth workers and a sizeable number work in both occupational sector roles.

The play and youth service seeks to provide a holistic person-centred approach that is responsive to the individual and developmental needs of children and young people in a diversity of contexts; the purpose of the work being to improve or enhance the life experiences of children and young people. In addition to this shared vision and values, there is an appreciation of the distinctiveness of play and youth work. The role of the playworker is to create environments to support or facilitate children's play. The youth worker designs and develops programmes with young people that help progress their personal and social development.

There is an understanding that a child will and should be able to access all manner of services that are appropriate to his/her developmental needs and contemporaneous circumstances. The methods and experiences offered by play and youth workers can be seen to have different, but equally important relevance in the lives of some children and young people, and should be present alongside other required services, provided by professionals in the children's workforce.

Such a view was clearly envisioned by one of the interviewees:

> That old expression that says, 'It takes a village to raise a child' – well, I think it takes a range of services to support a young person and sometimes one methodology will work more effectively than another and that rather than feeling precious about which is best, I think it's more about which is fit for the young person we have at hand at the moment.
>
> (Head of Play and Youth Service)

The organization of play and youth services in the authorities increasingly puts children and young people, even more centre stage in the configuration of services; this is particularly the case in relation to transitions. The developmental transition from childhood to adolescence coincides for most children with a move from primary to secondary school. Play and youth services are used to support this transition through providing continuity and offering some control and choice over where leisure/free time can be spent.

Adventure playground provision with its 5–15 age span is seen to provide continuous support to children through sometimes turbulent transitions. For example the adventure playground 'says' to children, 'Well you might now be going to secondary school, but you can actually use the same playground; and you might now be going somewhere completely different from your friends, but you can still meet up where you've met with them for the last five or six years'.

On some adventure playgrounds in one of the authorities, it has been possible to make specific provision for different age groups, within the same setting, providing some children with the opportunity to use both services. However, the officers interviewed stressed that care is needed in the multipurpose use of settings; it is imperative that the environment is perceived to be physically appropriate by those using it:

> It's all very well to say you can have mixed use of a building so that you have a nursery in, then play provision for 5–12s, and then the 'transitionals' 11–14 and finally the youths. Actually you can lose the last two groups, because going into a building with a home corner and tiny chairs and lots of kiddie arts and crafts equipment is not appropriate to what they are looking for.
>
> (Head of Play and Youth Service)

Where the provision of play and youth services, within the same setting or locale, isn't feasible, and indeed as an organizational strategy that maximizes choice, the age range of provision is offered on an overlapping basis; for example play centres for 4–13 years, and youth provision for 11–19 year olds.

However, increasingly in some areas, there has been an appreciation that 11–14 year olds have needs that might best be met through specific provision, designed to address their interests, in locations and at times of maximum appeal. This is currently being identified through consultation with young people and professionals.

The practice in both local authorities stresses the importance of children's rights and an inclusive integrated approach to play and youth work. Informal participation on the adventure playground is 'hands on' in terms of children's involvement and participation in the day-to-day running of the setting. Playworkers observe and listen to children, reflecting with colleagues on the implications of this for the day-to-day and longer-term running of the site. Direct conversations, requests and demands, can also ongoingly inform the life of the playground. More formal structures, such as children's committees, councils and parliaments are used locally and across the authorities to ensure that children and young people can be involved in influencing their play and youth services.

The services have put considerable emphasis upon encouraging older children to contribute to the running of the play and youth setting, with young people being encouraged into volunteering, training, and employment within the services. Training programmes and supported placements have become permanent and successful features of the authorities. An unanticipated consequence of this has been that both boys and girls have been encouraged to join the workforce, and the senior play officer from one of the authorities observed, 'We don't have the shortage of male staff working with primary school-age children that you find elsewhere'. It is anticipated that the provision of play and youth services, by former users, heavily involved through ethos, activity and consultation with their delivery, will ensure that future service provision is relevant to the interests and needs of local children and young people.

The reviews, visits and interviews with officers in both boroughs reflect an enthusiasm for the new ways of working, heralded in by the common core and the *Every Child Matters* agenda. There is much to be celebrated in terms of 'joined-up' integrated working, supporting children and young people with transitions, and the articulation of professional methodologies in the provision of rights-based, participatory child-centred services.

The factors that are perceived to have contributed to this 'work in process' in the authorities visited and as expressed by the managers interviewed include:

1. An approach to the delivery of services that stresses commonality of purpose and values, and ensures a structure of communication and information sharing that reaches all staff. This includes e-bulletins, newsletters and briefings, meetings, service days, conferences and other collective events.
2. A reflective management approach to service delivery that respects and preserves existing effective practice and seeks to build upon it; an appreciative approach that builds upon past successes in integrated working.

3. A structure of employment that seeks to recruit staff from within the users of services and sustains retention through volunteering and training opportunities and that provide for movement through a visible service structure that offers both horizontal and vertical progression.

4. Adopting a clear commitment to a rights-based approach that translates into material change at grass roots level.

5. A task-focused approach to management which acknowledges that 'when things are flagged up, they tend to slow down, it's best to just get on with it!'

6. And finally, an approach to change that embraces the *Every Child Matters* agenda as a means to enhance existing services and provides new ones where appropriate.

The reflective reader is encouraged to review critically such considerations in relation to their own practice settings.

39

MAUREEN O'HAGAN
The children's workforce: the early years and playwork

In order to explore the interface between early years and playwork it is necessary to explore understandings of play, learning through play, empowerment, freedom to choose and the *Playwork Principles* (PPSG 2005).

In the area of early years, the adult constructs play activities in order to ensure that the child achieves certain learning outcomes from the play activity. However, when we come to compare this with playwork definitions, as Rennie (2003: 19) points out, 'play suffers from an absence of clearly recognisable outcomes'. Is this because it is difficult to express in academic terms what a child may be gaining from an unstructured/child-structured activity?

Playwork outcomes relate to the child/young person's freedom to choose. This empowers the child or young person and enables them to undertake activities purely for pleasure or the exploration of their emotions. Brown (2003b) refers to the acronym SPICE (Social interaction, Physical activity, Intellectual stimulation, Creative achievement, Emotional stability) that is commonly used to describe playwork. He argues that while this is a useful terminology, it is too simplistic and adds the three Fs, which could offer a fuller description:

- Fun – risk, challenge, recreation; entertainment;
- Freedom – boundary testing, exercise of power and control;
- Flexibility – experimentation, investigation, exploration.

These are important aspects of a child/young person's all round development and need to be combined with the learning through play definitions. If children are really learning through play then why do they need breaks during the formal day, which are referred to as 'play time'? This point seems to imply that there are two types of play which exist side by side within a child/young person's day but which are seen as separate entities. These two timetabled aspects of a child's day mean there is recognition that both are important aspects of a child/young person's development.

Article 31 of the UN Convention on the Rights of the Child asserts: 'States parties recognise the right of the child to rest and leisure, to engage in play and recreational activities appropriate to the age of the child and to participate freely in cultural life and the arts' (UNICEF 1991). However, Newell (1991) states that in the UK the obligation to attend school at the age of 5 years interferes with the child's right to play, unlike other countries in Europe where children may not start school until the age of 6 or 7 years. However, nowhere in the Convention or in Newell's book does it actually define play as being different from learning through play.

The early years sector has well known pedagogues such as Friedrich Froebel (1888), Maria Montessori (1912), Margaret McMillan (1919) and Susan Isaacs (1954) who all advocated theories which refer to learning through play. However, the type of play they referred to was planned by adults and had definite learning outcomes.

More recent publications, for example the DfES consultation document on the Early Years Foundation Stage, has early learning goals and four columns labelled

- development matters,
- look, listen and note,
- effective practice,
- planning and resourcing,

leaving no room for children to determine and control the content.

However, Ryan (2005) argues for a child-centred education system where the emphasis is on personal choice, freedom from adult authority, and a developmentally appropriate curriculum which responds to individual differences and ensures success for all. Child-centred educators share authority with children in order to enable the children to become self-regulating and self-determining individuals. Ryan seems to be offering us a thesis which would combine the pedagogy of the educationalist with the values of playwork.

Where then does the interface come between early years workers and playworkers? The people who work in these fields are professionals and as such they have respect for each other's areas of work and the differences in definition and interpretation. Interestingly there are a number of people who work across both professions, for example working in an early years setting during the day and moving to the playwork area in the after-school period. One major area of agreement is that both early years workers and playworkers view the child's/young person's best interests as paramount.

The Children's Workforce Development Council (CWDC) has been trying to work towards developing a more multi-skilled workforce in order to enable people to work across existing boundaries. To this end it has promoted the development of Transition Modules for those who hold a Level Three qualification in Early Years and Child Care and want to work in Playwork, or those who hold a Level Three qualification in Playwork and want to work in Early Years and Child Care. These awards focus on the differences between the knowledge and skills of the two areas. The awards are linked with the National Occupational Standards (NOS) for

Children's Care Learning and Development and Playwork. These new awards have resulted in an interface between early years and playwork. At present it is too early to say how this will progress.

In the awards put forward by CACHE each award has two core units as follows:

1. Early Years for Playworkers:
- Unit 1 Theory and Practice in promoting children's learning and development
- Unit 2 Aspects of children's care, learning and development practice

The age group covered in this award is 0–4 year-olds.

2. Playwork for Early Years Workers:
The assumptions and values of playwork are clearly stated in the second section of the candidate handbook, which gives very clear messages about the differences in approach.
- Unit 1 Theory and Practice of children's and young people's play
- Unit 2 Issues in Playwork Practice

The age group covered in this award is not actually stated but the documentation all refers to children and young people.

So where is the interface between early years and playwork? What is really the difference for the childcare worker/playworker between formal and informal learning? This issue does not seem to arise in the Transition Modules, but it does need to be understood in order to ensure there is mutual respect and understanding of the two philosophies which underpin the work roles.

In conclusion I offer Tina Bruce's (2005) twelve features of free-flow play:
- It is an active process without a product.
- It is intrinsically motivated.
- It exerts no external pressure to conform to rules, pressures, goals, tasks or definite directions. It gives the player control.
- It is about possible, alternative worlds, which lift players to their highest levels of functioning. This involves being imaginative, creative, original and innovative.
- It is about participants wallowing in ideas, feelings and relationships. It involves reflecting on, and becoming aware of, what we know – meta-cognition.
- It actively uses previous first-hand experiences, including struggle, manipulation, exploration, discovery and practice.
- It is sustained and, when in full flow, helps us to function in advance of what we can actually do in our real lives.
- During free-flow play, we use technical prowess, mastery and competence we have previously developed, and so can be in control.
- It can be initiated by a child or an adult, but if by an adult he/she must pay particular attention to 3, 5 and 11 of the features.
- Play can be solitary.

- It can be in partnership or groups, with adults and/or children, who will be sensitive to each other.
- It is an integrating mechanism, which brings together everything we learn, know, feel and understand.

These twelve features can be summed up through the equation, 'Free-flow play = Wallow in past experiences + Technical prowess, competence, mastery and control acquired' (Bruce 2005: 261–62).

By definition 'free-flow play' would appear to reinforce both the early years and playwork philosophies particularly that children should not be put under external pressures in order to conform to rules. Play should be an enjoyable activity for children and young people offering them the opportunity to enter into formal or informal learning situations. I hope my colleagues in playwork would agree with me.

40

LOUISE TAFFINDER
Summer camp in Romania: playwork with volunteers

Some of the most disadvantaged children in Europe – the Roma children of Cold Valley village in Transylvania – have had the opportunity to attend summer camps for a few years now. The charitable trust Aid for Romanian Children (ARC) organize three camps every summer staffed by volunteers from the UK. They work with local villagers to provide a memorable experience for more than 150 children. The UK volunteers are mainly students and ex-students from Leeds Metropolitan University who each raise around £500 to cover their personal costs and those of five children. This includes providing each child with two clothing outfits, towel, toothbrush, toothpaste, soap, shampoo, comb and a pair of shoes.

The campsite is very well equipped, even by UK standards. It has a children's play area, with a good range of climbing equipment and swings, a football pitch and badminton net. There are wooden cabins to sleep in, a dining room where three meals a day are prepared for the camp, and two toilet and shower blocks. The campsite is also home to an orphanage operated by a foundation which relies on income from the site to keep running. So, the fees from the ARC camps not only provide a holiday for 150 Roma children, but also help to provide a secure home for 12 orphans.

Before a camp starts, the volunteers visit Cold Valley village to meet the children. The village is based on a hill, so children tend to congregate at the bottom and take the volunteers up the hill themselves. The village is across a busy main road from the rest of the town. It has a large dirt track which leads up the hill into the rest of the village. At the bottom, there are brick houses which are only small, but look quite clean and well cared for. Further up the hill though, the houses turn into much smaller wooden shacks. The top part of the village is altogether dirtier and poorer. The village has a class hierarchy just like the rest of society. The richer live in the brick houses, the poorer in the wooden shacks. Some of the villagers bring home a wage for their families by working as street cleaners. Other villagers work as farm labourers, or do odd jobs around the village such as house repairs, and then there are those who don't to work at all. There is a school, a church, a health centre and a couple of bars in the village, and ARC has recently completed a play area project, a playgroup and a youth club.

When volunteers enter the village, the children will run up to them and give them a hug and hold their hand. The children have very limited clothing; some wear no clothes at all, which is very shocking to see at first. The children are very friendly and affectionate, and appear very happy. This can all seem quite surreal to an outsider. Seeing children who have rags for clothes and dirt on their face and bodies, it's hard to believe how bright and cheerful they are. But of course their culture is a long way removed from ours in the UK. They are not born into a culture of money, where they are given what they want, so they never expect it. Nevertheless, they appreciate the attention shown to them and everything they are given.

As the volunteers walk further up the village, more children run to hold their hand, so there is always a bit of competition between the children to see who gets the hand first. The adults in the village may shout things out to them which they can't understand or may just stand and stare. This can be quite intimidating at first, but you learn to understand that the villagers are just being rightly suspicious of strangers, and curious about these very different-looking adults who are walking through their village. It's only what we would do if a group of strangers arrived to play with our children.

The children are mostly together in the village. It's not often you see them with their parents. They seem to get on with their lives and rely on themselves and friends to keep busy by playing games. This can be hand-clapping with singing, rolling carts down the hill and even play fighting.

The camps are a way to let the children be free of responsibilities and get back to being a child and having fun. The children are picked up from the village by coaches. They have tearful farewells with their families and head off to camp full of excitement and curiosity. Camp is where the children's individual personalities really shine.

The first day of camp is very hectic! After organizing the cabins for the children, each volunteer is assigned a cabin to look after which may include up to six children. Each child is then given their clothes and toiletries. The rest of the day is spent exploring their new surroundings and having the meals prepared for them in the dining room. Meal times are a joy to be part of: the children line up and sit down at the tables in an orderly fashion; a chosen child will say grace which the others will repeat (this is all said in Hungarian, their first language); the volunteers then help serve the food and drinks and help the children when necessary. The children are so well behaved at meal times. I was expecting food fights and bad manners!

The rest of camp consists of games and a lot of fun! Camp demonstrates some of the nine processes of playwork (Lester 2004), one of the most important ones being to facilitate the play process. This includes creating an environment in which children are motivated to develop their own play opportunities. The role of a playworker is to support all children and young people in creating a space in which they can play (PPSG 2005). Another process of playwork used on the camps is the organizational process, ensuring the most effective use of all available resources to promote a positive play environment, which is made all the more successful with strong teamwork. Also on camp, the playworkers promote opportunities for risk taking and challenge in the child's play, yet at the same time maintaining their physical, social and emotional safety (Lester's 'safety' process).

On a typical camp day, children rise around 8.00am, and play on the swings until breakfast. They then take part in the large games if they want to, as all the activities are based on choice. Play is a process that is freely chosen, personally directed and intrinsically motivated (PPSG 2005). This means the child should be able to determine and control the content and intent of their play, by following their own instincts, ideas and interests, in their own way, for their own reasons (Hughes 1996). The large games on camp include parachute games, football matches, water fights, and craft activities such as face painting. Some children choose not to take part, and instead prefer to stay in the cabins or wash their new clothes. All the children have the freedom and flexibility to enjoy what they like on camp. Sometimes the planned activities take off in a completely unexpected direction. For example, on one occasion a very successful puppet-making activity turned into an improvised music and dance session when children decided to use the scrap materials to make percussion instruments instead of puppets.

Even though it seems hard to believe that an English-speaking volunteer can play a game with a Hungarian-speaking child, it is easily possible, and usually successful. The children shout things to you in their language, which you usually learn to understand after camp. To some extent play has its own universal language, so communication is not much of a problem. One of the most successful ways to communicate is through body language and pictures. For example, when face painting, a child will show you a picture of what they want and the volunteer can easily copy it. The hardest time is usually during large group games when a volunteer needs to explain the rules to the children. This is where the adult helpers from the village come into their own. They become our half-way line of communication with the children, and the games are always more fun with them involved.

There are times on camp when the volunteers will play one on one with a child. This often involves card games, ball games and catch. This sort of play usually entails a complex interaction involving lots of play cues (Sturrock and Else 1998). For example if a child kicks a ball to you and walks away all the time holding eye contact, it's easy to understand the invitation to play ball. Conversely, if you kick a ball to a child, they can either respond to that cue by kicking the ball back or walking away, which will then show you they are not interested in playing that game. Play cues involve a lot of body language and facial expression. Much of a playworker's role on camp is to observe the children and to make informed assessments on the child's needs and use of play signals and so on. An effective playworker expects to pick up on signals rather than instigate them.

Throughout camp, volunteers become aware of basic language from the children including words such as 'yes', 'no', 'good', 'thank you' and the question, 'what is your name?'. These words are all you really need to get by on camp. At the end of a day on camp, the children all get washed and go to bed. The volunteers are a chaperone for this and keep the children company in their cabin before they are ready to sleep. I find the really difficult part of the language barrier is not having the opportunity for a really good conversation with the children at this time. The way to learn what they enjoy and what their life is like in the village is to ask others, which is unfortunate, because you can't learn about their personal fears and feelings. You can, however, still form a good bond with these children by showing them attention, playing with them and expressing similar interests such as dancing or football. It is one of the guiding principles of playwork that the child's agenda should be regarded as the starting point for child–adult interactions (Brown and Webb 2005). A playworker should be responsive to the child and choose an intervention style that enables the child to extend their play (PPSG 2005).

Dance and music are very important to these children as they are a key part of the culture of Cold Valley. The girls learn to shake their hips at a very young age and it's traditional for the boys and girls to dance together. A disco is held on the last night of camp, where the volunteers are encouraged by the children to dance. It is a great activity which shows a great talent in the children, and it is felt by all to be the best moment on camp.

Being a volunteer on camp is hard work, mostly due to the hours you are with the children every day. There is not a lot of time to oneself, but I often feel quite lost if the children are not around me. Camp is where we see the children at their best. The children rarely fight, and they are in a place where they don't have to go begging for money or be beaten by their parents. They have clean clothes, clean faces, and play like all other children of their age. They are happy and it is so much fun playing games with them. As a volunteer, I feel so rewarded by these children, and so appreciated. I hope to learn more of the language every year I return, as I know it will help, but mostly because I know the children will appreciate it. The camps are a great way to make new friends with the other volunteers, but mostly, they are a great boost to your self-esteem, because you are helping hundreds of children to boost theirs.

For several years, ARC has sponsored a full-time worker in the village, providing food, shelter and medicines for the children. A dispute between the pharmaceutical industry and the Romanian health service has resulted in a chronic shortage of drugs in the hospitals. Roma children suffer more than most. Their appalling living conditions (overcrowding, poor diet and lack of fresh water) make it more likely that they suffer illness. Life for these children is a constant struggle. The camps support the Playwork Principle No.1: 'All children and young people need to play. The impulse to play is innate. Play is a biological, psychological and social necessity, and is fundamental to the healthy development and well being of individuals and communities' (PPSG 2005). The camps offer positive moments in an otherwise bleak existence – powerful reference points in a child's life. It couldn't happen without the work of dedicated groups of volunteers.

Part 8

Contributing to the management and development of play settings

41

ADRIAN VOCE

Playing the policy game: promoting effective play strategies with government, and why we should bother?[1]

In 2005 the Children's Play Council was asked by the Big Lottery Fund (BIG) to set up a regional structure to support the development of area-wide play strategies. Play England, as we have called the project, is a key element of BIG's new Children's Play initiative, its response to the 2004 Play Review chaired by Frank Dobson MP (see Chapter 4).

One of the noticeable features of our work to date has been a certain scepticism within the playwork community about the whole project (one wag even likened it to the futility of trench warfare and warned us that Baldric was unavailable!). Another has been the continuing absence of strategic policy on play from the national (UK) government (the initiative is the Fund's, not the government's). These two phenomena are not unrelated.

Government publicists know that just as 'attractive' models effectively sell consumer goods without the purchaser's chance of romance being remotely improved, so images of happy, playing children help to sell policy, regardless of its substance. Children look their best doing what comes naturally – having fun, exploring the environment, concentrating like only they can on a creative engagement with their world – but such images also convey a powerful wider message. A summary of the local government White Paper (DCLG 2006) included 4 (out of 7) such images. The vision for the 'Strong and Prosperous Communities' of the document's title are not best conveyed, it seems, by depictions of commercial enterprise or even adult sporting prowess, but by children laughing while playing in the soil of a garden or climbing and swinging on ropes. The message is clear: 'these communities are safe and thriving: look at their children'. The document has nothing to say about play.

Playworkers and play advocates[2] are jaded by this phenomenon and what it signifies. We have seen countless policy and funding initiatives exploit such images only to pay mere lip service to the importance of play, or to neglect it entirely.

Children themselves were asked by the government (DfES 2001) to indicate what was most important to them from *seven* different 'aspects of their lives', including, as separate items, 'leisure: what you enjoy doing in your spare time' and 'achievement: your personal achievements in and out of school and college'. The results consistently showed a marked preference for more opportunities for parks, play and recreation. Formal education scored consistently low in comparison.

In a clever sleight of hand, these responses were conflated in the response summaries, and so 'Enjoy and Achieve' became one of the *five* outcomes 'that children and young people tell us are most important to them'. The *Every Child Matters* (ECM) Green Paper (DfES 2003) then had so little to say about the 'enjoyment' part of this outcome that many officials were heard to speak of 'enjoying achieving'. One minister, when challenged, responded that 'children tell us they *do* enjoy school'. The worst fears of play advocates were later realized when the extended schools programme, a major vehicle for the ECM agenda and an obvious opportunity to expand play opportunities, omitted play provision from the core offer of the prospectus (DfES 2005c).

Such manipulation can breed mistrust and disillusionment and many in the playwork community want nothing to do with the government and its strategies. A consequence though is a disengagement of the best play advocates from processes that can only be made less helpful by our absence. A siege mentality, while understandable, simply serves to reduce the likelihood of our principles being understood and our practice being supported. Even in Whitehall the play sector has many more allies than it may sometimes recognize and this number is growing. To take the view that all other professionals are 'crappy adults'[3] with no time for children, and that only playworkers truly understand what children need, is self-defeatingly elitist. While there is genuine concern, born of experience, that even within play strategies the real meaning of play will be lost or distorted by an agenda that up until now has not understood or valued it, this is a reason to be more, not less engaged. As the people with the greatest knowledge of what is being attempted, we should seek to have as much influence as possible.

Bob Hughes (2006: 132) has said the playworker 'is privileged like no other human beings ever before, to be subsumed into a culture that in the past human adults have only been able to intuit or nostalgically recall'. This privilege comes with a responsibility: to promote as widely as possible the environments and services that best enable that culture to flourish. To do this we will need to engage with those who have never studied, practised or even encountered playwork but, as a playwork advocate, Gordon Sturrock said at the launch of Hughes's book, 'the map is not the territory' and play is a domain that we have all inhabited. Most adults, if they care at all about children and allow any time for reflection, are able to 'intuit' its importance, to observe its beauty and to recall its magic. The challenge is to mine that rich seam and to harness it into collaborative action. Planners, parks and open-space managers, even highways engineers and traffic managers, are important allies in the project to roll back the dominance of economic interests over the common spaces where children should play. Health, social care and education professionals are equally important allies in the project to promote a culture of planning for children that sees them as agents in their own lives, needing space and time for their own domains, rather than a succession of services and interventions.

Current statements about playwork say that 'playworkers should maximise opportunities for play' (Else 2006) and 'inform the development of play policy (and) strategy ... (to) act as advocates for play when engaging with adult-led agendas' (PPSG 2005). This must mean promoting, being engaged in and engaging others in the development of play strategies However, the development and implementation of local strategies doesn't happen in isolation. With some local variations, national policy drivers like legislation, national strategies, government guidance, inspection regimes, and especially Public Service Agreements and targets, largely determine the priority that local authorities give to different objectives and, ultimately, which plans are funded. Because it is not a statutory service,[4] the degree to which play provision is a priority for local authorities will be largely dependent on other levers.

In its response to the *Play Review* (DCMS 2004), the government promised a 'more strategic, cross-departmental approach to play policy' (DCMS 2005). This announcement seemed hugely significant but play campaigners have been critical of the subsequent *Time for Play* (DCMS 2006) with its absence of specific policy commitments. Putting the onus on the play sector and local authorities to take advantage of the lottery funding and our new infrastructure, the government has, in spite of its promise, so far rebuffed the sector's long-standing call for the national play strategy that would ensure the long-term impact of both.

Nevertheless, the persistent campaign for government action on play, together with a growing awareness of the terrible impact of play deprivation, is beginning to have an effect, with specific policy on play becoming part of some important national strategies. For example, both DfES and DCMS have said that the outcomes around 'enjoyment' – play and informal recreation – are as important as any other and there are key judgements for this in the inspection framework. The recent White Paper on public health recognized play deprivation as a probable cause of childhood obesity (DoH 2004). Guidance on tackling the problem, published by the National Institute for Health and Clinical Excellence (NICE 2006), says that 'local authorities should work with local partners ... to create safe spaces for physical activity ... by providing safe play areas'. In a Planning Policy Statement (DCLG 2006), the government revised its planning regulations for housing, specifying the need to ensure adequate play space in all new developments.

How to ensure that such space and provision are right for the children who will use them (and, for example, terms like 'safe play area' are properly qualified) is the job of a play strategy that is underpinned by the knowledge and understanding that playworkers and play advocates can bring to the table. In the meantime, the investment of lottery funding, not just in local strategic development but also in our increased capacity to make the national policy case, means that there is every chance to build upon these developments.

Hughes (2006) suggests that unless children are allowed and enabled to express a comprehensive range of play behaviours, at least during their crucial first eight years, then we risk serious harm to their neurological development. This could be to their instinctive, emotional or rational brain function or to any combination of the three. Hughes's theory is also that these behaviours are so deeply innate and so fundamental to our development that play deprivation, that is, the significant denial of the child's experience of any one of at least 16 different 'play types' jeopardizes not only the individual child's well-being but the very future of our species.

The play types, Hughes posits, have developed and survived, passed on genetically through generations of humans from our distant, prehistoric ancestors. Indeed it may be the play types themselves that have charted the path of human evolution. Playing out from birth, and thereby becoming adept in the behaviours necessary to survive and then to thrive, individually and as communities in a predatory world, human children have led the evolution of the species. The play behaviours exhibited by children tell us about our evolutionary past and, to the extent that they are inhibited, distressed or changing, may provide the best clues to our future.[5]

Perhaps those government publicists, decorating their masters' policies with pictures of children at play, are intuitively tapping into a deeply resonant instinct within the communities they seek to persuade. What politician would not want to be associated with the aspect of human behaviour that contains the key to our survival on the planet?

Not everyone – even within playwork – fully agrees with Bob Hughes, and he himself admits to occasionally doubting his sanity in the face of his own inquiry. But even if he is half right, the question of whether or not we should have strategies for play is ridiculous. In a world whose space is, in evolutionary terms, suddenly dominated by the machinery for exploiting resources – and the resulting strife of that exploitation – at the expense of the natural earth which has been our evolutionary habitat over hundreds of millennia, it is like questioning the wisdom of planning for farms or houses.

The growing professionalism of playwork and the unmistakable signs that our society's intuitive awareness of play's significance is starting to find a reflection in some key policy areas are part of an essential response to a phenomenon that threatens our existence every bit as much as global warming, and may not be unrelated to it: large-scale play deprivation. It is, as yet, a very partial and inadequate response. The most recent theories about play suggest that children need more space and more time, not less, in which to explore and grow, than previously thought. All the indicators are that each of these continues to shrink and that we are denying children, collectively and individually, the opportunity to be not just who they are meant to be, but who society needs them to be.

I dislike the lazy cliché that 'children are our future' because it tends to lead to policies that only consider them as adults in the making; possibly the most self-defeating notion in social policy. But playworkers, of all professionals, while committed to the child's here-and-now reality, also know that time and space for play are vital to the future well-being of our species and its society. Play strategies should be integral to the plans for all communities, and if we are not to be their champions, then who?

Notes

1 The author has produced two practical guides to developing and implementing play strategies: *The Mayor of London's Guide to Preparing Play Strategies* (GLA 2005) and *Planning for Play* (Voce 2006). This chapter is not intended to replicate or paraphrase these publications, but rather to explore the concept of play strategies, their significance to the playworker and play advocate and the challenge of securing real strategic commitment to play from different tiers of government.

2 I use the term 'play advocate' to describe a genre of professional who is either qualified in playwork or who has an equivalent understanding and commitment to the playwork principles and emerging code of ethics but who no longer works directly with children.

3 A contributor to UK Playworkers on line discussion, November 2006.

4 The Children Act (2004), includes 'recreation', later explicated to include 'play and informal recreation', within the outcomes for coordinated children's services, the provision itself is not defined in law, unlike education, health, social care and, since the Childcare Act of 2006, childcare.

5 In attempting to briefly paraphrase a substantial theoretical work, I have inevitably oversimplified it and, no doubt, removed its subtlety and magic. The original material is highly recommended and if readers of this volume are inspired to search it out, I will have no need to apologize.

42

TONY CHILTON
Managing children's play provision

This chapter highlights the professional management requirements for those involved in play provision. It relies heavily on my experiences gained as a play-worker operating at local level, as a Regional and Senior Play Development Officer with two major national voluntary organizations, and as a Principal Play Development Officer for a local authority, supplemented through my experience as a County Councillor for 20 years!

As is expected of any other service designed to benefit children and young people, play provision should be professionally, sensitively and competently managed. In the first instance, there has to be a clear and underpinning principle that children's needs are at the very heart of the content, intent and result of the service. In this context it surely has to be the case that the quality and appropriateness of organizational structures and management systems, at whatever level they are operating, directly reflects the quality and relevance of play provision as determined by children's developmental needs. In relation to this, it should be abundantly clear that those involved in the delivery of play service need to have a comprehensive level of experience and understanding of children's play needs and the process of play development in the first instance, together with the knowledge, skills and personal qualities required to deliver a well-managed and high-quality level of provision.

In the past, the management of children's play provision has been subject to an approach that has relied too heavily on chance, and one which has been determined by convenience and staff availability, rather than professional and empathetic considerations. For instance, in times of local government reorganization, staff are all too often appointed to positions on the basis of continuous employment procedures, and/or new streamlined staffing structures, rather than on consumer and service needs. This has frequently resulted in those seen to have management experience in fields perceived as being related to children's services, but without the essential understanding of children's play, being given the responsibility for play development and play project management. On the other hand, we have sometimes witnessed those with direct face-to-face experience of working in play settings being designated as Senior Managers within local authority departments. However, many such appointments have been made on the basis that the person concerned at least has an understanding of play, while their lack of management skills is seen as less important. This would be acceptable to a degree, especially if in-service management training, appropriate to play provision, was an integral part of a staff development process. In too many situations however this has not been the case and staff have more or less been left to determine their own learning and development needs. Children's play and the quality of play settings is too important to be left to chance or to the inappropriateness of general management training.

In managing play provision, those directly responsible should be knowledgeable with regard to play as a developmental process together with all the related influences and requirements. They also need to be skilful in management techniques, practices and styles and have personal qualities that are responsive to the uniqueness of play development.

Many local authorities throughout the UK are establishing policies/strategies for children's play and in doing so it is vitally important that they adopt an appropriate, well resourced and informed management structure at every level of operation. In most instances play development officers have been appointed to lead this process, one that embraces the involvement of various departments of the local authority and the expertise and experience of other agencies, many of them external to the local authority.

Knowledge

To be effective in delivering play services it is essential for those with management responsibilities to be adequately equipped in terms of awareness, understanding, empathy, experience and the necessary expertise. The following provides some of the key elements required. While it is difficult to measure awareness and understanding, managers must be able to provide some evidence of these requirements together with recognition of the status of children and young people. Managers of play provision should have knowledge of:

- play and child development, and an understanding and awareness of play behaviour;
- all appropriate legislation particularly in relation to the status of all children;
- human rights legislation, especially the United Nations Declaration of the Rights of the Child;
- The Children Acts (1989 and 2004);
- health and safety matters and other related legislation;
- child protection procedures;
- childcare standards;
- cultural profiles;
- playwork operational principles and practices, including reflective practice;
- local authority services, structures, practices, operational systems and communication procedures;

- local and national political and social policies and strategies, which impact on children's lives;
- an awareness of local political dynamics and the personalities involved – the key drivers;
- an understanding of protocols between local members and officers of the local authority;
- an awareness of the position, role and status of other statutory agencies and voluntary groups, locally and nationally, and levels of interagency collaboration;
- an awareness of management styles and different practices;
- resources – sources of funding and access criteria;
- employment and staffing procedures, pay and conditions and disciplinary procedures;
- training opportunities and support, and staff development requirements;
- the damaging effects of play and stimulus deprivation;
- planning and development policies, and local plans and spatial standards;
- different types of play opportunities/settings and codes of practice;
- ethical, philosophical, moral and theoretical principles that underpin play provision for children;
- social/economic, environmental and demographic knowledge of the area together with the physical characteristics and the characters (the movers and the blockers!) of the area;
- local support mechanisms;
- policies for play settings (i.e. access, behavioural, confidentiality, disciplinary, grievance procedures, complaints procedures, risk assessment, exclusivity/ discrimination).

Skills

With regard to skills, managers at all levels should demonstrate a wide range of abilities which can be embraced by these particular areas: technical, organizational, interpersonal, creative, and analytical. These would be likely to show themselves in the following ways in practice:

- fluency in communication;
- operational expertise;
- motivational abilities;
- effective team and group work;
- successful problem solving;
- sensitive assessment and appraisal;
- awareness of, and appropriate support for staff development needs;
- resource management;
- conflict management;
- an ability to organize people and work environments;
- a creative and imaginative approach to the work.

Personal qualities

Playwork is a unique, complex and dynamic profession and it is therefore essential that managers are committed to reviewing and reflecting on practice. They also need to be flexible and responsive to changing circumstances. To be successful in any area of management it is necessary to be seen by others to have a human rather than purely bureaucratic approach to operational matters. It is important to possess a wide range of personal attributes which promote respect. In managing play provision it is obvious that for a large part of the time the manager will be engaged in human contact with other people in a variety of situations. The following should be qualities looked for when considering the management of play provision:

- reliability;
- non-judgemental attitude;
- sense of humour;
- honesty and trust;
- motivation;
- commitment;
- empathy;
- flexibility and versatility;
- a controlled passion;
- a responsive nature rather than a reactive one;
- durability/stamina;
- creativity;
- humility;
- receptive nature;
- belief in the value of play;
- confidence;
- good with ideas and opinions;
- original thinking;
- intellectual capacity;
- imagination;
- questioning attitude;
- courage to face up to challenges and risks;
- tolerance/patience;
- sound moral and ethical standards;
- sensitivity.

It may seem that I have described not only the perfect Playwork Manager, but almost the perfect human being. I make no apology for that. After all, the management of children's play provision is an enormous responsibility. Children learn and develop while playing, and it is not just at the face-to-face level that we need to get our approach to staffing right. If things are wrong at a senior level; if the knowledge, skills and personal qualities of the managers are inappropriate; if managers fail to take on board the magnitude of their task, then problems are likely to escalate further down the hierarchical chain, and the quality of provision available to the children will suffer.

43

MAGGIE HARRIS and VICKI HUNT
Voluntary community play provision:
a case study

Voluntary groups can take many forms and adopt several different roles to support a community. The Wakefield and District Play Forum (WDPF) is one example of a local, voluntary play organization. It was formed in 1992 as a registered charity with support from the Wakefield Metropolitan District Council who provided funding and a member of staff to work for the otherwise voluntary group. Charitable status enables access to sources of income and funding bodies not available to statutory organizations. The Forum's stated remit was to promote children's play opportunities in the district of Wakefield. It successfully raised and directed funds to a variety of play-related projects, including holiday playschemes and playwork training.

In 1996, Local Authority cutbacks resulted in withdrawal of the Council's funding and staff support. Funding is the lifeblood of voluntary sector organizations, the main resource on which their activities depend (Handy 1990). The staff worker had provided time and energy to projects and important links to Council management and administration structures. The haemorrhaging of these two critical resources had a large impact on the Play Forum and precipitated a lull in their activity. It highlighted the importance of variety and overlap in funding support, small and large, to enable continuity if some funding is removed (see Brown 2007 for a more extensive discussion of this).

The Forum resisted breaking up and went through a period of reforming and reassessing to adapt to the changes it faced. It maintained considerable commitment to the concept of children's play, the importance of developing play opportunities in the District and bringing additional play resources into Wakefield despite poor representation on the Forum from the statutory sectors. By 2002 larger amounts of longer-term funding for play projects were becoming available. The Play Forum adapted its strategy to make the most of these opportunities (Carter et al. 1984).

A decision was reached to seek funding for a full-time playworker. This would meet the criteria of the new, larger funding opportunities; enable the fullest use of the Forum's assets (members' local knowledge, connections and experience), and drive forward the stated objectives of the group, that is, to support local community play provision, promote understanding of the importance of play in children's lives and develop good playwork training.

The *Better Play* grant scheme, part of the Big Lottery Fund, offered a package that most closely met the Play Forum's needs. It provided two years' funding, including wages, and was specifically suited to play projects. The monitoring and evidence that was required related well to the Play Forum's aims and objectives and the identified play needs of the community.

The size and time scale of the funding were important. Play development is a long-term process. Appropriate long-term funding attracts good staff. It offers opportunities to identify accurately the community's own felt needs and develop appropriate responses, rather than short-term knee-jerk reactions. It provides the necessary time to build creative, sustainable partnerships with other organizations to support and strengthen individual local provisions. It allows workers and management the opportunity to embed fund-raising and other support into their work without sacrificing the more rewarding work of creating provisions that meet children's own felt play needs (NYA/NSF 2004).

The bid required a good job description, evidence of identified need, a well-planned structure for the project, and measured milestones to monitor and review the success of the project. It included a reasonable professional salary to attract qualified, experienced playworkers. The bid was successful, and in May 2003 the Play Forum appointed a play development worker from a strong field of applicants.

The Play Forum had no physical base. Desk space for the development worker was provided at a local Adventure Playground to ensure a supportive playwork workspace. A mentor was appointed, and Play Forum members shared experience and knowledge (Megginson and Clutterbuck 1995).

The new strategy, personified by the Play Development Worker, required new management and administration structures. Becoming an employer brings legal responsibilities, for example providing employers liability insurance, policies for staff, meeting tax law requirements. The Play Forum developed and adopted additional policies and procedures to support the new structure. The members collaborated to ensure good, organized line management, access to quality training and acceptable working conditions.

The WDPF is a registered charity, of which the officers are trustees: 'Trustees have and must accept ultimate responsibility for directing the affairs of a charity, and ensuring that it is solvent, well-run, and delivering the charitable outcomes for which it has been set up' (Charity Commission 2007: E). A local grant paid for trustees to have professional legal training and advice and the Play Forum opted to become a 'company limited by guarantee'. This is a suitable structure for a charity that limits member's liability to an agreed amount (often £1) and provides a sound basis for external funding bids.

The full-time Play Development Worker had a huge impact on the Forum's activities. The organization had a face, a contact point and a professional play advocate operating at a variety of levels in the community. Monthly Forum meetings discussed projects with visible outcomes that made a tangible difference to children's local play provision. Reports on new and existing projects, professionally supported, provided evidence of changes of view in other agencies. Change happened faster than before and the results fired enthusiasm and energy in the group. The perception of the Play Forum changed. Their knowledge was more welcomed, respected and sought in other organizations. The Forum's vision expanded as the possibilities afforded by the employment of professional staff became clear.

For an employee, working for a voluntary community group can be quite exhilarating. There was ample opportunity for the role to be shaped and directed by the post holder, working to their strengths within the job description. The Forum's knowledge and structure aided quick decision making with fewer tiers of approval than most statutory organizations.

In response to additional demand on the resources of the Forum, an approach to the funder increased funding from one full-time Play Development post to two part-time posts on three days a week each. The second Play Development Worker brought complimentary skills, knowledge and experience enabling new, diverse and innovative approaches to working with communities and organizations. Each worker was supported to develop their personal strengths to meet the Play Forum's objectives.

Examples of projects undertaken included:

- Administering Wakefield Children's Fund money for local free open access holiday play schemes.
- Working with established community groups to provide play opportunities for children and young people in their community.
- Developing new projects, including naturalistic play environments without standard play equipment. This involved introducing the community, local authority staff and partner organizations to the benefits of natural play environments.
- Staffing summer playschemes as a catalyst to engage and encourage local people to become involved in play provision.
- Providing support and training to community groups to increase children's access to local play provision.
- Consulting with children and young people to build detailed information and evidence of where they wanted to play, how they use and move around their communities and identify their play needs.
- Organizing children's visits to a range of play spaces to broaden their play experiences and inform their decision making.
- Facilitating platforms for children's voices to be heard in their communities.
- Sharing consultation feedback with local organizations to inform their plans.
- Working in partnership with local statutory organizations to develop appropriate play opportunities.
- Leading discussion of children's play and play issues, not previously prevalent in the authority. This work laid a foundation for a partnership to develop the Play Strategy for Wakefield District.

The Development staff and Play Forum members evolved into an effective fluid partnership. Feedback from the Play Development Workers informed the vision and planning of the Play Forum members whose own workplace knowledge fed into and informed the play development staff's work. Evidence gathered suggested the need for more direct play service delivery. Wakefield is a mixed district with urban towns, mining communities and large rural areas. The Play Development work exposed the lack of good appropriate play provision throughout the region.

Experience of good play provision highlights the immediate benefits to children and their communities and the potential benefits from permanent play provision. Play has close connections with, and can significantly contribute to, community development processes that facilitate and empower disadvantaged communities. Play activities that fully involve parents and adult activists can have far reaching impacts on the confidence of communities, encouraging the development of collective activity through the emergence of new groups and organizations addressing wider felt needs.

A mobile play ranger service appeared the best route forward. Different communities would experience, on their doorstep, a flexible play provision tailored to their particular community needs. A bid to the Community Fund (later becoming the Big Lottery Fund) was successful in September 2004, providing three years' funding for a Playwork Coordinator, two local Playworkers, a van and running costs. Smaller funding bids paid for equipment and resources. The Play Ranger project started in January 2005 targeting areas of serious play deprivation. Sessions ran after school, at weekends and during school holidays.

A well-established relationship with the Parks and Public Realm Department provided access to green open spaces and play areas. Visits to other successful mobile play services provided ideas for best practice. Local and personal contacts helped develop and resource a fast-growing provision. Knowledgeable, enthusiastic and energetic staff converted abandoned, neglected spaces into popular, free, safe community play provision. Additional funding bids provided 'play pods', placed at regular sites to enable all-year-round provision.

The Play Development Workers supported access to playwork, management committee and fund-raising training for local adults interested in taking over 'play pod' provision on a more full-time basis. The Mobile Play team offered lunchtime play session support in schools linked to playwork training for lunchtime supervisors. Close working between all areas of the Play Forum ensured interactive support for each area of play development.

Success can make moving forward easier. Funding from one source can help raise funds from another organization. Successful projects attract the confidence of other funding bodies, and groups with money will approach successful organizations to work in partnership (NYA/NSF 2004). In early 2005, the closing stages of the *Better Play* programme prompted a new, successful bid to increase the play development posts to one full time and one part time, plus an administrator post to support both projects.

Within two years the WDPF had grown from one play development post to six varied posts. This growth in service delivery prompted further reassessment of the organization, in particular the roles and responsibilities of Play Forum members and staff. An 'Away Day' provided the opportunity for all to discuss, debate and plan future directions. SWOT analysis (strengths, weaknesses, opportunities and threats) informed the future strategic plan to meet the aims and objectives. Identified strategies to support future sustainability include:

- To make regular, relevant applications to a wide range of funders.
- To seek commissions from a successful Wakefield Play Strategy. Local Area Agreements require Local Authorities to commission services from the voluntary and community sector (DCLG 2006).
- To advocate and encourage, through playwork and related training, community interest in running local play provision. The hoped-for take-over of 'Play Pods' has made a tentative start; one adult group has expressed an interest in running the play provision.
- To explore partnership funding with organizations and departments whose provision we naturally support and enhance, for example, the Play Rangers' upkeep and use of community leisure space.
- To maintain and build relationships with children, young people and their communities to support development of provisions that meet real play needs.
- To support training for Forum members and staff to ensure appropriate, flexible responses to the continuing changes in local community play provision.

The structure of the Play Forum has changed but its aims and objectives remain the same: to support local community play provision, promote understanding of the importance of play in children's lives and develop good playwork training.

44

NICK JACKSON
Somerford Grove Community Project and Adventure Playground

Background

Haringey Play Association (HarPA) (a charitable company limited by guarantee) started the development of Somerford Grove Community Project in 2001 in response to consultations in the Northumberland Park area of the borough. A MORI poll among local adults had highlighted the lack of local facilities for children and young people, and subsequently HarPA ran a consultation project, *Can I Say Something*, with children from local schools. Over the course of several workshops and visits to facilities around London, the children were encouraged to think about and design their ideal estate facilities. Top of the 'wish list' was an adventure playground, staffed with playworkers, and with outdoor play structures and indoor space for activities.

In the light of this consultation a partnership was formed with 12th Tottenham Scouts, who had a run-down scout hut on the Northumberland Park estate and were keen to work with HarPA to see it improved and to see more facilities for children and young people in the area. Capital funding was secured through the National Lottery New Opportunities Fund Green Spaces programme, via Sport England (£450,000); with contributions also coming from nearby Park Lane SureStart (£96,000); Joining Up Northumberland Park SRB6 (£101,000); DTI (£10,000 for solar panels); as well as other trusts and charities.

Following further extensive consultation, a large eco-friendly building and an adventure playground were designed and built (finished in July 2005). Somerford Grove Community Project sits on the site of the old scout hut, and is designed to be used by a variety of groups. The building has offices for HarPA, the playwork team and for the local Scouts, as well as a large activity hall and a meeting room. Several other local organizations, including Park Lane Sure Start, currently run services there.

From the start the local community has been fully involved in the development of the project. They feel a sense of belonging and ownership, which has always been one of our primary aims. This is especially true of the children and young people who use the adventure playground and building after school and in the holidays.

Somerford Grove Adventure Playground

Managed and run by HarPA, the free, open-access adventure playground for 5 to 15 year olds has been open since July 2005; every weekday after school and on Saturdays; as well as during the day in the school holidays. It is extremely well used with an average of 40 to 50 children term time, and a peak of over 100 in the holidays. Our ongoing feedback from users – children, young people and their parents – constantly tells us how much they value and like the free, open-access nature of the playground and the fact that they get to experience many play opportunities that are just not available to them anywhere else and that allow them to develop skills and understanding that they would otherwise not have.

Through this we meet many children and young people who may have significant issues to deal with as a result of the effects of deprivation in the area. In order to provide the holistic support that they need we have been developing our links with other agencies including schools, education welfare, social services, the local children's centre and others.

We built the outside playground and structures, using some of the designs and ideas from the *Can I Say Something* consultation; involving groups of children, where appropriate, in the physical building of the play structures. We feel it is important that the children develop a sense of ownership and belonging. The playground should feel like 'their space', providing opportunities to affect and change their play environment. This still carries on, on a daily basis, through den building, painting structures, and sometimes just digging holes.

The site incorporates some traditional adventure playground features such as rope swings and climbing platforms, as well as water play, a sand pit, climbing nets and most importantly during the winter, a camp fire area. There are natural features such as a pond and flowing water and rare and interesting trees have been planted. Most important is the ethos of adventure play and adventure playwork which is to let children play in an enriched environment, safe and supervised by playworkers who know if, when, and how to intervene.

Many children in today's urban environment just don't get the opportunities they need to explore and experiment in their own way, at their own pace and for its own sake. This is what we try to give them – access to nature and the elements, and many and constantly varying possibilities. We have a regular camp fire in the winter and cook on it; the hose pipe is on mostly all the time in the summer (hose-pipe bans permitting); we like playing out in the rain; we have a pond with fish in it; we plant fruit trees and berry bushes … most importantly, we give children the opportunities to take and assess risks.

The opportunity to be able to access a rich play environment, and assess and take risks, is paramount for the healthy development of all children, physically, mentally, emotionally, socially and creatively. Sadly, and increasingly, children are unable or not encouraged to play out. For many parents the risks from traffic, and fear of strangers, are perceived to be too great to let their children play out and engage freely in play activities that a generation ago would have been taken for granted. It is only by direct personal experience that children learn to assess and overcome danger and hazardous situations, and gain varied and flexible responses to the different physical and social situations they find themselves in. Playing on site promotes physical health and well-being, important to all children and particularly those who do not enjoy or participate in organized sport.

This is what a good adventure playground aims to achieve – opportunities to experiment and explore, providing risks that children can take but that are assessed and in a controlled environment, supervised by trained, professional playworkers, who know when to intervene and are always on hand to help out if needed, but also know when to stand back and let children work things out for themselves.

Funding

HarPA receives 'core' funding through the London Borough of Haringey (LBH) Corporate Voluntary Sector Team as a 2nd tier infrastructure organization providing support services to voluntary sector children's out-of-school service providers across the borough, and supplements this with grants from the Big Lottery Fund and other trusts and charities. HarPA also runs the very successful Play People In Parks project (funded by Haringey Children's Fund and now in its fifth year), and various projects to promote the importance of play for children and young people.

The adventure playground is an additional and new direct service provision, originally funded by the Big Lottery Fund, New Opportunities Fund (NOF), and the Local Network Fund. The NOF grant represented a subsidy for providing childcare places at the playground, to be supplemented by income from childcare fees, but this proved to be not financially viable so the service was temporarily curtailed from September 2006. The primary purpose of the adventure playground is for free, open-access provision, which is harder to find money for, so fundraising is a constant and ongoing task.

Community cohesion

A pilot project, 'Living Under One Sun', has been running with temporary funding initially through Joining Up Northumberland Park SRB6, and now from LBH Neighbourhood Management, that encourages and enables parents and local residents from the diverse cultures of the local community to get together to 'cook, eat and share' activities, based at Somerford Grove. This has enabled isolated groups and communities to gain the confidence to get out; many people have attended our Saturday 'Family Days' at the playground, together with local parents and their children. The project has also provided some training, identified by the participants, including food hygiene, first aid for children, and a 'keep fit' class. The group are now being helped to set up their own independent organization, so that they can continue with their activities and provide support to other parents and families in the local community.

Gradually, Somerford Grove is becoming a focal point for the community, a place where they belong, feel safe, comfortable, and that they can call their own, thereby promoting integration and social cohesion.

The future

Northumberland Park, the ward in which it is situated, is in the top 5 per cent most deprived in the country, and has a very diverse make up with communities from many different countries. Somerford Grove Community Project is a unique facility in Haringey, incorporating a free, open-access adventure playground. We hope that the Project will develop to be a living example of how children's play can be integrated into community life, and can improve the health, well-being and skills of children, young people and their families, meeting all five outcomes of the *Every Child Matters* (DfES 2005a) agenda.

Our long-term vision is to provide a service similar to the children centre model, where children, young people and their families can come and access the support and advice they may need in all aspects of their lives. The local Park Lane Children's Centre provides this type of service to families with children under five, but when children reach this age and start school, the support stops, at a time when families can then be faced with many new problems. This is especially the case for children starting secondary school and entering adolescence. A recent evaluation report highlighted that some children, especially the young teenagers, valued being able to come somewhere where they were not judged or told what to do, but felt safe and knew that there were friendly adults to talk to if they needed them.

While we carry on the struggle to secure long-term revenue funding to keep the playground open for as much as we would like, we are convinced that we are providing a necessary and vital service for the local community, and we will continue to do so.

45

STEPHEN RENNIE
Tell me an old old story: ICT and the play setting

The pace of development of communications media has been breathtaking in recent years. It is evidently accelerating. There is as yet no indication of an end point and there are significant differences in use of these new systems by young and old. All of the traditional ingredients of a fight over change are present and the arguments presented by each side are as true and as false as they always have been in relation to social change.

There is a key difference though. The new communications media are much more accessible to children than their predecessors. This is especially true in the developed world, but huge production volumes and decreasing costs have made them increasingly available in the developing world too. Through their play, children are finding ways to use this technology that its inventors had not envisaged.

As playworkers, we can look at this issue in two quite distinct ways, we can try to keep pace with the technology and its detailed application, or we can seek its roots and relate those to what we already know.

The first of those options is not as hard as it sounds. This is after all largely communications technology, so it works constantly to inform each of us of its abilities and potential. We don't have to know how an iPod works to know broadly what it does. The same goes for 3G phones. We do need to think through where we guess these developments are going, but there is a wealth of punditry to guide us (Love 2005). In an attempt to convey that, all of the sources offered in support of this chapter are electronic and can therefore be accessed while you are reading.[1]

Technologies tend to be convergent, that is they tend to develop towards each other, often from very different start points. The new communications media seem to be doing this faster and more effectively than most. As processing devices get smaller, wireless signals more compressed and file sharing protocols more sophisticated, we can readily anticipate a single wearable device that we instruct by voice (or even by thought) that will hold our music, films, diaries and writings. It will also be our link to the world at large for all forms of communication and of course will let us play games (Roco and Sims 2003).

Children will use emerging technologies in ways we will fail to predict. They will tell their stories in new and different ways, many of which we will find disturbing. That is natural, normal, utterly essential and a part of childhood we can trace back millennia. Our grumbles about mobile phones exactly echo those of Socrates about street puppet theatre.

That leads to our second set of options. We can let technological changes wash past us, catching only such flotsam and jetsam as we are able and as suits our immediate purposes. Meanwhile, we can focus on the stories being told and their implications for the happiness and well-being of the children. Playworkers have always been superb at understanding children's stories and this generation is no exception. Children have always welcomed stories told by adults, even where the medium is not cutting edge. Tales around a camp fire still find a good audience, well over 6000 years since they were first devised. Neanderthal man buried at least some of his dead and that implies story. Cro Magnon man told more and better stories to judge from his burials, jewellery and body decorations – and he survived to become our direct ancestor, while poor old Neanderthal died out (Kurten 1995; Pettit 2000).[2]

Story lies at the root of every child's development, it shapes what we think and do, how we perceive others and ourselves and how we judge situations. Story is developed through play, rarely if at all in any other way, so play is the core process both of our becoming who we are and who we are perceived to be by others.

We are very quick to adopt artificial ways of enhancing our story. Like all animals, we start with voice, physicality and behaviours, but while almost all other animals stop there, we go further. We learn to wear clothing, to decorate our bodies with pigments, to alter the appearance of our hair. We carry weaponry, tools and jewellery, all artefacts we want others to see as precious and desirable and that enhance our status. These are all truly ancient behaviours, originating way before recorded history, but the lessons of their success are still with us.

Leaving aside developments in clothing, weaponry and make-up for another discussion, our development of artefacts to enhance our stories makes sense of our adoption of particular forms of information technology. The latest versions are extensions of very evident past choices.

As intensely social animals, it is crucial to us that we are accepted and valued by others, first by family, then peer group then wider society. Good choice in use of IT is not very relevant to the first, but it is highly relevant to the second and is crucial in relation to the last.

It is interesting that music plays such a large part in peer-group socialization. This is not in any way a new phenomenon, but it is one that has taken full advantage of every development in communications technology, from the crystal radio on. The resentment of adults and their resistance to this process is evident in the promotion of teaching of more ordered music than that adolescents tend to choose (Arnett 1995).[3]

There are parallels for this in other behaviours and the message older children and adolescents appear to want to send is complex. Part is 'hiding in plain sight', very much along the lines of the Sherlock Holmes story, 'The Purloined Letter'. The child's story has grown with his or her physical stature and felt maturity. There is need to send a message that adults must work to understand them and should be appropriately cautious in coming to conclusions. Use of recent advances in IT supports this need. Children and young people tend to learn faster than adults, particularly if what they are learning lacks an accessible body of knowledge. They tend too to be more dexterous manually. SMS messaging is a good example of this (Reid and Reid 2004).[4]

So, how should playworkers react to new technologies and their adoption by children and young people? Not by seeking to keep pace with them, that is for sure. There is little more embarrassing than an adult vainly trying to follow young people's trends in language, dress, dance, music or use of technology. Like the invisible inks of children long ago, many of these developments are designed to deny adults access. They work well for that purpose. On the other hand, enough knowledge for unobtrusive oversight is essential. There are risks in what children and young people do to find privacy. Chat Rooms and other internet facilities are no different to secret dens in this respect. They are places where children explore who they are and who they might be. They are vulnerable at these times, but there seems to be no alternative if they are to develop healthily (Berson 2003; Larson 1995).[5]

Historically, playworkers are good at unobtrusive oversight, their ability to reflect on behaviours they have seen in children at play lets them spot where secrets are becoming uncomfortable. They can train to do this better by reading up on body language, so that clues in voice, posture and gesture reveal more to them. Children and young people using the very latest Bluetooth almost-invisible headset and communicating with friends or strangers locally or worldwide primarily by image and music swapping, are still children and young people shaped by their far distant ancestry. They will still blush, look round anxiously, move uncomfortably and show in so many ways that they are being faced with unwelcome choices. Sensitive intervention will work to distract and deflect (Last and Aharoni-Etzoni1995).[6]

Playworkers can use new technologies just as they have used older technologies. Provided the roots in story telling are recognized, it is all just glorious play. Children do not need playworkers to be IT experts. They do need playworkers to be aware (and appropriately approving) of their newly developed skills. We all need to keep in mind that if we fail to cope with the present, the future is ever more scary. We are on the verge of finding practical ways of delivering machine/human telepathy. How will we cope with that? (Kulkami et al. 2005).[7]

Notes

1 www.en.wikipedia.org/wiki/ipod; www.three-g.net/3g_standards.html#USA; www.idea-group.com
2 worldcatlibraries.org/wcpa/isbn/0520202775; www.britarch.ac.uk/ba/ba51/ba51feat.html
3 www.springerlink.com/content/v8416262r0434m25/
4 www.160characters.org/documents/SocialEffectsOfTextMessaging.pdf
5 www.springerlink.com/content/l0w718026472k236/; www.cs.auckland.ac.nz/~john/NetSafe/I.Berson.pdf
6 www.ncbi.nlm.nih.gov/entrez/query.fcgi?cmd=Retrieve&db=PubMed&list_uids=7798078&dopt=Citation
7 www.ocf.berkeley.edu/~anandk/neuro/bci-vertex-abstract.pdf

Part 9

Legislation and rights

46

TERRY THOMAS
The history of child protection, present procedures and practices

Introduction

The history of child protection in the UK can be traced to Victorian times. Ill-treated children could be removed from abusive situations and the adults concerned duly prosecuted. Today the same powers exist but the focus of attention has widened to include the general welfare and safeguarding of *all* children under the rubric that 'every child matters'. We are more likely to support families to care for their children rather than just remove them when abused. We also now look beyond the family to protect children from abusers in the community.

The modern era of child protection

Although child protection has its own history from the 19th century through to the post-Second World War period, it is the 1970s that sees the start of child protection arrangements in its modern form. In 1971 the new local authority Social Services Departments came into being and the local authority social worker became the new profession at the centre of interventions. The growth of the social sciences in the 1960s, and a better understanding of family dynamics, made this a time of general optimism.

It was to be an optimism that would be short lived. In 1973 the death of Maria Colwell, aged seven, at the hands of her stepfather was followed by a major inquiry in to why social workers – and other agencies who knew the family – had failed to take appropriate action to protect her.

The inquiry revealed a lack of communication between the various agencies involved with the family (Secretary of State for Social Services 1974). These other agencies now included social workers, the police, health visitors, paediatricians, GPs, teachers and others, all of whom were seen as part of the state response to children at risk of abuse. The outcome was the implementation of a series of non-statutory 'mechanisms' to ensure these agencies worked better together and did not 'miss' abused children in future; they included the production of local procedures, the introduction of case conferences, registers of children at risk and Area Child Protection Committees of high level officers from all the agencies to coordinate strategies for a given geographic area.

These localized 'mechanisms' or arrangements continued into the 1980s subject to periodic refinements often following the death of a child and a subsequent enquiry into what had gone wrong. The report into the death of four-year old Jasmine Beckford, for example, was a particularly high-profile inquiry at the time (London Borough of Brent 1985). At the opposite extreme was the inquiry in Cleveland where seemingly overzealous child protection practitioners had removed too many children from their families (Secretary of State for Social Services 1988).

The Children Act 1989 (Part 5) incorporated all the lessons of experience, and the enquiry reports over the years into new child protection laws and is still the current law in this area. Local authorities, through their Social Services Departments, had a duty to assess the welfare of children brought to their attention, and 'emergency protection orders' replaced 'place of safety orders' as the means to remove children now said to be at risk of 'significant harm'; care proceedings still led to long-term 'care' for children. The Act also strengthened the equivalent duty on local authorities to prevent the need to remove children. 'Family support' was to be offered to 'children in need' who were children with emotional and developmental needs who fell short of being at risk of 'significant harm'.

The Children Act was accompanied by guidance on how agencies should be 'working together' in their child protection work and outlined how the local arrangements for conferences, registers, procedures and Area Child Protection Committees would be revised and continued (Home Office et al. 1991).[1]

As the Children Act 1989 embedded itself into child protection work in the 1990s other concerns for the safeguarding of children came to light. While these new arrangements were premised on abuse *within* families and household, children could still be abused *outside* the family by strangers – even though this was statistically less likely. Practitioners also had to face the unpleasant truth that children could be abused in care settings such as children's homes and foster homes, where they had ostensibly been removed to for protection.

Every Child Matters

Research on the working of the Children Act published in 1995 revealed an uneasy tension in child protection work, between the two conflicting duties to assess and remove children where necessary and to support families and prevent removal where possible. Social workers in particular seemed far better at mastering the legalities of removal than they were at providing preventive services to 'children in need'. They appeared to be missing the logic that if you got it right with 'children in need' then children might not move into situations where they were at 'significant harm'. They were also missing the fact that 'family support' was not a discretionary option, but a legal duty placed on local authorities (DoH 1995). Renewed guidance was produced on how to properly assess 'children in need' (DoH 2000).

When another child death inquiry in 2003 revealed a catalogue of missed communications between agencies (Laming Report 2003) an opportunity was taken to again rethink child protection. The report into the death of Victoria Climbie was the trigger for the new White Paper *Every Child Matters* (Chief Secretary to the Treasury 2003).

The essence of *Every Child Matters* was that we should not just be trying to identify 'children in need' and children at risk of 'significant harm' and putting them on a register, but had to look at *all* children and their needs. Instead of having around 30,000 children on the child protection registers as at present, we would use the latest information technology to effectively put *all* 11 million children in the country on a giant register or database and then 'flag' those who were known to the different agencies so that those agencies could talk to each other.

The Children Act 2004 provided the legislative base for the new arrangements and pilot schemes started to run an Information Sharing Index – later renamed as 'Contact Point'. The Children Act 1989 still provided the law for child removal and care proceedings but the 2004 Act did recast the Area Child Protection Committees as Local Child Safeguarding Boards and put them on a statutory footing for the first time, and did alter the law on parental smacking of children. One of the paradoxes for some observers had been the fact that throughout the evolution of our child protection measures, parents in the UK had always been legally allowed to hit their children as long as it was judged as 'reasonable chastisement'. The Children Act 2004 now tightened the law, and brought us into line with many other countries, by saying that such smacking was now illegal and an offence was committed if a mark was left on the child.

With all these changes, the local authority services to children were now taken from Social Services Departments and given to new Children's Services. In a way we had come full circle back to the old post-war Children's Departments (Parton 2006).

'Stranger danger'

The abuse of children *outside* the family had always been given greater media coverage than abuse *within* the family despite the fact that most abuse was within the family and the child protection services premised on the idea of protection within families. This so called 'stranger danger' was also probably easier for journalists to write about than the unpalatable truth that more abuse was intra-family. The spectre of the unknown person (male) moving in our midst and sexually preying on children made 'the paedophile' the folk devil and hate figure of the late 1990s.

In 1997 a sex offender register was introduced that required all convicted and cautioned sex offenders to notify the police of changes in their circumstances for a given period of time. The aim was to make communities safer because the authorities knew where these people lived and could therefore monitor them better (Thomas 2004). Some people thought that the public should also know where they lived – not just the authorities.

When eight-year old Sarah Payne was abducted and killed in the summer of 2000 the *News of the World* newspaper started a campaign to empower the police to reveal the whereabouts of all sex offenders in the community. The newspaper named such 'community notification' powers as Sarah's Law after a similar law implemented in the USA called Megan's Law. The government was not persuaded, especially after public demonstrations in Paulsgrove, near Portsmouth got out of hand, and preferred to build on its existing Multi-agency Public Protection Arrangements known as MAPPA (Parton 2006: 126–131).

MAPPA had been introduced by the Criminal Justice and Courts Services Act 2000 and brought together local police, probation service and others to oversee the progress of sex offenders and violent offenders living in the community. Mostly those on the sex offender register but also some who were not (Bryan and Doyle 2003).

The idea of Sarah's Law re-emerged in 2006 and a Home Office Minister dispatched to the USA to see how it worked there. A review document followed but still held back from a full Sarah's Law (Home Office 2007).

'Unsuitable to work with children'

A backcloth to all aspects of child abuse was the growing awareness of abuse of children by workers in schools, children's homes and other sites where children were. These workers used their access to children to offend against them and measures to exclude them as 'unsuitable to work with children' were now put in place.

In 1986 all workers with substantial access to children started to be screened by criminal record checks before they could start work. These original localized arrangements were later centralized through the new Criminal Records Bureau (CRB) that started operations in March 2002. The CRB check is now an embedded part of recruiting and selecting new staff to work with children. Employers use the disclosed records (if any) to inform their appointment decision (Thomas 2002).

Apart from criminal records other non-conviction information held by the police can also be disclosed if it is considered relevant. After the conviction of Ian Huntley for the murder of two children in Soham in 2002 it came to light that he had been working as a school caretaker. Huntley had no convictions for offences against children, but the police did have a good deal of non-conviction information to suggest he was not suitable to be working near children; this information had never been passed to the employers and improvements in the system of vetting were now called for (Bichard 2004).

Conclusion

Child protection has slowly evolved from a focus on the few children needing to be identified and then 'rescued' or 'removed', to a wider perspective of family support where 'every child matters'. Protection in the community and protection in the workplace have been added to the traditional forms of child protection. In a risk-averse society every loophole must be seen to be closed to safeguard children, even if no 100 per cent guarantees can ever be given. In the meantime the bigger questions as to why certain adults (especially men) want to abuse, injure, exploit and kill children remain to be answered.

Note

1 This guidance was updated in 1999 and again in 2006 and is now HM Government (2006).

47

MAUREEN PALMER
Health and safety: a playwork perspective

> They're saying it's not safe, then there's one question I would want to know, if
> it was safe for me all those years ago, why isn't safe today?[1]

It's hard to escape from information, publications and a wealth of web sites that provide anything and everything about health and safety. Local authorities, specialist companies and all kinds of consultants providing health and safety training abound. Some issues are pertinent to this.

First, all health and safety legislation and regulation relates to the workplace (Health & Safety at Work Act (1974)). Although play has been described as a child's work, it has to be noted that children do not come to the play space 'on the cards' and 'working for the firm'! All things considered, it's hard to find any connection between children playing, and abiding by a myriad of regulations, and related policies and procedures that relate to adults at work. Indeed it's valid to ask, why should there be?

In my experience, much of playwork is more concerned with the emotional safety of children, and with the idea that children should be allowed to encounter risk and perceived danger and thereby develop risk-assessment skills and be empowered to take care of their own physical safety. Playworkers remove dangers; children engage in risky play, assessing what they can do, what they want to do and what kind of risk they want to engage in – if they are allowed to of course!

Hughes describes the child's approach to risk as conscious and chosen, contrasting this with danger and environmental hazards, that are unassessable to the child. He asserts, `there is a developmental legitimacy in injuring ourselves as we attempt to stretch our limits and evolve our abilities' (2001a: 9). Following from this, it is clear that risk is children's business to sort, and danger is playworkers' business to sort.

Moreover, there is the question, how much impact does health and safety training have in terms of changing behaviours in the workplace or play setting? Some professionals in the health and safety field have commented that training tends to have little impact on attitudes or behaviours in relation to safety. I suggest it's analogous to having anti-bias-anti-discriminatory practice events in an organization and expecting it to solve deep-rooted institutionalized issues such as racism. Helpfully, the *Playwork Principles* (PPSG 2005) provide strong professional guidance, stressing the importance of putting learning and control into the children's hands if it is to have real-life impact and significance (i.e. health and safety is learned and applied in the play setting, rather than externally introduced through training).

Let's consider some examples from an adventure playground.

So you're here!

Joe McIver ('give us a fiver') ten years of age is talking to a group of children by the entrance gates to the site. He spots me crossing through the public park coming to do my session on the playground, and shouts with glee, 'Mo nana, Mo nana are we going to get on with our business tonight?'. Joe has become my key partner in our work exploring 'risk personality'. He now sees this as 'what we do'! Joe can focus and concentrate well, but when things, for whatever reason are not to his liking he can 'go off on one'. Playworkers have to learn to read Joe and go with the flow. This evening Joe lasts a while in the process and engages several children in discussions about their own 'risk personality' and that of other well-known children on site. The majority are assessed and then confirmed they are risk reducers, some are risk optimizers, very few emerge as risk avoiders. These three risk types, derived from work by Cathy Gordon (1999) on Riskogenics, are useful tools, ensuring that the risk personalities of individual children can be built into a full risk assessment of the play setting.

At this point everyone is ready to do something else and we go our separate ways – Joe and I to brief one of the staff on risk assessment. At the end of the session Joe says, 'Can I have one of those?' He is pointing to a bit of a large pack called *The Risk Assessment Pack, Young People's Services*. He points out the worker has been given one. Quite right, I give him his. Lord knows what his family will think when he gets home with that exciting document!

I've got your back!

The following week we continue the process. Joe 'goes into one' and begins standing up on the benches and running up and down them. There are cries of complaint from the children I'm working with, but in a very accepting way; they know Joe too. Joe dashes off. Five minutes later he jumps up on the benches and it is disrupting, so I ask him if he could come down. Joe is carrying a huge thick lump of wood hardly appropriate as a gun and he is struggling to hold it in two hands. I realize Joe is in another play space now, as he takes a machine gun like stance, spraying the site in front of us with gunfire. He doesn't hear me and says, 'Don't worry Mo nana I have you covered'. Clearly Joe has joined in gunplay with others on the site and as a sideline thought he might give covering fire to the people discussing Riskogenics at the benches.

Accidents and ...

On another session Joe and others are discussing accidents. Children love to tell you bad news, particularly if it involves someone getting damaged.

Joe takes the lead and describes in great detail, stage by stage, his most recent accident, falling off a plank connecting two play structures. Joe re-enacts in some detail what happened and why. He is highly descriptive and plays it out dramatically; he seems disappointed that his injuries were not more serious! He considers how he could have done things differently. He suggests that an old mattress should be put underneath the plank. This meets with general approval, and it becomes clear that the accident is getting turned into a fun, risk-taking opportunity as everyone imagines lots of children crossing the plank and leaping off onto the mattress below.

If you're not locked up don't have to escape

Over the next few weeks, Joe and I are joined by a different group. They too are keen to discuss and to inform me about their accidents and the need for risk and Riskogenics assessments.

The issue under discussion today is inclusion, and a concern that the open gate of the adventure playground might pose a risk for some children; for example those that can't see well, don't understand danger, have no concept of fear, might run out and be at risk from adults. Someone, a football fan, suggests 'turnstiles' to slow down the children with complex needs who may be at risk if they get off site alone! Someone else offers a different perspective on the perceived risk posed by open access for a child who was perceived as a 'runner'. When placed on an adventure playground to play, they stopped running, as there was nowhere to escape from any more – this was open access!

Reflection

I would argue that it's essential that playworkers should know the implications of the health and safety legislation thoroughly. If the craft of playwork wants to preserve, promote and enhance children's opportunities to play, we need to be informed and able to meet and challenge the health and safety tidal wave that is infecting children's play opportunities and restricting good playwork practice.

It is the duty of the playworker to deal with hazard, what we call danger, because if we do this, it provides the safe space that truly enables children to explore risk and risk taking and as Joe does, turn much of it into a fun, risky activity rather than what all too often happens in many contexts, for example schools, where the plank and the play structure would probably have been removed.

As playworkers we need to support children in what they do and how they do it, by engaging and enabling them to take control of their own world and be the risk assessors. Children love to talk about the real things that happen, those that are worth retelling. They are clearly the things worth reflecting on, and they are probably the areas of key intelligence and importance.

Health and safety is about what you can do, not what you can't.
(Saying, said regularly, at Barnard Park Adventure Playground)

Note

[1] Sam Smyth-Cavey asking why her children aren't able to do the things she did
as a child on an adventure playground (Palmer 2002).

48

ISSY COLE-HAMILTON
Children's rights and play

To play is not only a developmental imperative but also a basic children's right. The United Nations Convention on the Rights of the Child (UNICEF 1991) confers on children the right to 'engage in play and recreational activities appropriate to the age of the child' (Article 31). The key articles underpinning the Convention – non-discrimination; the best interests of the child; the right to express a view and to be listened to; freedom of expression; freedom of association and the right to protection from abuse and neglect – all affect children's play provision. Additional articles, supporting the rights of specific groups of children, for example disabled children, children from minority ethnic groups, child refugees and asylum seeking families and those in public care must also be respected. For example, disabled children have the right to take their place in mainstream society as well as to services to meet their own specific needs; children from minority ethnic groups have the right to use their own language and be brought up understanding their own culture and heritage; refugee and asylum-seeking children should be given special protection and children unable to live with their own families must be given the best possible care, protection and life chances.

The UN Convention on the Rights of the Child (UNCRC)

The UNCRC is the most widely ratified UN convention with all but two member states (the USA and Somalia) having agreed to implement its principles. The Convention was first agreed by the UN in 1989 and was ratified by the UK government in 1991. In ratifying the Convention the government agreed to translate the rights in the convention into reality for all children and young people (with some agreed opt-outs).

In order to assess whether or not a country is taking its obligations under the Convention seriously, and respecting the rights of all children and young people, the UN Committee on the Rights of the Child meets regularly and governments are required to report on their progress at regular intervals. In scrutinizing a country's progress in implementation the Committee also receives reports and evidence from other organizations in that country, and can question the government about issues highlighted in these reports.

The rights of all children and young people

The Convention sees children as people who have the same basic human rights as adults but who also have additional rights because they are children. The rights are often grouped into three types:

- Rights to active *participation* in their own lives and in society.
- Rights to *protection* from neglect, harm and abuse.
- Rights to *provision* of services, which meet their needs.

All the rights in the Convention are conferred on all children and young people from birth to 18 years old, wherever they are in the world, whatever their background and circumstances, and whatever they have done. The rights are defined in the main 41 Articles, and there are an additional 14 Articles referring to the way in which governments should implement the Convention.

Children's rights and play

Although not all the Articles are relevant to playworkers many of them are – perhaps the most important being Article 31, the right to leisure, play and participation in cultural activities.
    Article 31 states:

1. States parties recognize the right of the child to rest and leisure, to engage in play and recreational activities appropriate to the age of the child and to participate freely in cultural life and the arts.
2. States parties shall respect and promote the right of the child to participate fully in cultural and artistic life and shall encourage the provision of appropriate and equal opportunities for cultural, artistic, recreational and leisure activity.

This means that all children and young people in the UK have the right to play and recreation and that the government, and its agencies at national, regional and local level, should encourage provision for this.
    However, Article 31 is not the only Article with implications for playworkers. Tables 48.1 and 48.2 summarize the key articles of relevance to playwork and how a full understanding of these might influence playwork practice.

Table 48.1 Children's rights and the implications for play providers

Child's right	Short description	Implications for playwork
Underpinning articles		
Article 2: non-discrimination	All rights apply to all children without exception and the State must protect children from any form of discrimination	All children have the right to play and should be protected from all types of discrimination
Article 3: the best interests of the child	All actions concerning the child should take full account of his or her best interests	Playworkers must always consider what is best for children above other considerations
Article 12: the right to express a view and be listened to	The right to express an opinion, and to have that opinion taken into account, in any matter or procedure affecting the child	Children should be consulted on all matters that affect them and should be given the chance to be active participants in decisions about the play opportunities offered to them
Article 13: freedom of expression	The child's right to express his or her views, unless this would violate the rights of others	Children should be able to express their views but if these are discriminatory or violate the rights of others they should be challenged by playworkers
Article 14: freedom of thought, conscience and religion	The right to freedom of thought, conscience and religion, subject to appropriate parental guidance and national law	Playworkers should respect the religious traditions of children in their playwork practice
Article 15: freedom of association	The right to meet with others and to join or set up associations, unless the fact of doing so violates the rights of others	Unless they are violating the rights of others children should be allowed to gather and meet with their friends
Article 16: protection of privacy	The right to protection from interference with privacy, family, home and correspondence, and from libel or slander	Playworkers must respect children's privacy and right to confidentiality unless this will put the child in danger
Article 19: protection from abuse and neglect	The government's duty to protect children from all forms of maltreatment perpetrated by parents or others responsible for their care, and to undertake preventive and treatment programmes in this regard	Child protection policies and procedures and the need to safeguard children are as important in play settings as in any other places where children are in the care of adults

Table 48.2 The rights of specific groups of children and young people, and the implications for play providers

Child's right	Short description	Implications for playwork
Underpinning Articles		
Article 20: protection for children without families	The duty of the government to provide special protection for children deprived of their family environment and to ensure that appropriate alternative family care or institutional placement is made available to them, taking into account the child's cultural background	Children looked after by local authorities have the same rights as other children but should also be offered additional care and protection. This might include opportunities to play with others of similar ages and backgrounds
Article 22: refugee and asylum seeking children and young people	Special protection for children who are refugees or seeking refugee status, and the government's obligation to ensure them protection.	Children in refugee and asylum seeking families, or who have entered the country as unaccompanied refugees, may need additional support and services from local play providers to support their development and integration into their new communities
Article 23: children and young people who are disabled	The rights of disabled children to special care, education and training designed to help them achieve as far as possible self-reliance and to lead a full and active life in society	All play provision should be inclusive and ensure it is welcoming and accessible to disabled children. Playworkers have an important role in supporting disabled and non-disabled children playing together
Article 30: children and young people from minority ethnic groups	The right of children of minority communities to enjoy their own culture and to practise their own religion and language	The recruitment of playworkers from local community groups is an important part of ensuring that children are able to practise their own religion and play in ways appropriate to their own culture

Conclusion

Although there are no international sanctions for countries failing to implement the Convention it does act as a valuable benchmark for the assessment of services for children and young people and for each country to assess and monitor progress in respect of children and young people and their rights. It also offers a valuable framework for the practice of all those working with children and young people including playworkers.

49

HAKI KAPASI
Being an anti-racist

If I was anti-racist I would notice that:
Most speakers and workshop facilitators at conferences were White
Most delegates were White
Most of those in significantly senior posts were White.

If I was an anti-racist I would notice that:
Few talked openly about racism
And when racism was discussed White people tried to convince Black[1] people that
they were not racists
and worked hard to include Black people
although they
perpetuated the institutional discrimination that they
claimed to challenge.

If I was an anti-racist I would notice that:
The only Black people who were noticed spoke like White people
Black playworkers who spoke and behaved differently
were patronized and treated like children.
Black playworkers felt vulnerable
and White workers were defensive about the fact that
Black playworkers felt vulnerable and discriminated against.

If I was an anti-racist I would notice that:
The world often looked fair and decent for White people
and unjust for Black people
and Black people sometimes got angry and seemed unreasonable
and White people got hurt and sulked about this unreasonableness.

If I was an anti-racist I would notice that:
White people often denied the experiences and anger of Black people
and could not tolerate discussion on these experiences because
it was more important
to make things
better, there, there.

If I was anti-racist I would notice that:
Black people sabotaged their own path to success because they
lacked confidence and experience
Black people preferred to stay in places and spaces they knew
and felt comfortable in
rather than expose themselves and venture into the
unknown
or rather the too familiar
territory occupied by
White people.

If I was an anti-racist I would notice that:
Black people convince themselves they do not want
Any responsibilities and would rather work
directly with children than have the hassle of
management jobs.

If I was anti-racist I would notice that:
Instead of fighting racism Black people get embroiled
in cultural prejudices until
the common
fight
is forgotten.

If I was an anti-racist I would notice that:
Black people are often employed in jobs that require specific
cultural knowledge
or language
Trying to get Black people to apply for other jobs was almost
impossible
and few questioned why this was
the case.

If I was an anti-racist I would notice that:
Three-year playwork courses rarely explore the impact
of Racism waiting instead
for Black people
to educate the White students who will
get better paid jobs than the Black people who
helped the White lecturers educate them.

If I was an anti-racist I would notice that:
Anti-racism is very, very difficult for White people
It needs a lot of
pondering
pondering
pondering
so that we all get it
just right ...

If I was an anti-racist I would notice that:
Black people also deny the impact of racism
and believe, despite
all evidence to the contrary
that they don't experience
any racism.
And I wouldn't use this to defend myself against
anti-racists.

If I was an anti-racist I would notice that:
There were those who stood up as anti-racists despite
being told they were
wrong to rock the boat and to
make unfair judgements.

If I was an anti-racist I would notice that
Being anti-racist requires a commitment
to fairness and justice
without compromise
and requires listening, without
self-centredness or
prejudice.

If I was an anti-racist I would
notice
and act.

Note

[1]   For the purpose of this article, the term Black is used to describe all those people
who are not White and include people of African, Caribbean and East and South
East Asian heritages.

50

PENNY WILSON
... and inclusion

The title of this piece is ironic. Inclusion should never be an add-on. By the nature of our craft, playworkers are ideally suited to have inclusive practice at the core of our work.

In my interview for Chelsea Adventure Playground, I was asked why adventure play was important to 'handicapped children and their siblings?' It seemed as simple and obvious to me then as it does now. In an adventurous play setting nothing matters but the playing. One side-effect of this is that children find a commonality, and they play beyond difference.

The same is true of inclusive playwork. We focus on the playing of the children while at the same time meeting their individual needs so that we remove disabilities. By this we mean that children come to us with impairments that in everyday society create obstacles. We meet the specific needs arising from the impairment so that there are no obstacles and the child can play. An illustration of this, from good employment practice, is the diabetic playworker who needs to be given a reliable lunch break at a reliable and appropriate time, to do blood tests, take an injection and eat. Without this meeting of the specific needs of her impairment, she would be disabled.

This meeting of need is not always a simple process. It would be impossible to come up with a definitive 'How to provide inclusive play'. Such a set of guidelines would be formulaic and incompatible with the Playwork Principles. Because the playing of children is the core of our work, it is from this playing that we best learn our craft.

By telling stories of inclusive play, we build a library of experience; a commonality of shared experience that we can enjoy and learn from. We too can play beyond difference.

If you are a good play practitioner within a well-run playground then all you really need to work inclusively is an ability to expect the unexpected and reflect upon the stories that roll out in front of you.

Introduction

When I first looked at this child on paper, he seemed so fragile I thought he would crumble away in the breeze.

Remembering this, I watched the playworker stride away from him, leaving him securely harnessed with lengths of lycra onto the tyre swing, which had been pulled back as far as it would go, as if for a mighty swing, and then lashed to a tree. Child, ten feet high, was weak with laughter.

I'll be your mirror, reflect who you are

For Winnicott the child first begins to recognize 'self' and 'other' when, in his mother's arms, they mirror each other for example by sticking out tongues. The same principle can be used to establish a play relationship with a child with autism.

- Watch what the child is doing.
- Mirror this playing within the peripheral vision of the child.
- Talk about what you are doing and how it feels to you,
- Discover something of the flavour of the child's playing for yourself.
- Assimilate it so that you understand something of it.
- The child will see you as someone who understands and shares his passion.
- He will begin to make moves towards you, possibly to correct your mistakes or joining your play.
- His true self is playing in the big wide world.

Trying to explain to an Ofsted Inspector that ...

... We have a no swearing policy to apply to 'that child', without breaching his confidentiality by telling her he has Tourettes Syndrome.

Hair

She reaches out to the little one and grabs two handfuls of hair twisting and pulling.
The worker softly and with a gentle voice places her own hands in front of the eyes of the grabbing child who then has to untangle herself from the hair to take the playworker's hands away so she can see again.
Afterwards is always difficult.
Hurt is never intended, but hurt is felt.
The older girl cannot change her patterns easily. She is compulsively and innocently drawn to the sensuality of hair.
There is no one solution.
'Disability doesn't go away just because we want it to. We have to keep working with it.'

Play cues

He uses a wheelchair but can support himself, with help, for short periods.
He does not see or hear much. He doesn't speak.
As a baby he never grasped his toes and looked at them.
How does he recognize his playing?
As playworkers we puzzled for ages about how we could discover his freely chosen play with him.
By holding his body as he stood, we realized that his excitement or disinterest could be felt through the muscle tone of his back.
We *felt* his desire to be close to the sound system.
His hands planted on a solid table, the speakers close to his ear and we watched as the music flowed through his body and he danced until his legs could stand no longer.
Then we laid him on the sofa, speakers near enough to feel the music, and he went on dancing lying down.

Communication

He's profoundly deaf and a fluent singer. He has been removed from the family home without signed counselling or explanation.
He knows that the playground is a safe place to explore his feelings and that our British Sign Language skills are basic.
This visit feels significant.
He stands trembling in the cold and pours a bucket of dry powder paint over his head, then goes back for another colour to take outside and tip again.
We watch as layer after layer of colour covers him.
He stands alone knowing he is observed.
He trusts that he will not be interrupted by playworkers.
He is matted with layers of colour, pure and mixed. He has shown himself to be a mess. Layered in confusion; not knowing how to communicate this to himself, let alone anyone else. He doesn't know the signs for the feelings he has, just as hearing kids do not have the words for these concepts.
So he paints it all over his body.
When he is ready we shower, clothe and comfort him as he needs.

Personal care

Some of us will never be able to control bowel or bladder movements.
Changing a pad, not a nappy, nappies are for babies, can be the best playtimes.
A lad of 14 has soiled himself. Two playworkers whoop with delight, grab his wheelchair and race to the loo. They are ages in there. Three voices howl with laugher. He has been lifted, changed and cleaned and re-dressed; all in a continuation of the playframe.
We are playworkers who also have an element of care work in our brief – but playworkers most of all.

If a child goes home, having had a great playday, but soiled, or missing their medication or having had a seizure or a bump to the head that we have not told home about, then the day is not good enough.

Quirkiness

A busy day in a public park, with an inclusive playscheme running in it. Our work on this public park has changed the site.
There's a mix of children, some with complex needs, autism or behaviour that challenges us and non-disabled children.
Today we had a new resource. A dressing-up box with stuff bought from charity shop trawls.
The children pounced on the box and dressed up like games of Consequences. Tiara, moustache, snorkel, police coat, ball gown, duck feet.
All the children dressed up.
Disability disappeared.
They all looked equally quirky and began to play more quirkily too.
Playing was the common ground.

Rough and tumble

We bought crash mats, which we dragged outside.
Older, adolescent lads took to these immediately.
They set up wrestling championships with the disabled kids; playing tenderly, pretend-roughly with them, choreographing the whole scenario so that all the fun and none of the hurt was there.
Then these older boys made a den from the mats and the playing moved on.
Another day we put the crash mats below the spider's web structure so that children, disabled or not could jump onto it. They were hooked on the danger.
Some could manage a jump of two feet. Others much more.
All were applauded by their peers.
Eventually a beanbag burst and a flurry of polystyrene balls eddied across the safety surface, blown by the light summer gusts.
The children with autism spotted this at once. A miracle. Self-scrabbling, bouncing stuff that begged you to chase it as it billowed through the site. The other children quickly joined in – adults too.
Why was there such a uniform response to this small happening?

We added sand to this site

All at once tiny kids experimented; older kids buried each other; kids with complex needs found moments of stillness to overlap and model their playing with other children in complete calm and comprehension.

Loose parts

The play building cost a couple of million and is furnished with blonde wood, glass and chrome. There are designer home corners, shiny books and toys.
The twins are unimpressed to the point of disinterest, disengagement.
Both of them sneak off to a sink, pull the plug from its fixing and twirl and spin it with complete absorption for the whole afternoon.

She's quick

She experiences the world through her mouth.
She was with the worker she had chosen to link arms with.
His attention flits to another child for a split second.
In that time, she spots an AAA battery, dropped by a member of the public, stoops, plucks and swallows it.
Litter picking is now on her risk assessment.

Setting precedents

Both boys are considered to have learning disabilities enough to attend special school.
'Look. There's John' (a member of the park staff team).
'John Washing Machine' (he was installing a washing machine on site).
'He was a President of America'.
'Who was?'
'John Washing Machine'.
'Don't be silly. That was George Washing Machine'.
The humour was deliberate and shared.

Transitional bear

Barely five and already abused severely enough that he is very challenging, the boy digs angrily in the sandpit.
He finds a tiny buried bear and with surprising tenderness brushes the sand away, cradling and cooing to it.
'He was alone, I found him – paint my face like a teddy!'
Does the lost teddy remind him of himself – buried alone under the weight of the world? A hurt innocent?
At the end of the session, he reinterred the bear, who had been free for a short while, but must now return to his real world.
We made sure that the bear was there for him to find on his next visit.

Neophilia

He stops abruptly and begins rocking to-and-fro, eyes locked in the middle distance.

This is uncharacteristic. Why is he doing it?

From a distance, I mirror his poise and actions and understand.

Other staff and children notice and do the same.

He has spotted a sunburst around a tree trunk – broken shards of rainbow.

Seeing this glory once was not enough. So he rocked back and forth to see it again and again.

Now we could all see it too.

51

MARIANNA PAPADOPOULOU

Gender and play: the development of gendered identities and their expression in play

A group of 5-year-old boys and girls are engaged in role-play at the home corner in a reception class setting. They play the family. The mum arranges some bottles. She touches her son's forehead to check his temperature. She is cooking and she stirs the food with a spoon. She offers a drink to her daughter. Then she stands by the sink and starts washing the dishes. A group of children are sitting on the bench. These are her sons and daughters. Another girl is holding a tray with plastic plates and cups and the mum asks her if she wants to be the maid. Dad comes back from work and everybody asks him how work was and whether he is tired. Dad sits down and mum serves food. The son leaves the house pushing a pram and says that he is taking the baby out. Dad tells him to take care of the baby and to dress it well because it is chilly outside.

(Papadopoulou 2003, Appendix 1, p. 273)

This extract can be a rich source of information about children's sense of gender identity and gender-appropriate roles. They act out a scenario where girls play the roles of women or daughters, and boys perform male roles. This indicates that these five year olds have an awareness of their gender, that is, that they belong in one of the two categories: male or female. Each character performs certain duties and interacts with others in specific ways, based on his/her gender. Girls can be mums, who are responsible for the household and take care of their family; they can be maids who help with household chores, or daughters, who are taken care of. Boys can be dads who work outside the house. When they are back at home they have dinner and a chat with other family members. They advise their children and shelter them from harm, or the cold. Boys can also be sons who are taken care of, but also take care of younger siblings.

In order to carry out their gender-specific roles these children must already have some sort of understanding of their own gender, the others' gender and the appropriate behaviours associated with being *male* or *female*. This chapter explores the ways children arrive at this understanding about gender identities and gender roles by giving a brief account of different theoretical approaches on gender development. It also examines the significance of role-play in gender identity formation, as the context where children communicate their understandings but also construct their gender identities.

Theories about gender development

Theories in the area of gender development can be divided into two main domains: the 'social' and the 'cognitive'. Social perspectives focus upon the role of nurture; the social processes involved in children's learning about gender. For cognitive approaches understanding of gender develops gradually and is driven by children's thought, or cognitive, processes.

Social learning approaches

One of the theories that supports the significance of social processes in gender development is Behaviourism. According to this view children learn through *conditioning, rewards, punishments* and *observation* (Ding and Littleton 2005). Children adopt the gender behaviours that are appreciated and encouraged by their environment, and avoid disapproved behaviours. Through rewards and punishments the social world shapes children's behaviours into gender-appropriate ways. Rewards and punishments do not necessarily have to affect the learner directly in order to be effective. Children can learn by observing others being punished or rewarded for their behaviours. Television and book heroes, as well as (other) 'real' people in the children's lives that exhibit certain male, or female, attitudes and receive attention, admiration, prestige, or ridicule, can give the child clear cues about gender-appropriate ways of acting.

The role of observation has also been examined by Bandura and Walters (1963). According to their approach, learning is achieved through *observation, imitation* and *modelling*. *Observation* involves watching others behaving in gender-specific ways, which is followed by the child's attempt to *imitate* these roles through *modelling*. Children tend to observe the way others behave and actively try to incorporate, or model, the roles they have observed. Bandura points out that children do not observe and model everything they see around them. Instead, they choose *role models* they identify with, or else, they select role models they perceive as similar to themselves (Woodhead and Montgomery 2003). This process of *selective imitation* and *modelling* is put forward to explain the reasons girls tend to observe, imitate and act out the roles of their mothers (or other females), whereas boys choose their fathers (or other males) as role models.

According to the Social Learning perspective the group of children playing the family, in the introductory scenario, acquire an understanding of gender through interactions in their social worlds. Others influence their gender development through rewards, or punishments, or through offering role models for observation, imitation and modelling.

Cognitive approaches

A common theme among cognitive approaches is the importance placed upon children's active and self-directed engagement with their social world. Children are seen as 'detectives' who actively try to make sense of the information they encounter in their everyday lives (Martin and Ruble 2004). The social world is seen as the setting that poses problems and challenges that children seek to understand. This understanding develops along with the child's cognitive, or thought, processes. Cognitive theorists study children's thought structures, that is, the ways they organize information in their minds and then use it to make sense of the world and to inform their behaviour. In order to make sense of gendered identities and associated behaviours children construct *stereotypes*. Stereotypes serve an important function; they help children organize a vast amount of information they perceive in their social world by attributing it to the two main categories: male and female (Powlishta et al. 1993). The formation of stereotypes is based on the assumption that all members of one category are alike, or they share common attitudes, behaviours, interests, and so on.

Kohlberg's (1966) Cognitive Developmental Theory supports that children's understanding of gender concepts develops in a sequence of three discrete stages. The first stage, '*Gender Labelling*', is reached around the age of three. Children make a basic distinction between the two categories of people, male and female, and identify themselves as belonging in one of the two groups. Their distinctions are based on superficial physical characteristics, such as length of hair and clothing, and gender is seen as something that can change in time, or when appearance changes. By the age of five children are said to reach the stage of '*Gender Stability*', where they appreciate that gender will remain stable over time, but not if one's appearance, or activity, changes. During '*Gender Consistency*' six to seven year olds comprehend that gender remains stable over time and across different situations (Ding and Littleton 2005). When they reach this last stage they start employing gender concepts and stereotypes to organize their action.

Gender schema theory claims that gender development is based on the formation of cognitive structures (*schemas*). These are organized knowledge structures that involve gender-related conceptions. Children form and apply these cognitive schemas to themselves and others (Martin and Halverson 1983). Children construct mental categories with associated characteristics and use those to organize the information they perceive in their world. They only need a very basic understanding of gender divisions in order to start constructing and developing gender schemas that guide their thinking and behaviour. This point contrasts Kohlberg's claim that a much more developed appreciation of gender is required in order for gender concepts to start influencing behaviour (Martin and Ruble 2004).

There are two main schemas that start developing as soon as the child gets a basic understanding of being a boy, or a girl. The first, *in-group-out-group schema*, includes a distinction of characteristics and attitudes as being attributable to one of the two genders, either for boys, or for girls. The second, *own-sex schema*, involves more specific and detailed information about the child's own gender and its associated characteristics (Martin and Halverson 1981). Children use the two schemas to make sense of and predict others' behaviours, as well as organize their own actions.

According to the cognitive accounts on gender development, in their search for meanings, children construct gender categories – schemas – that help them organize the information they perceive. These cognitive structures are created and developed through interactions with others, in everyday settings. One such setting is role-play.

Gendered identities at role-play

Mead's (1934) analysis of play considers the significance of play for the child's emerging sense of self and others. As the child develops s/he becomes increasingly able to play with others and act out a role in collaboration with others' roles. While in role-play each participant needs to keep in mind, not only his/her role, but also the roles played by all the other participants. This involves the skills of perspective taking and the ability to conceive each role in imagination.

In order to role-play gendered characters each participant would need to have an awareness of his/her own role and contribution. This would involve the activities, tasks, and manners of behaving in ways appropriate to the role and to the setting. An awareness of one's contribution to the scenario gives a sense of self in collaboration with other selves. In this particular instance this would be a sense of a gendered identity at play with others' gendered identities and an awareness of the way all gendered roles are organized into a unit – the family.

The role-play activity enacted by this group is a fictional scenario that was devised and performed by the participants themselves. When children are in play they create fictitious situations and perform actions in order to assign meaning to their worlds. 'Play worlds' may be inspired by 'real-world' situations and are purposefully constructed by children in order to experience situations and explore emotions that would otherwise not be possible (Vygotsky 1995).

While engaged in role-playing children construct a fictional setting where they can adopt male and female identities and act out gender-appropriate roles. They perform based on their understanding of what being male and female are about. At the same time they experience their new identities and construct their own meanings of what gendered identities involve.

Children become aware quite early in their lives that the world is divided into two genders – male and female. In order to 'fit into' their society they need to adopt a gendered personality and behave in gender-appropriate ways (Davies 2003). Play, thus, becomes the context where they explore meanings, construct their gendered identities and rehearse their future, adult, roles.

52

JACKIE KILVINGTON and ALI WOOD
The enigma of the missing female perspective in playwork theory

This chapter will consider whether there may be a missing female perspective in current playwork theory and if so why and how this perspective may add to our playwork thinking. Herein 'male' and 'female' will not equate to 'men' and 'women'; however, it is recognized that generally men have more 'male' traits and women more 'female' traits. Neither male nor female traits are considered better, just different.

Over time, women in playwork have shared feelings about aspects of playwork theory, including possibly missing play types; social empathy and emotion displayed in play; the nature of 'choice' versus 'negotiation' or 'dominance' during play; the role of caring in playwork; gender differences in play; alternative play environments. A recurring theme in these discussions has been the possibility of male dominance or male bias in playwork thinking and theorizing. Although there are some women who have 'influence' in the playwork world they are usually espousing theories developed by men. The numbers of women involved in face-to-face playwork compared to the numbers of men does not compute: men heavily outweigh women in research; women heavily outweigh men in playwork practice.

Why is this? How has this enigma come about? Current research suggests that the brains of males and females have a number of differences. These are 'anatomical' (Sabattini 2000) and 'morphological' (structural) (Gabriel 2001). For example females use both hemispheres to solve problems; males use one (Nadeau 1997); female brains are 'hard wired' for empathy; male brains for understanding and building systems (Baron-Cohen 2004). The documented main differences are summarized in Table 52.1.

In conversation many playworkers also note differences in the play behaviours of boys and girls. The causes of these differences are 'complex and interrelate and will include biology, psychology, religion, culture, socialisation, politics, fashion, media, peer pressure, play context' (Wood and Kilvington 2007, p. 94). However, as play contributes to children's development (PPSG 2005) these differences will have an experiential and developmental effect on boys and girls' perceptions of the world and their own place within it. This effect, together with the concept that male and female brains think and communicate differently, gives us a basis for potentially missing female perspectives in playwork theory. Whether these perspectives are 'female' or whether they are just 'missing' is still an enigma.

Table 52.1 Differences in male and female brains

Male	Female
Brain types	
Understanding and building systems	Empathy
How do things work?	How are people feeling?
What are the underlying rules?	How to treat with care and sensitivity
Brain differences	
Greater spatial awareness	Hear higher frequencies
Visualize 3D objects	More vocal
Greater mathematical reasoning	More skilled in reading/vocabulary
More skilled in gross motor movement	Wider range of vision
Thinking	
Action-focused	Detail focused
Problem-solving	Making connections
Immediate	Internal debate
Compartmental	Global
Intuitive/reactive	Analytical/perceptive
Systemizing	Empathizing
Communicating	
Few words	Many words
About things	About people
Gives information	Seeks information
Competitive	Cooperative
States point straight away	Paints whole picture before reaching point

The following are the germs of some of these perceived 'female' perspectives that are currently being explored by some playwork women.

1 Current playwork theory is wholly based on the assumption that play is 'freely chosen, personally directed and intrinsically motivated' (Hughes 1996: 16). We do not wish to lose this, as it is the central premise that supports children's freedom and right to play without adult intervention or *adulteration* (Sturrock and Else 1998). However, we would want to expand on it, based on the collective reflections of playwork women, to include the perspective that it can be equally important to play with others in their chosen way as to play in your own way. The play cycle (Sturrock and Else 1998) has been very influential in playworkers' understanding of play, but to date it has focused on the individual. Sutton-Smith (1997: 44) suggests that 'children are so motivated to be

accepted in play that they make sacrifices of egocentricity for membership of the group'. We would go further: women (and many men, when prompted) report happily making this 'sacrifice', and indicate that the play drive is weighted and motivated towards a *collective* consciousness and experience regardless of who is choosing and directing the play.

2   The 16 original play types listed by Hughes (2002a) describe observable actions as their basis. However, what they do not describe is the feeling and thinking aspects of playing, and in our view this has led to a greater emphasis on the 'doing' elements of play within the playwork sector. But what else is going on cognitively and emotionally when children are involved in various play types? Can a child 'feel' different play types without necessarily be seen to be doing anything? How do the facets of thought, emotion and action relate to, or stimulate each other in the context of play? The Choice Theories of William Glasser (2007) are based on the idea that behaviour is composed of four simultaneous components: deeds, ideas, emotions, and physiological states. Sutton-Smith (2001: 166) suggests that play may be 'a solution to the paradox of the conflict between the involuntary and voluntary systems of emotional release'. Thus, is it not possible to think that the play types of which Hughes speaks are emotionally driven and that there could be 'feeling' types whose physical manifestations, if any, are merely embodiments of far more complex emotional needs; examples are 'nurture' play, 'sadistic' play, 'sexual' play, 'empathetic' play. Elsewhere we have explored whether play frames can be primarily emotional and whether play cues are emotional acts (Wood and Kilvington 2007).

3   The Integral Play Framework, adapted from Wilber's model in Sturrock et al. (2004), provides a way of looking at the world from a holistic viewpoint (Table 52.2). When focusing on developmental play it demonstrates how four quadrants of the model integrate the subjective feelings of self and others from the viewpoint of psychologists and anthropologists with the objective facts of self and others from the viewpoint of biologists and sociologists. Much current playwork theory focuses on the biological and psychological approaches that relate to 'self'. Far less is being explored in relation to the socio-cultural and socio-emotional dynamics in play, as noted by Wendy Russell who says that, 'there has been a resistance by some in playwork to draw from these disciplines, based on a questionable assumption that any analysis that stems from the influences of society and culture will use that understanding to socialise and acculturate' (Sturrock et al. 2004: 23). We would argue that our sector's understanding of social play and the social dynamics in play is consequently lacking.

4   Hughes (1996: 36, 48) talks of 'environmental modification' and about 'creating an ambience' and ensuring that 'spaces are varied and integrate with a range of moods and activities'. He refers to 'mood descriptors' (Hughes 2001b: 39) – that are interestingly mainly positive – and when he goes on to discuss the playwork curriculum, he refers to the importance of the senses. Brown (2003: 56) talks of creating, 'a flexible environment', mainly described in physical terms, although in his explanation of a 'positive spiral' he talks of

creating an environment that affects positive feelings. We would go further and contend that an environment should be 'effectively affective', and the ambience should knowingly support the exploration, experimentation and experience of a full range of emotions and feelings, both positive and negative. Braun (2004) suggests that the stimulation of the emotions is more important than stimulation of the senses in relation to brain development and perhaps this is also true in play. Creating an affective play space requires thought, planning, observation and plenty of appropriate props as well as attitude. Current theory in playwork does not fully explore what stimulates emotion in play or how and why this is worth while. Kilvington et al. (2006) have expanded on this, exploring the importance of children freely expressing their feelings in play and giving suggestions as to the kinds of resources and playworker behaviours that might facilitate this.

Table 51.2 The Integral Play Framework

	Feelings	Facts
Me	Feelings and thoughts	Physical ability and skills
	(Psychological and cognitive development)	(Physiological development)
Others	Belief and culture	Relationships, power and control
	(Cultural development)	(Social. Political development)

Source: Sturrock et al. (2004).

The conversations of women raised a number of other questions and ideas worthy of further playwork exploration. These include:

- Are adventure playgrounds male-biased and disliked by some children?
- What difference in playwork practice might there be if playworkers placed more emphasis on feeling rather than doing?
- What are the gender differences in play and how does play relate to gender development? Harris (1998) and Thorne (1993) have explored this but not from a playwork perspective.
- What are the roles, style and impact of male and female playworkers on children's play in supervised settings?
- How does emotional risk taking manifest itself in play, and how can it best be supported?
- What are the best methods for communicating playwork theory to playworkers and to other professionals?
- How do boys and girls play with power?

Is there a missing female perspective? Do readers accept that this enigma exists? Can we tempt more women playworkers to become involved in theorizing and presenting their ideas? If the imbalance is to be properly addressed then both female and male playworkers will need to recognize and accept both the strengths and weaknesses with which their gender imbues them and then cooperatively use the strengths that they possess to overcome the barriers that are manifest.

Part 10

Research and methods

53

SUE PALMER
Researching with children

Playwork practitioners find themselves at the interface with children and the expectations of society. In recent times the requirement for playworkers to engage with research practices has increased. This has included evaluating the impact of provision supported by public money, the demonstration of 'value added' by play projects, and the encouragement to add to the body of knowledge underpinning playwork practice. These pressures lead to the need to consider what the value of research is for the playwork community of practice. It also highlights the need for reflection as to how ethical models of research may be incorporated into playwork.

There is a growing body of literature on the need to consider research practices that engage children as co-researchers (for example Farrel 2005; Greig et al. 2007). This has led to a shift in the research paradigm from a model of researching *on* children to a growing acceptance of the value placed on research *with* children. However, the need to consider what this shift means for those engaged in research practice, for playworkers and for children has not been fully explored.

Playworkers have a role in supporting and engaging children in seeking opportunities to enhance the play environments and to build the cultural landscape to support play and playfulness. Webb and Brown (2003) suggest that this places them in a unique position to engage in research with children. Playwork relationships with children are built on models of facilitation enablement rather than external goals as in education, sports or other practices. The logic that such a role can be exploited to meet the outcomes of a research project will need to be carefully examined to ensure that the relationship does not become overly conditioned by adult agendas.

To examine the processes of research that can enhance playwork practice the following models for research informed practice may be applied: ethnographic research, action research, case study and narrative construction.

Ethnographic research

This is research that takes place within natural settings and seeks to set out meanings by observing and reflecting on the socio-cultural aspects and relationships within the community. Emond (2005) explores the implications of this approach for researching with children in some depth.

Playwork is about engaging children in the creation of play environments and so models of ethnography can be applied to research within the playwork practice arena. Ethnographic research would seek to describe or to analyse the play community. Involving children in the process of data collection for an ethnographic study could be of value to the playwork setting in offering the child's perspective on the experiences of childhood as well as providing the playworker with the analytical tools to investigate the impact of their own practice on children.

Action research

The model for Action Research is familiar to many playworkers in that it has at its core the action learning cycle of 'Plan, Do, Review', a fundamental part of the High/Scope (2007) approach. This learning cycle is repeated through successive stages of the research process allowing the researcher to develop new responses in a continuous process of change so that the impact of relatively small changes can be mapped over successive cycles and reflections.

Children may be fully involved within an action research project in suggesting changes to their playwork provision, gathering information on the impact of changes and feeding back to the playworkers and everyone involved about how this is affecting their play experiences. Such inclusive approaches to research practice become a part of the ethos of the play setting and can enhance the playwork provision over time. A risk of this approach to developing playwork practices is the need to guard against the 'We did that four years ago and it didn't work then' syndrome. However, this is a risk readily reduced by the use of qualified playworkers sensitive to the issue.

Action research can provide a basis for risk taking at the playwork setting. It supports the development of practice over time with the children as an integral part of the group. The action research cyclical model fits neatly against models of reflective practice and can allow for the children to develop their own reflections on the value of the playwork provision and their place within it.

Case studies

The case study approach allows for an in-depth description or analysis of chosen cases (Denscombe 1998). Case studies may consider an individual child within a play setting, a group of children or the whole setting itself. Brown (2007) provides a good example of this in his case study of *The Venture*, a long-standing, and extremely successful adventure playground in Wrexham.

The choice of a case to study may represent one or more of four forms. The typical case allows an investigation into the base for practice within a play setting, describing and analysing typical child behaviours and play can offer rich material for the researcher concerned with engaging in widening provision and practices. On the other hand, a study of an extreme case explores the boundaries for both play behaviour and playwork interventions.

Some case studies may be concerned with supporting or establishing theory. Case study work investigating the approach of agencies framed by theory could include analysis of children's homes basing their practice on Winnicott's theory of integrated personality for example. There are also adventitious situations when playworkers may find themselves at the centre of unexpected events or outcomes such as riots or natural disasters, when the opportunity to investigate practice forms a part of ongoing playwork (see Chapter 56 for an example of this).

Narrative construction

Telling the stories of a playwork setting allows children and playworkers to share expectations and to describe how the setting has become what it is today. There is also an element of describing how the playwork setting may develop in the future.

Narratives may be linear or non-linear in form. When collecting material from the children it is important to be aware of the dream-like and non-linear formats that may be used by children when describing both their present experience of a play setting and their future expectation of such places and people. Narrative methods also imply that the personal and group narratives of participants are woven into the story of the setting (see Chapter 27 for an example of this).

Gathering the data with children

Data collection methods are fully covered in much of the literature on research methods (for example Bell 2005; Rugg and Petrie 2007). The construction of observation sheets, questionnaires and interview schedules is clearly set out in the literature for most small-scale research projects. It is however worth considering the need to be aware of children's use of language when using verbal or written means to gather data.

The involvement of children in the data collection process needs to be carefully considered. Some researchers suggest visual methods of data collection such as photographs, mobile phone, child-guided tours (Mizen 2005) or the Mosaic approach proposed by Clark and Moss (2005).

There has also been a growth in research conducted over the Internet through chat rooms and other services where researchers have corresponded with groups of children. The involvement of children in joining such groups as researchers needs to be carefully considered in relation to the ethics of such work.

So, what about the ethics?

Given the earlier suggestions which propose that researching with children can be a positive approach for enhancing playwork practice, there needs to be a clear consideration of the ethical stance taken by those involved. Although a number of ethical considerations have been touched upon already, it is still worth examining some of those issues in greater depth. In February 1990 the Council of the British Psychological Society approved a statement entitled *Ethical Principles for Conducting Research with Human Participants* (BPS 1990). The statement covers a range of issues, including:

- participants having confidence in the investigator;
- considering the investigation from the standpoint of all participants;
- gaining the informed consent of participants;
- avoiding deception, unless absolutely unavoidable;
- debriefing participants whenever possible;
- the participants right to withdraw;
- offering confidentiality.

These are difficult issues when the participants are adults. When they are children, the problems are compounded (Alderson 1995).

Ethical practice requires playworkers to be concerned with the question of how far the children involved as co-researchers, as supporters or even as subjects of a research project are fully aware of the impact of their involvement. Children joining in with research projects should be informed about the purpose, methods and possible uses of the research. Researchers need to take care that children involved in research to establish the benefit of forms of playwork practice do not believe that they are responsible for the outcomes of the research.

In a media-driven world, we are becoming unsympathetic to the new celebrities who complain about the media intrusion into their lives after appearing on reality television shows such as Big Brother. However, the use of Internet and visual media can mean that children's involvement in playwork research can be longer lived than expected at the time of recording. This persistence of the material collected needs careful consideration as it can potentially cause harm to those involved in the research at a later date.

The issue of confidentiality and anonymity needs to be clearly considered in the light of the Children Act (2004). While it may be reasonable to offer anonymity in the reporting of research findings, the concern of playworkers to safeguard children may require action should the research process reveal instances of risk or real danger for the children concerned. Therefore, confidentiality can never be entirely guaranteed.

Children involved in research should know that they can remove themselves from the project at any time. This voluntary participation along with the notion of informed consent should be at the core of playwork research.

Questions for playworkers undertaking research with children

Finally, here are five questions for any playworker considering research with children:

- How will it enhance playwork practice?
- Is it ethical – do you have an agreed ethical code?
- Does it fit with playwork values?
- Does it have a positive impact on play, if not, then why are you doing it?
- Will the children involved in the research project benefit?

If you can answer 'Yes' to all of these, then go ahead, research away!

54

JACKIE JEFFREY
Storytelling and the reflective playworker

This contribution is based on the premise that with the emergence of a clearly defined professional identity for playworkers, we need to consider carefully how we engage the whole playwork community in contributing to growing examples of praxis. It recognizes the important role that reflective practice has to play in this endeavour but suggests that current tools may not be enough to bridge the gap between theory and practice. It offers a rationale for viewing storytelling as a natural reflective tool for playworkers.

After many years of having to fight to be recognized, a new language of playwork theory is emerging that firmly establishes playwork as a profession in its own right. This is good news. However, I believe that we will only become fully accepted as a profession and the theories deemed relevant when all playworkers are able to accept and use the language as part of their everyday practice. As practitioners, we all need to contribute to the creation of a professional identity that 'involves fostering self-descriptions consistent with the performance of the values and skills of *playwork*' (Winslade 2003: 4, emphasis added).

At this time, reflective practice is seen as an approach that facilitates such descriptions through using tools such as diaries, critical incident reviews and question techniques such as the ASKE model (Attitude, Skills, Knowledge and Emotions). These techniques do help us to describe our practice; however, they may only just touch the surface of what we know about what we do. There are several possible reasons for this. One of the most obvious may be the fact that some people do not like to be pushed to reflect in specific ways. Another could be linked to the 'preoccupation of those new to theory with acquiring a set of "know-that" rules which may mean they have neither the desire nor capacity to engage in productive reflection' (Haigh 2002: 52). Add to this the fact that reflection tends to be on practice 'rather than broader contextual issues that shape *our* role and determine *our* working conditions in relation to practice' (MacFarlane 2004: 19), and we have potential explanations for why current tools may fail to deliver the praxis we need. Whatever the reason, in order to avoid a surface approach to reflection, we need to be reflexive in our thinking and use methods that enable us to explore the complexities of our work and provide our own evidence 'rather than blindly accepting reality as described by others' (Ghaye and Lillyman 2000: 66).

One solution is to use methods that build playwork traditions. Some of the best reflections have taken place around a fire in the dark with no books or papers or in a pub over a drink. I would argue that we are not making the most of such opportunities and that we need to pay more attention to our discussions, especially if 'professional knowledge' is formed through a reflective conversation (Hartog 2004: 65). Such conversations enable the exchange of knowledge and understanding in a way that connects and builds on the understanding of those involved. They represent our stories of practice to which theoretical models can be explored, critiqued and understood. It is for this reason that I would advocate adding storytelling to the playworker's repertoire of reflective tools. Ellyatt (2002) suggests that storytelling most likely has its origin in the quality of human playfulness, and as such presents as a natural and appropriate choice for the reflective playwork practitioner. Storytelling also eliminates some of the concerns expressed earlier as analysis of experience is 'easier to understand when seen through the lens of a well-chosen story and can of course be used to make explicit the implications of a story' (Denning 2007).

Much is written about the value and potential for understanding within storytelling. Bruner (1986, in Mello 2001: 20) says that 'storytelling is part of how humans translate their individual private experience of understanding into a public culturally negotiated form'. If we accept Winslade's (2003) view of how professional identities are formed then such translations are essential because 'our thinking is constituted in the way we use language' (Chen 2004: 181). It also provides 'cognitively complex and culturally potent systems for conveying the way we think about, feel about and make connections in experience (Amulya 2003: 3). This is particularly important if the theory is to become real 'as opposed to something that is abstract and disembodied contemplation' (Hartog 2004: 29). But what I find particularly attractive about storytelling is that no one has to teach us how to tell a story. It is the way we make sense of our experiences. It is inclusive and open to all playworkers irrespective of their setting, previous experiences or education. It reduces the gap between the theorists and practitioners, seeing all of us as having important stories to tell as storytellers in our own right.

Over the past three years, I have been using storytelling to explore and reflect on my practice. This has involved meeting with a number of critical friends within a community of practice and sharing our stories. I have also visited a number of playwork websites that provide some rich examples of stories that reveal 'patterns and larger truths' (Cognitive Edge 2006) about current playwork practices and challenges. I also encourage my students to tell stories and through the use of open questions unpick the key themes and learning, linking principles and theories to practice.

So much can be learned from the briefest of stories. Below is a story told by a playworker having difficulty understanding how to balance risk with the developmental benefit and well-being of children as expressed in the new Playwork Principles:

She was determined to climb the tree. Every time she fell or slipped, she would pick herself up and start again. We watched from the sidelines willing her silently to achieve her goal. We watched as her knees become grazed, her hands sore, but did nothing. I am sure I felt more pain than she did. At one point we asked her if she wanted some help, suggesting that there would be no shame in stopping. She resented our intervention, she told us to go away. She was on a mission and would not stop until she had climbed the tree ...

During the discussion that followed I employed Heron's (1992) framework to facilitate an exploration of this story considering the playworker's feelings, viewpoint, thoughts, decisions and actions she took. We discussed her fear of getting told off by the child's parents for the grazed knees, her awareness of others (not playworkers) watching, and about what she had learnt about herself and that child that day. What emerged as we began to analyse the story was a clearer sense of what it means to be a playworker. Now she spends more time observing and noticing. The quantity and quality of her storytelling continues to improve and so does her confidence in her professional role.

A number of key learning points have emerged since I began to use storytelling. I have learnt so much about myself, my motivations and how my life experiences have shaped my current thinking. I have been reminded that it is my perception of the world, the way I choose to represent my reality, my personal constructs and the stories I tell myself that define my reality. To improve my practice I have needed to understand the thinking that drives my actions.

I have also learnt that when we share our stories we 'share knowledge and create understanding constructed out of the process of interaction' (Weick 1995: 20). This is what we as a community need because the development of a professional identity is a social action. It cannot be gained by individuals working in isolation. Through the process of sharing our stories, we gain access to the tacit knowledge and understanding held within all of us.

Many practitioners accept rather than question the theories they encounter because they find the language challenging and do not want to show their 'ignorance'. This is creating deeper gaps between those seen as 'theorists' and 'practitioners'. In exploring these ideas with students we found it easier to relate theory to practice using our stories. We accepted the personal risks involved when we opened ourselves up to others, and that, as Casterton (2005) suggests, when we told our own stories we would create our own myths, and that these figures would all be aspects of our own psyche. We acknowledged that this could cause a gap between the 'espoused theory' and 'theory in use' (Argyris and Schön 1978: 13), that is, the gap between what we say and what we do.

Argyris (1991) suggests that people try to avoid embarrassment or threat by isolating their mental models or theories from critical scrutiny. When a story is held up for examination it can present a very different picture from the one originally painted, bringing to the surface our deeply held personal assumptions and values that may conflict with our professional self. Think of workers who, due to their religious beliefs, deprive children of access to particular play types, or separate children to play only in their 'age groups', or due to their own preferences and habits intervene inappropriately, ignore particular play cues or destroy play frames. In these examples the outcomes may have been unintentional but still result in a child not being able to control the direction and the intent of their own play.

These and other 'living contradictions' (Whitehead 1993: 2) can be addressed through the analysis of stories because when we 'notice ourselves as living contradictions we imagine a way forward through which we may resolve this tension and improve our practice, thus learning to live our values more fully in our practice' (Hartog 2004: 25). We all need to be willing to participate in the level of reflective practice that moves us beyond reflective logs designed for someone else to assess our practice. Irrespective of what we think we know, or our length of service, we need to recognize that all we are doing is operating from a perspective bounded by our own perception of reality.

So I would like to leave you with the following conclusions:

- As the new theories continue to emerge we need to find ways of engaging all playworkers in conversations that encourage the type of debate that will provide valid and reliable evidence that supports or refutes current thinking.
- When used for reflection storytelling is a human process that provides opportunities for levels of dialogue and understanding not afforded by other reflective tools.
- This thinking requires all those who call themselves playworkers to celebrate and take ownership of the opportunities afforded at this time and become more engaged, observant and reflexive in their thinking encouraging others in the discussion of practice.
- We need to accept that we may need to move outside our comfort zones and enter into new debates with different people and different contexts.
- For this reason the language we use needs to allow access to all, rather than being something that negates sharing and the social action needed to create a professional identity – through storytelling we come to appreciate how language conveys meaning.

I look forward to a future where all playworkers are able to participate fully in the creation of a professional identity that is sustained through communities of storytelling playworkers. So let's build on what already exists. What stories will you tell after reading this chapter? What will they tell you about your practice? I hope a lot.

55

BECKY COLE
An exploratory study into practice and attitude towards child-led play

The question, 'Do playworkers' own childhood play experiences affect their practice in relation to child-led play?' has been considered in playwork circles for the last few years, and in 2006 a small team of professionals decided to conduct a pilot research project to investigate.

The piece came about when playwork tutors, based in Cardiff, began to notice that, on asking their younger students, 'What sort of childhood play experiences did you have?', the answers did not contain the same sort of freedom to roam and wild variation that had been sighted in previous years, that is: climbing trees, playing in woods, making up games and hanging out with big groups of friends. Furthermore the younger playworkers who were not recalling such experiences tended to feel uncomfortable facilitating child-led play.

The research team looked for any published work already carried out in this area. Only one research paper was found, *Preschool Teachers' Play Experiences Then and Now* (Sandberg and Pramling Samuelsson 2003), which investigated how pre-school teachers view play exhibited by pre-school children now and their own play experiences. This study showed that there were two views held by the pre-school teachers. One was the 'pragmatic' view where they felt that play was the same today as it was when they were children, and the other was the 'idealized' view where play was not seen as the same today, because the pre-school teachers remember their childhood through 'rose-tinted' glasses.

From this initial search, which revealed the dearth of subject literature, the research team felt it was important to begin the process of exploring, with playworkers of this generation, the reality of the assumptions made about younger playworkers' play experiences, and if a change is present, how these changes are affecting their practices and attitude towards child-led play. The research was performed with the view that the data could highlight any need to develop playwork training materials to meet the changing needs of the next generation of playworkers.

A mixed-method approach was used, utilizing a triangulation of quantitative (anonymous questionnaires) and qualitative (semi-structured interviews) research methods. We sent out 390 self-completion questionnaires across five large local authorities to statutory and voluntary sectors. Of these, 49 questionnaires were returned, and on initial analysis there was a clear shortage of 16–25-year-old respondents. It was concluded that, as it was this age group whose play experiences and practices were in question, it would be useful to have a larger amount of respondents for data analysis and comparison. Therefore, 100 questionnaires were sent to holiday playworkers and 19 responded within a short time frame. This is why the results appear over-represented in this age bracket. Otherwise, respondents reflected the cross-section of age and play setting worked in, comparable to the SkillsActive (2005c) report (see Figure 55.1).

Figure 55.1 Age range and work setting of participants in comparison with SkillsActive (2005) estimates for playworkers across England

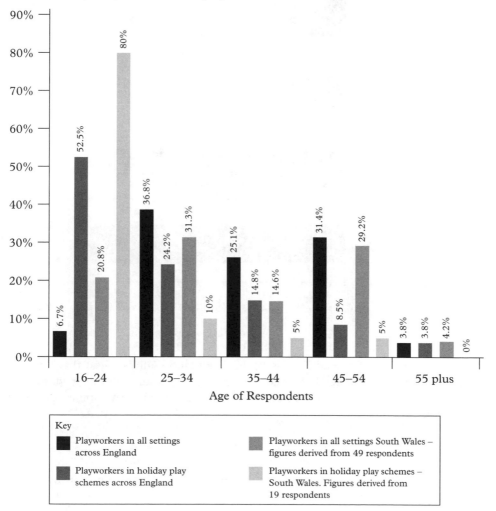

The gender balance of respondents within the complete sample was 10 males and 58 female (14.7% and 85.3% respectively) which roughly correlates with what SkillsActive (2005c) estimated for England at 18% male and 82% female workforce.

The sample also covered a cross-section of experience within the field (see Figure 55.2).

Figure 55.2 Duration of participants' career in playwork

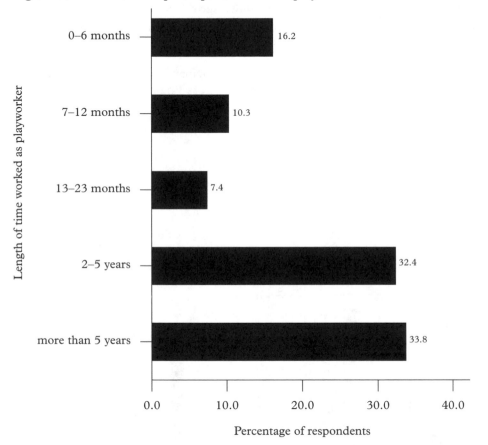

The demographics of respondents is encouraging and could suggest that a representative cohort of playworkers were present in the study, although without a professional register this cannot be verified, so none of the information in the study can be taken in this way.

Results

Participants were asked to recall what and where they played. The top five most remembered play activities reported were den making (28%), football (18%), imaginary play (18%), climbing trees (18%), and bike riding (18%). Table 55.1 shows that respondents under 29 years cited playing in formal settings, indoors and outside near to home more than respondents of 30 years and above. Interestingly, the respondents aged 17–29 years reported to have spent more time playing outdoors further field. A statistical test was undertaken and it was found that there was no relationship between age (now) and location of play as a child. The individual interviews also demonstrated the richness of play experience regardless of location.

Table 55.1 Current age of participant and location of childhood play

Play location	Respondents aged 17–29	Respondents aged 30–58
Indoor	34.5%	32%
Formal settings	14%	7%
Outdoor near to home	31.5%	36%
Outdoor further afield	20%	16%

Initial findings indicate that while the 30+ age bracket recall a higher percentage of time in child-led play before the age of 11, the 29 and under age bracket recall a higher percentage of child-led play after the age of 11, suggesting that although there may be increasing restrictions on play for children in today's society, such as safety, their experiences do become balanced after the age of 11, when these restrictions may not be so heavily imposed (see Figure 55.3).

The interviewees were asked, 'What does play mean to you personally?', and five core themes appeared: playing without adults; playing with little constraint; making up the rules; play instigated by the child without reward; and developing physical and emotional well-being.

When asked, 'What is the role of a playworker?' we had a mixed response. Playworkers were seen as a constant reflector of practice, a provider of a set of play opportunities, an entertainer, and as an enabler of inclusion.

All but one interviewee felt that their own childhood play experiences had an impact on their practice. Respondents also discussed other factors which influence their practice such as the variation of intervention styles within a team, fear of litigation, the organization and value placed on playwork training.

Playwork practices were proven to be varied depending on the individual. Health and safety was often stated as hindering child-led play, and some stereotypes were sited when interviewees were recalling settings they have worked in, such as male playworkers always doing sport, teachers not being very good in non-structured environments, older playworkers being too strict and 'mothering'. Respondents worked in a variety of open and closed play settings and there was no significant correlation found between the type of setting and the ratio of child-led play perceived by the playworker. However, there was some correlation between playwork qualification and the amount of perceived child-led play. It seems from this research that playworkers who hold a play qualification perceive there to be a high ratio of child-led play present, and that the ratio was about right or needing to be greater.

Respondents felt there were outside factors that influenced the depth, intensity and amount of child-led play they experienced, and that these same factors were influencing the way children play today. These fell in to five major categories: geographical locality (where they lived and played); resources (lack of provided resources was seen both as an opportunity for a greater amount of child-led play, and as a hindrance to child-led play opportunities); safety concerns and exposure to risky play (freedom to roam and lack of awareness/adults' fear projected from the media); variety of play; and the pace of change (children having a consumer attitude and seeming to get dissatisfied or bored more easily).

Figure 55.3 Age of participant and time engaged in non-adult-led play during childhood

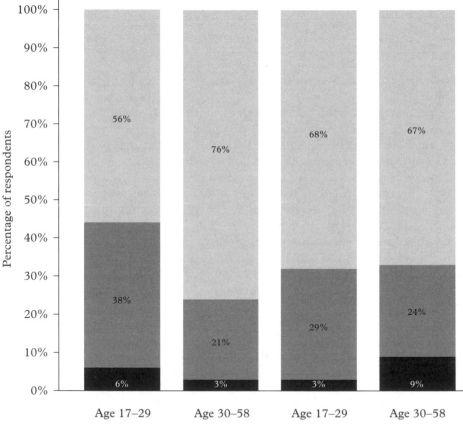

The research shows that 35 per cent of respondents held a recognized play qualification, 75 per cent have attended training in the last five years and 22 per cent stated that they would like further training. All respondents felt that training had assisted them in their development, and feel it had been necessary in enabling them to practise effectively. Alongside this, interviewees also stated that their practice has been greatly influenced by their colleagues and by formal training they have received. They also highlighted that problems could arise when there are differences in approach within a team, when training is going over old ground and does not progress, and when exposed to ineffective practices at introduction stage to playwork.

This exploratory study has only just begun to unravel the finer points about what factors lead to a playworker developing attitudes and practice that discourage non-adult-led play. What it does suggest is that there are few generational differences, given that there was no significant relationship found between age and amount of time spent engaged in child-led play, or between location and the amount of child-led play.

It could therefore be suggested that the hypothesis was derived from idealized viewpoints of childhood, as all memories are subjective and the same everyday experiences of working in play are shared across the ages. As demonstrated in this study playworkers of all ages have different intervention styles and approaches to child-led play, the interviews reveal that age and youth can both be seen as a facilitator of child-led play. When asked, 'Do you think age is a factor?', one female 19-year-old interviewee responded:

> I don't think there is (a difference) because I've seen older people, some of the them are more directing … a bit more strict but then some of (them) just get involved with the kids, and they're less strict, and then there's the same with young people as well. There are just different types of people at every age.

There are eight recommendations in the full report which highlight important factors to be considered in future studies into this subject, while also highlighting the respondent's views of what impacts on the ability for a play setting to truly facilitate child-led play.

Acknowledgement

This research was funded by 'Ifanc' and a full report is downloadable from: http://www.cardiff.gov.uk/childrensplay/content.asp?nav=2868%2C2971% 23874%2C3894&parent_directory_id=2865&positioning_article_id= &language=&sortkey

56

FRASER BROWN and SOPHIE WEBB
Children without play: a research project

The following extract is taken from an article originally published in the *Journal of Education*, March 2005. It focuses largely on the background and methods employed in conducting a specific playwork research project. The detailed outcomes from the project are addressed elsewhere (Webb and Brown 2003).

Introduction

We recently completed a small-scale research study examining the impact of a playwork project on a group of abandoned children living in a Romanian paediatric hospital (Webb and Brown 2003). The children, ranging in age from 1 to 10 years, had suffered chronic neglect and abuse. They had previously spent most of their lives tied in the same cot in the same hospital ward. They were poorly fed and their nappies were rarely changed. Although able to see and hear other children, they experienced little in the way of social interaction. The focus of our study was the children's play development, which we assessed using an instrument developed for a previous study (Brown 2003c). During a period when nothing changed in their lives, other than their introduction to the playwork project, the children themselves changed dramatically. Their social interaction became more complex; physical activity showed a distinct move from gross to fine motor skills; the children's understanding of the world around them was improved; and they began to play in highly creative ways. They no longer sat rocking, staring vacantly into space. Instead they had become fully engaged active human beings.

It is our contention that playwork practice includes elements of both play and care, so we did not attempt to isolate the play elements from the care elements of the project. That would have been an impossible task, given the restrictions on our time and resources, quite apart from a number of ethical issues, and basic human sensitivity. We have subsequently been asked, was it playwork method itself, or the relationships that developed through the method, that benefited the children? That is not a useful distinction, since the development of relationships (both child–adult and child–child) is one of the basic aims of playwork. Our conclusion was straightforward, that is, the children's developmental progress was clearly identifiable, and apparently made possible through their experience of the play-work project.

Background

The playwork project started in the summer of 1999 and continues today. It started as a result of the concern of the newly appointed Director of the Sighisoara Paediatric Hospital, Dr Cornel Puscas. When confronted with a ward full of disturbed children sitting rocking in their own solitary worlds, he was reminded of one of the most powerful conclusions from Harlow's studies: 'play is of utmost importance for the subsequent social well-being of the individual and those around him' (Suomi and Harlow 1971: 493). Hoping to help the children recover some sort of 'normality', he approached the White Rose Initiative[1] for funding to employ someone to play with the children. They employed Edit Bus, the first Romanian playworker, and brought her to Leeds Metropolitan University for a specially designed training course. Upon her return to Romania, Edit worked with the children for four months, before being joined by Sophie Webb for an extended period, and later by Fraser Brown for briefer periods. During the first year of the WRI project, the two Leeds Met researchers spent more than 500 hours working with Edit, and studying this small group of children. At this point it is worth re-emphasizing the distinction between the ongoing WRI Therapeutic Playwork Project, which eventually employed four Romanian playworkers; and the research study conducted during the first year of that project.

Methods

Our original intention was to help alleviate the suffering of the children, but it quickly became apparent that remarkable changes were occurring, and so we resolved to conduct a research study of the outcomes of the playwork project. Thus, the research project evolved out of the WRI project. The aim of the research was to assess developmental change during the first year of the project. It was possible to observe the children each day, noting the details of their play behaviours and social interaction. Observations had to be unobtrusive for two reasons: first to avoid disrupting what the children were achieving in their play, and second to enable the recording of detailed notes at close quarters. In the early stages of the study we used a form of participant observation where the participant's role is partially concealed (Steckler 1999). Although our dual role was understood by the Romanian playworker and the Director of the hospital, everyone else would have seen us as visiting playworkers from the UK. The ethical implications of this, especially in relation to 'informed consent' and privacy (Alderson 1995), are not significant since the nurses had very little input into the lives of the children, and the Director of the hospital had given permission for the study to take place. Although we had permission to use the children's medical records, in the subsequent write-up their names were changed for reasons of confidentiality. In the later stages of the study we employed a slightly different observation technique (i.e. rotated peer observation), which saw us alternating tasks and roles – one hour working with the children, one hour non-participant observation, and vice versa.

The issues of language and culture, and the pros and cons of these methods in terms of their specific application to this study, have been explored in some depth elsewhere (Webb and Brown 2003). However, it is worth restating our view that the role of the playworker is particularly appropriate with regard to participant observation. It is one of the guiding principles of playwork that the child's agenda should be regarded as the starting point for child–adult interactions (Hughes 1996: 51). This means that playworkers naturally adopt Corsaro's (1985: 28) *reactive strategy*, which encourages researchers to avoid dominating the adult–child relationship. Corsaro suggested that the adult's tendency to take control of the child's world often has a detrimental affect on research outcomes. Instead, Corsaro recommended adult researchers should be responsive to the child, and set aside their adult prejudices. This is reflected in a second guiding principle of playwork, namely 'negative capability' (Fisher 2002), which is discussed in Chapter 35. An effective playworker expects to pick up on signals rather than instigate them, which means the playworker is adopting an approach similar to that of the classic Tavistock Model (Greig and Taylor 1999). This encourages researchers to interact with the subjects, and record the behaviours and feelings of all the participants, including themselves. In the Romanian context we made extensive use of reflective diaries, not simply as a memory aid, but also to provide raw data.

All this enabled us to complete independent assessments of the play development of the children. Assessments were made using a variation on a system developed during an earlier study of children's play behaviours (Brown 2003c). One hundred and fifty-four assessment questions, largely derived from play and playwork theory, were grouped under 11 general headings covering the full range of children's play behaviours and/or characteristics of play:

- Freedom
- Flexibility
- Socialization
- Physical activity
- Intellectual stimulation
- Creativity and problem solving
- Emotional equilibrium
- Self-discovery
- Ethical stance
- Adult–child relationships
- General appeal

The children were assessed in February, April and August 2000, using the questions in the assessment tool. Three separate forms were completed for each child.

Outcomes

There was evidence of change in all the children, albeit to differing degrees, presumably according to a combination of their individual genetic make-up and their life experience. A detailed breakdown of each child's progress has been provided previously elsewhere (Webb and Brown 2003). This was extremely encouraging in terms of its implications for the recovery potential of abused and neglected children. It was also slightly chilling, since the medical records described most of the children as 'retarded'. We were told informally, although this was not confirmed in the medical records, that most of them were waiting for places in a children's mental hospital. Thankfully their remarkable progress meant that 14 out of the original 16 children were eventually either adopted or fostered. Sadly, the other two were eventually transferred to a children's mental hospital.

Although it was not feasible to conduct a longitudinal follow-up study of all the children, it has nevertheless been possible to retain contact with those who were fostered through the Luminita Copiilor Foundation.[2] Six years later, most of the children were progressing well (always allowing for the extreme disadvantage of their start in life). One is receiving extra tuition to help him catch up with school work. One has sadly regressed for reasons too complex to explore here. However, overall, there is nothing in the present condition of the children to lead us to change our original conclusion, namely that the children's developmental progress was clearly identifiable, and apparently made possible through their experience of the playwork project.

Notes

[1]   For further details, contact White Rose Initiative, 1 Stonebridge Grove, Leeds LS12 5AW

[2]   For further details see the Fundatia Luminita Copiilor Website: http://www.luminitacopiilor.org/

Appendix 1

ANNA KASSMAN-McKERRELL
Annotated bibliography of selected playwork texts

The following annotated bibliography of 30 highly relevant and commonly used texts is typical of the service offered by the Children's Play Information Service (CPIS).

Allen of Hurtwood, Lady (1968) *Planning for Play*. London: Thames and Hudson.
Looks at how to create exciting play provision for children, particularly in housing schemes, with examples from England, Denmark, Sweden and the United States.

Armitage, M. (2000) The ins and outs of school playground play: children's use of 'play places', in J.C. Bishop and M. Curtis (2000) *Play for Today: Approaches to Contemporary Children's Playground Culture*. Buckingham: Open University Press.
Explores the relationship between what children do at playtime and where they do it, and looks at the implications for the design of school playgrounds. Based on fieldwork in primary school playgrounds.

Blatchford, P. (1994) Research on children's school playground behaviour in the United Kingdom: a review, in P. Blatchford and S Sharp (1994) *Breaktime and the School: Understanding and Changing Playground Behaviour*. London: Routledge.
Reviews research on children's behaviour in school playground and looks at two contrasting views on the nature of playground behaviour.

Brown, F. (ed.) (2003) *Playwork: Theory and Practice*. Buckingham: Open University Press.
Presents a range of theoretical and practical perspectives of playwork, with examples of playwork in practice, including adventure playgrounds, establishing play in a local authority, and a therapeutic playwork project with abandoned children in Romania.

Brown, F. and Webb, S. (2005) Children without play. Journal of Education, 35: 139–58.

Reports on a small-scale research study conducted during the first year of a playwork intervention with abandoned children living in a Romanian paediatric hospital. Includes quotes from reflective diaries kept during the study in order to identify some of the most significant therapeutic elements of playwork.

Bruner, J.S., Jolly, A. and Sylva, K. (eds) (1976) *Play: Its Role in Development and Evolution*. New York: Basic Books.

Brings together philosophical, scientific and literary studies of play to set play in an evolutionary context. Looks at play in animals and humans, play and the use of objects and tools, play in the social world, and play and the world of symbols.

Caillois, R. (1961) *Man, Play and Games*. New York: Free Press.

Defines play as a free and voluntary activity, and looks at the relationship between culture and categories of children's play. Examines the means by which games become part of daily life, and contribute to customs and institutions.

Cole-Hamilton, I. and Gill, T. (2002) *More than Swings and Roundabouts: Planning for Outdoor Play*. London: National Children's Bureau (Children's Play Council).

A practical guide to creating and improving play opportunities for children and young people, which emphasizes the need to start with children's needs and wishes, and the importance of local partnerships. Includes case studies, a practical play space checklist and a discussion of key policy issues.

Davis, L. (2008) *Policy Summary. The Children's Plan: Building Brighter Futures*. London: Play England.

Davy, A. and Gallagher, J. (2006) *New Playwork: Play and Care for Children 4–16*. 4th edition. London: Thomson Learning.

This textbook covers the key areas of practical playwork. Topics covered include child development, playwork principles and the role of the playworker, policy and legislation, creating play spaces, relationships with children and parents, behaviour, inclusion, reflective practice, teamwork, child protection, health and safety, and playwork and the wider community

DCFS (Department for Children, Schools and Families) (2007) The Children's Plan: Building Brighter Futures. CM.7280 London: HMSO.

DCMS (Department for Culture, Media and Sport) (2004) *Getting Serious About Play: A Review of Children's Play*. London: DCMS.

The report of the government's review of children's play chaired by the Rt. Hon Frank Dobson, MP. Sets out how to best invest the £200 million from the New Opportunities Fund, pledged in 2001, for improving children's play opportunities.

DfEE (Department for Education and Employment) (1998) *Meeting the Childcare Challenge: A Framework and Consultation Document*. London: The Stationery Office.

Describes the government's aim of ensuring good quality, affordable childcare for children aged 0–14 years in every neighbourhood, and sets out the national strategy, to be run locally, that will achieve this aim.

DfES (Department for Education and Skills) (2005) *Every Child Matters: Change for Children*. London: The Stationery Office.
Sets out the national framework for local change programme, underpinned by the Children Act 2004, to build services around the needs of children and young people.

Erikson, E. (1963) *Childhood and Society*. New York: Norton.
Classic study of the social significance of childhood, which looks at the relationship between childhood training and cultural accomplishment.

Garvey, C. (1991) *Play*. London: Fontana.
Analyses the way in which play helps the child to learn about the self, about others, and about the world. Describes the various manifestations of play, and looks at their origins.

Goldstein, J. (1993) *Play Value: A Review of Research*. London: British Toy and Hobby Association.
A summary of research and theory on the role of toys and play in learning and memory, motor skills, thought, creativity and problem solving, language, communication and literacy, and social development.

Hart, R. (1992) *Children's Participation: From Tokenism to Citizenship*. Florence: UNICEF International Child Development Centre.
Identifies eight levels of young people's participation, and looks at the roles of play and work in children's lives internationally.

Hayes, N. (1994) *Foundations of Psychology*. London: Routledge.

Hughes, B. (2001) *Evolutionary Playwork and Reflective Analytic Practice*. London: Routledge.
Explores the complexities of children's play, and its meaning and purpose. Considers the fundamentals of evolutionary playwork, and looks at some key theoretical concepts underlying playwork.

Hughes, B. (2002) *A Playworker's Taxonomy of Play Types*. London: Playlink.
Defines 16 play types, with indicators of how each play type is manifested in play, and suggestions on how to modify play environments to help children engage in that type of play.

Hughes, B. (2006) *Playtypes: Speculations and Possibilities*. London: London Centre for Playwork Education and Training.
Analyses the playtypes as they appeared in the original 'Taxonomy of Playtypes', and suggests that there may be more playtypes than previously proposed.

Huizinga, J. (1949) *Homo Ludens: A Study of the Play Element in Culture*. London: Routledge and Kegan Paul.
Illustrates with many examples, from the fields of law, science, philosophy and arts, that culture first appears under the form of play.

Millar, S. (1968) *The Psychology of Play*. Harmondsworth: Penguin.
Discusses psychological theories about play, and reviews observational and experimental studies of play in animals and children.

Moyles, J.R. (ed.) (2005) *The Excellence of Play*. Maidenhead: Open University Press.
> Examines the importance of play as a tool for learning and teaching for children and practitioners, and argues that a curriculum which uses play is beneficial for children now and in the future.

Nicholson, S. (1971) How not to cheat children: the theory of loose parts, *Landscape Architecture Quarterly*, 62(1): 30–4.
> A theory which suggests that 'loose', moveable parts in an environment will empower creativity, inventiveness and discovery.

Opie, I. and Opie, P. (1959) *The Lore and Language of Schoolchildren*. New York: Oxford University Press.
> Based on information collected from five thousand children in England, Scotland and Wales, this book is a record of children's language, culture, customs and beliefs.

Petrie, P. (1994) *Play and Care out of School*. London: HMSO.
> Presents an overview of services which provide for children's care and recreation out of school. Examines the values and objectives of service providers, the management and funding of such services and issues of quality and evaluation.

Sturrock, G. and Else, P. (1998) The playground as therapeutic space: playwork as healing, in *Proceedings of the IPA/USA Triennial National Conference, Play in a Changing Society: Research, Design, Application*. June 1998, Colorado, USA.
> Presents an argument that as natural play space is gradually being eroded to the detriment of children, the role of the playworker is changing to encompass a more therapeutic function.

Sutton-Smith, B. (1997) *The Ambiguity of Play*. London: Harvard University Press.
> An examination of play which suggests that play theories are rooted in seven distinct rhetorics – the ancient discourses of fate, power, communal identity, frivolity, and the modern discourses of progress, the imaginary and the self.

United Nations (1991) *Convention on the Rights of the Child. Adopted by the General Assembly of the United Nations on 20 November 1989.*
> The international human rights treaty that grants children and young people a comprehensive set of rights, including the right to 'engage in play and recreational activities'.

Winnicott, D.W. (1971) *Playing and Reality*. London: Tavistock.
> Classic psychology text on how the nurturing of creativity in young children will give them an opportunity to enjoy a rich and rewarding cultural life.

Vygotsky, L.S. (1966/1976) Play and its role in the mental development of the child, in J.S. Bruner, A. Jolly and K. Sylva (eds) *Play: Its Role in Development and Evolution*. New York: Basic Books.
> Analyses the role of play in children's development, and suggests that imaginative play is a preparation for the development of abstract thought.

Note

Children's Play Information Service is based in the offices of the National Children's Bureau, 8 Wakley Street, London EC1V 7QE
Tel: 020 7843 6303 / 6026
Email: cpis@ncb.org.uk
www.ncb.org.uk/cpis

Appendix 2

The Playwork Principles

1. All children and young people need to play. The impulse to play is innate. Play is a biological, psychological and social necessity, and is fundamental to the healthy development and well being of individuals and communities.
2. Play is a process that is freely chosen, personally directed and intrinsically motivated. That is, children and young people determine and control the content and intent of their play, by following their own instincts, ideas and interests, in their own way for their own reasons.
3. The prime focus and essence of playwork is to support and facilitate the play process and this should inform the development of play policy, strategy, training and education.
4. For playworkers, the play process takes precedence and playworkers act as advocates for play when engaging with adult-led agendas.
5. The role of the playworker is to support all children and young people in the creation of a space in which they can play.
6. The playworker's response to children and young people playing is based on a sound up to date knowledge of the play process, and reflective practice.
7. Playworkers recognise their own impact on the play space and also the impact of children and young people's play on the playworker.
8. Playworkers choose an intervention style that enables children and young people to extend their play. All playworker intervention must balance risk with the developmental benefit and well being of children.

The Playwork Principles (PPSG 2005) were developed after a lengthy consultation exercise, and have been officially recognized by SkillsActive (the lead body for education and training in playwork).

They are intended to replace the previous statement of assumptions and values contained in: SPRITO (1992) *National Occupational Standards in Playwork*. London: Sport and Recreation Industry Lead Body.

References

3G Phones Limited http://www.three-g.net/3g_standards.html#usa (accessed on 14/08/07)

Abbs, P., Attenborough, L., Balbernie, R. et al. (2006) *Modern Life Leads to More Depression Among Children*. Open letter from more than 100 professionals and academics to the *Daily Telegraph*, 12 September 2006

Abernethy, D.W. (1968) *Playleadership*. London: National Playing Fields Association.

Abernethy, D. (1974) *Playleadership*. London: National Playing Fields Association.

Abernethy, D.W. (1977) *Notes and Papers: A General Survey on Children's Play Provision*. London: National Playing Fields Association.

Adams, J. (1996) *Risk*. London: University College London Press.

Adams, J., Gill, S. and McDonald, M. (1991) Reducing fear in hospital. *Nursing Times* 87(1): 62–4.

Alderson, P. (1995) *Listening to Children: Children, Ethics and Social Research*. Ilford: Barnardos.

Allen of Hurtwood, Lady (1968) *Planning for Play*. London: Thames & Hudson.

Allman, J.M. (1999) *Evolving Brains*. New York: Scientific American Library.

Amulya, J. (2003) What is reflective practice? *Centre for Reflective Community Practice MIT*. Available from: crcp.mit.edu/documents/whatis.pdf

Anti-social Behaviour Act (2003) London: The Statinery Office Ltd.

Argyris, C. (1991) Teaching smart people how to learn. *Harvard Business Review*, May–June.

Argyris, C. and Schön, D. (1978) *Organisational Learning: A Theory of Action Perspective*. Reading, Mass: Addison-Wesley.

Armitage, M. (2000) The ins and outs of school playground play: children's use of 'play places', in Bishop, J.C. and Curtis, M. (2000) *Play for Today: Approaches to Contemporary Children's Playgroud Culture*. Buckingham: Open University Press.

Arnett, J. (1995) Adolescents' use of media for self-socialization. *Journal of Youth and Adolescence* 24(5): 519–33.

Athey, C. (2001) *Extending Thought in Young Children.* London: Paul Chapman.

Axline, V. (1969) *Play Therapy.* New York: Ballantine Books.

Axline, V. (1989) *Play Therapy.* Boston, MA: Houghton Mifflin.

Bancroft, D. and Carr, R. (1995) *Influencing Children's Development.* Oxford: Blackwell.

Bandura, B. and Walters, R.H. (1963) *Social Learning and Personality Development.* New York: Holt, Rinehart and Winston.

Baron-Cohen S. (2004). *The Essential Difference: The Truth About the Male and Female Brain.* London: Penguin.

Battram, A. (1998) *Navigating Complexity: The Essential Guide to Complexity Theory in Business and Management.* London: Industrial Society.

Battram, A. (2007) *Retune to the Edge: Playwork at the Edge of Chaos in the Zone of Complexity.* Matlock: The Ludelic Press.

Battram, A. and Russell, W. (2002) The edge of recalcitrance: playwork, order and chaos. Paper presented at the '*Spirit of Adventure Play is Alive and Kicking*', Play Wales conference, Cardiff, June.

Beck, U. (1992) *Risk Society: Towards a New Modernity?* London: Sage.

Bell, J. (2005) *Doing Your Research Project.* Maidenhead: Open University Press.

Bengtsson, A. (1972) *Adventure Playgrounds.* London: Crosby Lockwood.

Benjamin, J. (1974) *Grounds for Play: An Extension of In Search of Adventure.* London: Bedford Square Press of the National Council for Social Service.

Berlyne, D.E. (1960) *Conflict, Arousal and Curiosity.* New York: McGraw-Hill.

Berson, I. (2003) *Grooming Cybervictims: The Psychosocial Effects of Online Exploitation for Youth.* Tampa, FL: University of South Florida.

Bichard Report (2004), *Inquiry Report*, HC 653, London: TSO.

Blatchford, P. (1994) Research on children's school playground behaviour in the United Kingdom: a review, in Blatchford, P. and Sharp, S. (1994) *Breaktime and the School: Understanding and changing playground behaviour.* London: Routledge.

Boal, A. (1995) *The Rainbow of Desire.* London: Routledge.

BPS (British Psychological Society) (1990) *Ethical Principles for Conducting Research with Human Participants.* Leicester: BPS.

Braun, A. (2004) in The Future of Play, Learning and Creativity; *Documentation of a LEGO Institute*, symposium held in Hamburg, Germany, January 2004. Available from http://www.legolearning.net (accessed 21/05/07).

Bretherton, I. (1989) Pretense: the form and function of make-believe play. *Developmental Review* 9: 383–401.

British Market Research Bureau (2005) *Playday 2005 Survey for the Children's Play Council and The Children's Society.* London: Children's Play Council.

Brown, F. (1989) *Working with Children: A Playwork Training Pack.* Leeds: Children First.

Brown, F. (2000) Compound flexibility (S.P.I.C.E. Revisited). Paper presented at the Play Education's 2nd Theoretical Playwork Meeting 'New Playwork – New Thinking?' 21 March 2000, Maltings Conference Centre, Ely.

Brown, F. (ed.) (2003a) *Playwork Theory and Practice.* Buckingham: Open University Press.

Brown, F. (2003b) Compound flexibility: the role of playwork in child development, in F. Brown (ed.) *Playwork: Theory and Practice*. Buckingham: Open University Press.

Brown, F. (2003c) An evaluation of the concept of play value and its application to children's fixed equipment playgrounds. Unpublished PhD thesis, Leeds Metropolitan University.

Brown, F. (2006) *Play Theories and the Value of Play*. London: National Children's Bureau.

Brown, F. (2007) *The Venture: A Case Study of an Adventure Playground*. Cardiff: Play Wales.

Brown, F. and Webb, S. (2005) Children without play. *Journal of Education* 35: 139–58.

Bruce, T. (1997) *Time to Play in Early Childhood Education*. London: Hodder & Stoughton.

Bruce, T. (2001) *Developing Learning in Early Childhood*. London: Paul Chapman.

Bruce, T. (2001) *Learning Through Play: Babies, Toddlers and the Foundation Years*. London: Hodder & Stoughton.

Bruce, T. (2005) Play, the universe and everything!, in J. Moyles (ed.) *The Excellence of Play*. Maidenhead: Open University Press.

Bruner, J.S., Jolly, A. and Sylva, K. (1976) *Play: It's Role in Deveopment and Evolution*. Harmondsworth: Penguin.

Bryan, T. and Doyle, P. (2003) Developing multi-agency public protection arrangements, in A. Matravers (ed.) *Sex Offenders in the Community: Managing and Reducing the Risks*. Cullompton: Willan.

Burghardt, G.M. (2005) *The Genesis of Animal Play: Testing the Limits*. London: MIT Press.

Caillois, R. (1961) *Man, Play and Games*. New York: Free Press.

Caputo, J. (2001) *On Religion (Thinking in Action)*. London: Routledge.

Cardiff Council (2007) *Do Playworkers' Childhood Play Experiences Affect Their Playwork Practice?* available from http://www.cardiff.gov.uk/childrensplay/content. asp?nav=2868%2C2971%2C3874%2C3894&parent_directory_id=2865& positioning_article_id=&language=&sortkey

Carse, J.P. (1986) *Finite and Infinite Games*. New York: Free Press.

Carter, R. et al. (eds) (1984) *Systems, Management and Change: A Graphic Guide*. London: Harpers & Row in association with the Open University.

Casterton, J. (2005) *Creative Writing: A Practical Guide*. London: Palgrave.

Chambers)1998) *The Chambers Dictionary*. Edinburgh: Chambers Harrap Publishers.

Champion K., Vernberg E. and Shipman K. (2003) Nonbullying victims of bullies: aggression, social skills, and friendship characteristics. *Journal of Applied Developmental Psychology* 24(5): 535–51.

Charity Commission (2007) *CC3 The Essential Trustee: What You Need to Know*. Liverpool: Charity Commission Direct.

Chen, V. (2004) The possibility of critical dialogue in the theory of CMM. *Human Systems: The Journal of Systemic Consultation and Management* 15(3): 179–92.

Chief Secretary to the Treasury (2003) *Every Child Matters*. Cm 5860. London: TSO.

Child Accident Prevention Trust (CAPT) (2001) *Safe Kids Campaign: Parents' and Children's Poll*. London: CAPT.

Children Act 1989 London: HMSO.

Children Act 2004 London: HMSO.

The Children (Northern Ireland) Order 1995. SI 1995 No.755 (N.I. 2). London: The Stationery Office.

Children Now (2006) Extended schools: play will be left out of the core offer. *Children Now*, 30 August.

Children's Society (2007) *The Good Childhood Inquiry*. Available from: www.childrenssociety.org.uk/what+we+do/The+good+childhood+inquiry/

Christensen, P. (2003) Play, space and knowledge: children in the village and the city, in P. Christensen and M. O'Brien (eds) *Children in the City: Home Neighbourhood and Community*. London: RoutledgeFalmer.

Clark, A. and Moss, P. (2005) *Spaces to Play: More Listening to Young Children Using the Mosaic Approach*. London: National Children's Bureau.

Cognitive Edge (2006) *Communities of Practice*. Available from: www.cognitive-edge.com/2006/10/communities_of_practice.php

Cole-Hamilton, I. (2002) Something good and fun: children's and parents' views on play and out-of-school provision, in I. Cole-Hamilton, A. Harrop and C. Street (eds) *Making the Case for Play: Gathering the Evidence*. London: National Children's Bureau.

Cole-Hamilton, I. Harrop, A. and Street, C. (2002) *Making the Case for Play: Gathering the evidence*. London: National Children's Bureau.

Cole-Hamilton, I. and Gill, T. (2002a) *Making the Case for Play: Building Policies and Strategies for School-aged Children*. London: National Children's Bureau.

Cole-Hamilton, I. and Gill, T. (2002b) *More Swings Than Roundabouts*. London: Children's Play Council, National Children's Bureau.

Conway, M. (2004) Professional playwork practice, in F. Brown (ed.) *Playwork: Theory and Practice*. Buckingham: Open University Press.

Conway, M. and Farley, T. (2001) *Quality in Play: Quality Assurance for Children's Play Providers*. London: London Play.

Corsaro, W. (1985) *Friendship and Peer Culture in the Early Years*. Norwood, NJ: Ablex.

CPC (Children's Play Council) (2006) *Play Naturally: Survey of Children's Views*. London: National Children's Bureau. Available from: www.playday.org.uk/view.asp?ID=55 (accessed 22/09/2006).

Cranwell, K. (2003) Towards a History of Adventure Playgrounds 1931–2000, in N. Norman(2004) *An Architecture of Play: A Survey of London's Adventure Playgrounds*. London: Four Corners

Cranwell, K. (2007) Adventure playgrounds and the community in London (1948–70): an appreciation of the ideas and actions that shaped the spirit of the 1960's play movement, in W. Russell, B. Handscomb and J. Fitzpatrick (eds)

Playwork Voices: In Celebration of Bob Hughes and Gordon Sturrock. London Centre for Playwork Education and Training.

Cross, G. (2004) *The Cute and the Cool.* Oxford: Oxford University Press.

Csikszentmihalyi, M. (1992) *Flow: The Psychology of Happiness.* London: Random House.

Damasio, A. (1994) *Descartes Error: Emotion, Reason and the Human Brain.* New York: Putnam.

Davenport, G.C. (1994) *An Introduction to Child Development.* London: Collins Educational.

Davies, B. (2003) *Frogs and Snails and Feminist Tales: Preschool Children and Gender.* Cresskill, NJ: Hampton Press.

Davis, L. (2008) *Policy Summary, The Children's Plan: Building brighter futures.* London: Play England.

Davy, A. and Gallagher, J. (2006) *New Playwork: Play and Care for Children 4–16.* 4th edition. London: Thomson Learning.

DCLG (Department for Communities and Local Government) (2006) *Strong and Prosperous Communities: The Local Government White Paper.* Norwich: The Stationery Office.

DCMS (Department for Culture, Media and Sport) (2004) *Getting Serious About Play: A Review of Children's Play.* The Report of the Review of Children's Play chaired by the Rt. Hon. Frank Dobson MP, London: DCMS.

DCMS (Department of Culture Media and Sport) (2005) *Response to the 2004 Play Review by the Secretary of State of Culture, Media and Sport.* Available from: www.culture.gov.uk/NR/rdonlyres/612631B7–11FE-4A83-B2AB-A5AEA7F44A14/0/govtresponsegsap.pdf.

DCMS (Department of Culture Media and Sport) (2006) *Time for Play: Encouraging Greater Play Opportunities for Children and Young People.* London: DCMS.

DCSF (Department for Children, Schools and Families) (2007) *The Children's Plan: Building Brighter Futures.* CM7280 London: HMSO.

DCSF (Department for Children, Schools and Families) (2007a) *Staying Safe: A Consultation.* Nottingham: DCSF Publications.

DCSF (Department for Children, Schools and Families) (2007b) *The Children's Plan: Building Brighter Futures,* CM 7280. London: HMSO.

Denning, S. (2007) *Storytelling Complements Abstract Analysis.* Available from: www.stevedenning.com/intro.htm

Denscombe, M. (1998) *The Good Research Guide: For Small-scale Social Research Projects.* Buckingham: Open University Press.

DfES (Department for Education and Skills) (2001) *Building a Strategy for Children and Young People: Consultation Document.* London: DfES Children and Young People's Unit.

DfES (Department for Education and Skills) (2002) *Birth to Three Matters: A Framework to Support Children in their Earliest Years.* Available from: www.standards.dfes.gov.uk/primary/publications/foundation_stage/940463

DfES (Department for Education and Skills) (2003) *Every Child Matters.* Green Paper, CM560. Norwich: The Stationery Office.

DfES (Department for Education and Skills) (2005a) *Every Child Matters: Change for Children*. London: The Stationery Office.

DfES (Department for Education and Skills) (2005b) *Common Core of Skills and Knowledge for the Children's Work Force: Every Child Matters, Change for Children*. Nottingham: DfES.

DfES (Department for Education and Skills) (2005c) *Extended Schools: Access to Opportunities and Services for All: A Prospectus*. Nottingham: DfES Publications.

DfT (Department for Transport) (2002) *Child Road Safety: Achieving the 2010 Target*. London: Department for Transport.

DfTE (Department for Training and Education) (2005) *The Childcare Strategy for Wales*. Cardiff: Welsh Assembly Government.

Dietz, W. (2001) The obesity epidemic in young children. *British Medical Journal*, 322(10): 313–14.

Ding, S. and Littleton, K. (eds.) (2005) *Children's Personal and Social Development*. Oxford: Blackwell Publishing Ltd in association with the Open University.

Dockar-Drysdale, B. (1991) *The Provision of Primary Experience*. New Jersey: Aronson,

DoH (Department of Health) (1995) *Child Protection: Messages from Research*. London: HMSO.

DoH (Department of Health) (2000) *Assessing Children in Need and their Families: Practice Guidance*. London: TSO.

DoH (Department of Health) (2004) *Choosing Health: Making Healthy Choices Easier*. Public Health White Paper, CM6374. London: HMSO.

DoH (Department of Health) (2006) *Health Challenge England*. London: HMSO.

Donald, M. (1991) *Origins of the Modern Mind*. Cambridge, MA: Harvard University Press.

Douglas, M. (1992) *Risk and Blame: Essays in Cultural Theory*. London: Routledge.

Douglas, M. and Wildavsky, A. (1982) *Risk and Culture: An Essay on the Selection of Technological and Environmental Dangers*. Berkeley: University of California Press.

Douglas, S. (2003) Establishing Play, in F. Brown, Playwork Theory and Practice. Buckingham: Open University Press.

DTE (Department for Training and Education) (2005) *The Childcare Strategy for Wales*. Cardiff: Welsh Assembly Government.

Edelman, G. (1994) *Bright Air, Brilliant Fire: On the Matter of Mind*. London: Penguin.

EDM (1983) *Early Day Motion 363*. Hansard. London: HMSO.

Elkind, D. (2001) *The Hurried Child: Growing Up Too Fast Too Soon*. Cambridge, MA: Perseus.

Ellis, M. (1973) *Why People Play*. Englewood Cliffs, NJ: Prentice-Hall.

Else, P. (2001) *What Is Therapeutic Playwork?* entry on the UKplayworkers website, 23 November.

Else, P. (2006) *Draft Statement of Ethics for Playworkers*. Unpublished paper for the Joint National Committee on Training for Playworkers.

Ellyatt, W. (2002) *Action Guide: Storytelling and the Power of Narrative*. Available from: www.pathsoflearning.net/library/storytelling.cfm#wendy

Emond, R. (2005) Ethnographic research methods with children and young people, in S. Green and D. Hogan (eds) *Researching Children's Experience: Approaches and Methods*. London: Sage.

Erikson, E. (1963) *Childhood and Society*. 2nd edition, New York: Norton.

Erikson, E. (1977) *Toys and Reasons*. New York: Norton.

ESRC Research Ethics framework, available from www.esrc.ac.uk/ESRCInfoCentre /Images/ESRC_Re_Ethics_Frame_tcm6-11291.pdf (accessed on 16/07/07).

Ewen, R. (1998) *An Introduction to Theories of Personality*, 5th edn, Mahwah, NJ, Lawrence Erlbaum Associates.

Farley, T. and Williams, P. (1992) *Aiming High: Quality Assurance Programme*. London: National Out of School Alliance (now 4 Children).

Farmer, C. (2005) *Citizenship Survey: Top Level Findings from the Children and Young People's Survey*. London: Home Office and Department for Education and Skills.

Farrel, A. (2005) *Ethical Research with Children*. Maidenhead: Open University Press.

Finkelstein, V. (1996) 'Modelling disability'. Breaking The Moulds. Paper presented at the conference, Dunfermline, Scotland 16–17 May.

Fisher, K. (2002) It Was Magic! Unpublished BA(Hons). Playwork dissertation, Leeds Metropolitan University.

Fjortoft, I. (2001) The natural environment as a playground for children: the impact of outdoor play activities in pre-primary school children. *Early Childhood Education Journal* 29(2).

Foley, P., Roach, J. and Tucker, S. (eds) (2000) *Children in Society*. Basingstoke: Palgrave Macmillan.

Freud, S. (1900/1974) The interpretation of dreams, in S. Freud (ed.) *The Standard Edition of the Complete Psychological Works of Sigmund Freud*. London, Hogarth Press.

Freud, S. (1922/1974) Beyond the pleasure principle, in S. Freud (ed.) *The Standard Edition of the Complete Psychological Works of Sigmund Freud*. London: Hogarth Press.

Froebel, F. (1888) *The Education of Man*. New York: Appleton.

Frost, J.L. and Klein, B.L. (1979) *Children's Play and Playgrounds.*, London, Allyn and Bacon.

Furedi, F. (2002) *The Culture of Fear*. London: Cassell.

Gabriel, J. (2001) *The Truth about Boys and Girls*. Available from: www.brainconnection.com

Garvey, C. (1977) *Play*. London: Fontana.

Ghaye, T. and Lillyman, S. (2000) *Reflection: Principles and Practice for Healthcare Professionals*. Wiltshire: Mark Allen.

Giddens, A. (1991) *Modernity and Self-identity*. Cambridge: Polity Press.

Gill, T. (2004) Bred in captivity, *The Guardian*, 20 September.

Gill T. (2005) *Cycling and Children and Young People: A Review*. London: National Children's Bureau.

Gill T. (2006) Home zones in the UK: history, policy and impact on children and youth. *Children, Youth and Environments* 16(1): 90–103.

GLA (Greater London Authority) (2005) *Mayor of London: Guide to Preparing Play Strategies.* London: GLA.

Gladwin, M. (2005) Participants' perceptions of risk in play in middle childhood. Unpublished MA dissertation, Leeds Metropolitan University.

Glasper, A., Roberts, T. and Venn, C. (1992) *Preparing Children for Hospital.* Report to the Consumer Association. London: Cascade.

Glasser, W. (2007) *Choice Theory.* Available from: www.wglasser.com/whatisct.htm

Goldstein, J. (1993) *Play Value: A Review of Research.* London: British Toy and Hobby Association.

Gopnik, A., Meltzoff, A.N. and Kuhl, P.K. (1999) *How Babies Think: The Science of Childhood.* London: Weidenfeld & Nicolson.

Gordon, C. (1999) Riskogenics: an exploration of risk, in Theoretical Playwork and the Research Agenda. Proceedings of PlayEducation Conference, March 1999, Ely: PlayEducation.

Green, J. (1997) Risk and the construction of social identity: children's talk about accidents. *Sociology of Health and Illness* 19(4): 457–79.

Greenfield, J., Jones, D., O'Brien, M., Rustin, M. and Sloan, D. (2000) Childhood urban space and citizenship: child-sensitive urban regeneration. *Research Briefing, No.16, July 2000, part of the Economic and Social Research Council's Children 5–16 Research Programme.* Available from: www.hull.ac.uk/children5 to16programme/details/obrien.htm

Greenhalgh, L. and Worpole, K. (1995) *Park Life: Urban Parks and Social Renewal – A Report by Comedia in Association with Demos.* London: Comedia.

Greig, A. and Taylor, J. (1999) *Doing Research With Children.* London: Sage.

Greig, A., Taylor, J. and MacKay, T. (2007) *Doing Research with Children.* London: Sage.

Grof, S. (1998) *The Cosmic Game.* Dublin: Newleaf.

Groos, K. (1901) *The Play of Man.* London: Heinemann.

Guss, F. (2005) Reconceptualizing play: aesthetic self-definitions. *Contemporary Issues in Early Childhood* 6: 233–43.

Haigh, M.J. (2002) Internationalization of the Curriculum: designing inclusive education for a small world. *Journal of Geography in Higher Education* 26(1): 49–66.

Handy, C. (1990) *Understanding Voluntary Organizations.* London: Penguin.

Harris, J.R. (1998) *The Nurture Assumption: Why Children Turn Out the Way They Do.* London: Bloomsbury.

Harris, T.A. (1970) *I'm OK, You're OK.* London: Pan Books.

Hart, R. (1992) *Children's Participation: From Tokenism to Citizenship.* Florence: UNICEF International Child Development Centre.

Hartog, M. (2004) A *self study of a higher education tutor: how can I improve my practice.* Unpublished Ph.D Thesis, University of Bath.

Harvey (1980) The Case for Play In Acute Hospitals, in *Early Childhood* December 1980.

Hayes, N. (1994) *Foundations of Psychology.* London: Routledge.

The Health and Safety at Work Act etc. 1974 London, HMSO.

Heron, J. (1992) *Feeling and Personhood: Psychology in Another Key.* London: Sage.

High/Scope (2007) *The High Scope Approach*. Available from: www.high-scope.org.uk.

Hill, M. and Tisdall, K. (1997) *Children and Society*. London: Longman.

Hillman, M.., Adams, J. and Whitelegg, J. (1990) *One False Move: A Study of Children's Independent Mobility*. London: Policy Studies Institute.

Hillman, M. (1999) Children's development in a civilised society. *IN Play Action*, Autumn: 13–21.

Hobsbawn E. (1994) *Age of Extremes: the Short Twentieth Century 1914–1991*. London: Michael Joseph.

Hofkins, D. (2006) 'The answer lies in Bexley', *Times Education Supplement* (18/05/2007: p.22)

Home Office (2007) *Review of the Protection of Children from Sex Offenders*. London: COI.

Home Office and Department for Education and Skills (DfES) (2005) *2003 Home Office Citizenship Survey: Top Level Findings from The Children and Young People's Survey*. London: Home Office and DfES.

Home Office, Department of Health, Department of Education and Science and the Welsh Office (1991) *Working Together under the Children Act 1989: A Guide for Arrangements for Interagency Co-operation for the Protection of Children from Abuse*. London: HMSO.

HSE (Health and Safety Executive) (2006) 'Get a life' says HSC. Press release, 22 August. London: HSE.

Hughes, B. (1975) *Notes for Adventure Playworkers*. London: Children and Youth Action Group.

Hughes, B. (1996) *Play Environments: A Question of Quality*. London: PLAYLINK.

Hughes, B. (2000) A dark and evil cul-de-sac: has children's play in urban Belfast been adulterated by the troubles? Unpublished MA dissertation Anglia Polytechnic University, Cambridge..

Hughes, B. (2001a) *Evolutionary Playwork and Reflective Analytic Practice*. London: Routledge.

Hughes, B (2001b) *The First Claim … A Framework for Playwork Quality Assessment*. Cardiff: Play Wales, and Ely, Play Education (held in trust jointly).

Hughes, B. (2002a) *A Playworker's Taxonomy of Play Types*. London: PLAYLINK.

Hughes, B. (2002b) *The First Claim: Desirable Processes: A Framework for Advanced Playwork Quality Assessment*. Cardiff: Play Wales, and Ely, Play Education (held in trust jointly).

Hughes, B. (2003) Play deprivation, play bias and playwork practice, in F. Brown (ed.) *Playwork: Theory and Practice*. Buckingham: Open University Press.

Hughes, B. (2006) *Play Types Speculations and Possibilities*. London: The London Centre for Playwork Education and Training.

Hughes, B. and Williams, H. (1982) Talking About Play 1–5. *Play Times*, Nos 31–35 London, NPFA.

Huizinga, J. (1949) *Homo Ludens: A Study of the Play Element in Culture*. London: Routledge and Kegan Paul.

Huttenlocher, P.R. (1992) Neural Plasticity. In: Asbury, A.K., McKhann, G.M. and McDonald, W.I. (eds) *Diseases of the Nervous System* 1: 63–71.

Huttenmoser, M. and Degan-Zimmermann, D. (1995) *Lebenstraume fur Kinder*. Zurich: Swiss Science Foundation.

iPod, Wikipedia, available from http://en.wikipedia.org/wik/iPod (accessed on 14/08/07).

Isaacs, S. (1954) *The Educational Value of the Nursery School*. London: British Association for Early Childhood Education (BAECE).

James, J., Jenks, C. and Prout, A. (1998) *Theorising Childhood*. Cambridge: Polity Press.

Kahn, P.H., Jr. (2002) Children's affiliations with nature, in P.H. Kahn Jr. and S.R. Kellert (eds) *Children and Nature: Psychological, Sociocultural and Evolutionary Investigations*. London: MIT Press.

Kahr, B. (1996) *D. W. Winnicott: A Biographical Portrait*. London: Karnac Books.

Kane, E. (2003) The development of professional competence in playwork in Northern Ireland: an evaluation of current practice. Unpublished MSSc thesis, Queen's University, Belfast.

Kant, I. (1800) *Anthropologie in Pragmatischer Hinsicht abgegasst*. Konigsberg.

Katz, E. (2007) *Favourite Quotations: Play*. Available from: www.daily celebrations.com/ play.htm

Keats, J. (1817) *Letter to George and Tom*. Available from: www.mrbauld. com/negcap.html

Kilvington, J., Wood, A. and Knight, H. (2006) Affective play spaces. Unpublished paper presented at the 'New Directions in Children's Geographies' Conference, Northampton University, 8 September.

Kohlberg, L. (1966) A cognitive developmental analysis of children's sex role concepts and attitudes, in E.E. Maccoby (ed.) *The Development of Sex Differences*. London: Tavistock.

Kolb, D. (1984) *Experiential Learning: Experience as the Source of Learning and Development*. London: Prentice-Hall.

Kulkami, A. Simler, K. Storer, A. and Vareth, M. (2005) *Technology-mediated Telepathy: A Natural Language Brain-Computer Interface. Vertex-Bases Innovators' Challenge Competition*. Berkeley, CA: University of California Press.

Kurten, B. (1995) *Dance of the Tiger: A Novel of the Ice Age*. Berkeley, CA: University of California Press.

Laming Report (2003) *The Victoria Climbie Inquiry: Report of an Inquiry by Lord Laming*, Cm 5730, London: TSO.

Larson, R. (1995) Secrets in the bedroom: adolescents' private use of media. *Journal of Youth and Adolescence* 24(5).

Last, U. and Aharoni-Etzoni A. (1995) Secrets and reasons for secrecy among school-aged children: developmental trends and gender differences. *Journal of Genetic Psychology* 156(2): 191–203.

Lazarus, M. (1883) *Uber die reize des speils*. Berlin: Dummler.

Lester, S. (2004) *9 Processes of Playwork*. London: SkillsActive.

Lindon, J. (2003) *Too Safe for Their Own Good? Helping Children Learn About Risk*. London: National Early Years Network/National Children's Bureau.

London Borough of Brent (1985) *A Child in Trust: Report of the Panel of Inquiry Investigating the Circumstances Surrounding the Death of Jasmine Beckford*. London: London Borough of Brent.

London Play (2007) www.londonplay.co.uk (accessed 06/07)/

Louv, R. (2005) *Last Child in the Woods: Saving Our Children from Nature-deficit Disorder.* Chapel Hill, NC: Algonquin Books.

Love, S. (2005) Review of the mobile connection: the cell phone's impact on society. *International Journal of Technology and Human Interaction* 1(4): 101–4.

LPYCA (Leasowe Play, Youth and Community Association) (1987) *Thirteen Years Hard Labour and Ten Years Joint Management.* Unpublished document.

Lupton, D. (1998) *The Emotional Self: A Sociocultural Exploration.* London: Sage.

Lupton, D. (1999) *Risk.* London: Routledge.

MacFarlane, B. (2004) *Teaching with Integrity: The Ethics of Higher Education.* London: RoutledgeFalmer.

McMillan, M. (1919) *The Nursery School.* London: J.M. Dent & Sons.

McNiff, J. and Whitehead, J. (2005) *All You Need to Know About Action Research.* London: Sage.

Mannello, M. and Statham, J. (2000) *The State of Play: A Review of Open Access Play Provision in Wales and the Play 2000 Grant Scheme.* Cardiff: Welsh Assembly Government.

Manwaring, B. and Taylor, C. (2007) *The Benefits of Play and Playwork: Recent Evidence-based Research (2001–2006) Demonstrating the Impact and Benefits of Play and Playwork.* Available from: www.skillsactive.com/resources/ research/ CYWU_Research_Complete.pdf

Martin, C.L. and Halverson, C.F. (1981) A schematic processing model of sex typing and stereotyping in children. *Child Development* 52: 1119–34.

Martin, C.L. and Halverson, C.F. (1983) The effects of sex-stereotyping schemas on young children's memory, *Child Development* 54: 563–74.

Martin, C.L. and Ruble, D. (2004) Children's search for gender cues: cognitive perspectives on gender development. *Current Directions in Psychological Science* 13(2): 67–70.

Maslow, A. (1973) *The Farther Reaches of Human Nature.* Harmondsworth: Pelican.

Mayall, B. and Hood, S. (2001) Breaking barriers: provision and participation in and out-of-school centre. *Children and Society* 15(2): 70–82.

Mead, G.H. (1934) *Mind, Self and Society.* Chicago: University of Chicago Press.

Megginson, D. and Clutterbuck, D. (1995) *Mentoring in Action.* London: Kogan Page.

Meggit, C., Stevens, J. and Bruce, T. (2000) *An Introduction to Childcare and Education.* London: Hodder & Stoughton.

Mello, R. (2001) The power of storytelling : how oral narrative influences children's relationships in the classroom. *International Journal of Education and the Arts* 2(1).

Melville, S. (1999) Creating spaces for adventure. *Built Environment.* 25(1) Oxford, Alexandrine Press.

Mental Health Foundation (1999) *Bright Futures: Promoting Children and Young People's Mental Health.* London: Mental Health Foundation.

Middleton, J. (2001) Practitioner review: psychological sequelae of head injury in children and adolescents. *The Jounal of Child Psychology and Psychiatry and Allied Disciplines* 42(2): 165–80.

Millar, S. (1968) *The Psychology of Play*. Harmondsworth: Penguin.

Mizen, P. (2005) A little 'light work'? Children's images of their labour. *Visual Studies* 20(2): 124–39.

Montessori, M. (1912) *The Montessori Method: Scientific Pedagogy as Applied to Child Education in 'the Children's Houses'*. New York: Frederick A. Stokes.

Moon, J. (1999) *Reflection in Learning and Professional Development: Theory and Practice*. London: Kogan Page.

Moore, R.C. (1990) *Childhood's Domain: Play and Place in Child Development*, Berkeley, CA: Mig Communications.

Morgan, E. (1996) *The Descent of the Child*, London: Penguin.

Morris, D. (1964) The response of animals to a restricted environment. *Symposia of the Zoological Society of London* 13: 99–118.

Moss, P. and Petrie, P. (2002) *From Children's Services to Children's Spaces: Public Policy, Children and Childhood*. London: Routledge Falmer.

Moyles, J.R. (1989) *Just Playing: The Role and Status of Play in Early Childhood Education*. Buckingham: Open University Press.

Moyles, J.R. (ed.) (2005) *The Excellence of Play*. 2nd ed. Maidenhead: Open University Press.

Mussen, P., Conger, J. and Kagan, J. (1974) *Child Development and Personality*. New York: Harper International.

Nadeau, R.L. (1997) Brain sex and the language of love, *The World and I Online Magazine*.

The National Assembly for Wales. Policy Unit (2000) *Extending Entitlement: Supporting Young People in Wales*: Cardiff: The National Assembly for Wales.

National Statistics (2002) Available from: www.statistics.gov.uk/CCI/nscl.asp? ID=8155

Naylor, H. (1986) Outdoor play and play equipment, in P. K.Smith (ed.) *Children's Play: Research Developments and Practical Application*. London: Gordon & Breach.

Nebelong, H. (2004) Nature's playground. *Green Places*, May: 28–31.

Neill, A.S. (1968) *Summerhill*. Harmondsworth: Pelican.

Newell, P. (1991) *The UN Convention and Children's Rights in the UK*. London: National Children's Bureau.

NFPI (National Family and Parenting Institute) (2003) *Making Britain More Family Friendly*. London: National Family and Parenting Institute.

NICE (National Institute for Health and Clinical Excellence) (2006) *Obesity: Quick Reference Guide 1, for Local Authorities, Schools and Early Years Providers, Workplaces and the Public*. London: TSO.

Nicholson, S. (1967) United Kingdom: whose playgrounds? *Interbuild/Arena*: 12–19.

Nicholson, S. (1971) How not to cheat children: the theory of loose parts. *Landscape Architecture Quarterly* 62(1): 30–4.

NPFA (2000) *Best Play: What Play Provision Should Do for Children*. London: NPFA/Children's Play Council/PLAYLINK and Department of Culture, Media and Sport.

NYA/NSF (2004) *Making It Last*. Leicester: National Youth Agency.

OED (2006) *The Concise Oxford English Dictionary.* Oxford: Oxford University Press.

Opie, I. and Opie, P. (1959) *The Lore and Language of Schoolchildren.* Oxford: Clarendon Press.

Orr, D.W. (1994) *Earth in Mind.* Washington, DC: Island Press.

Ouvry, M. (2000) *Exercising Muscles and Minds: Outdoor Play and the Early Years Curriculum.* London: National Children's Bureau.

Palmer, M. (2002) *Reflections on Adventure Play.* DVD, available from Maureen Palmer or Chris Taylor.

Palmer, S. (2003) Playwork as reflective practice, in F. Brown (ed.) *Playwork: Theory and Practice.* Buckingham: Open University Press.

Papadopoulou, M. (2003) An attempt to establish a developmental phenomenology employing a case studies' approach to 'understanding' and 'organised learning'. Unpublished PhD thesis, University of Portsmouth.

Parkinson, C.E. (1985) *Where Children Play: An Analysis of Interviews About Where Children Aged 5–14 Normally Play and Their Preferences for Out-of-school Activities.* Birmingham: Play Board.

Parton, N. (2006) *Safeguarding Children: Early Intervention and Surveillance in a Late Modern Society.* Basingstoke: Palgrave Macmillan.

Petrie, P. (1994) Play and Care Out of School. London; HMSO.

Pettit, P. (2000) Odd man out: Neanderthals and modern humans. *British Archaeology* 51.

Piaget, J. (1951) *Play, Dreams and Imitation in Childhood.* London: Routledge and Kegan Paul.

Piaget, J. (1959). *The Construction of Reality in the Child.* London: Routledge.

Pinker, S. (2002) *The Blank Slate: The Modern Denial of Human Nature.* London: Allen Lane.

PlayBoard (2004) *Policy Delivery Through Playcare.* Belfast: PlayBoard.

PlayBoard (2007) *A Play Manifesto.* Belfast: PlayBoard.

Playday (2006) *Children Want More Natural Outdoor Play, says Playday Survey.* Available from: www.playday.org.uk/view.asp?ID=56

Play Safety Forum (2004) *Managing Risk in Play Provision: A Position Statement.* London: National Children's Bureau.

playtrain (2000) Article 31 C.C.S. (Children's Consultancy Scheme). Unpublished final report on Lambeth Borough Councils Children's Consultancy Project, September–November 2000.

Powlishta, K.K., Serbin, L.A. and Moller, L.C. (1993) The stability of individual differences in gender-typing: implications for understanding gender segregation. *Sex Roles* 23: 223–40.

PPSG (2005) *Playwork Principles* held in trust as honest brokers for the profession by the Playwork Principles Scrutiny Group Available from: www.playwales.org.uk/ page.asp?id=50

Pyle, R.M. (1993) *The Thunder Tree: Lessons from an Urban Wildland.* Boston, MA: Houghton Mifflin.

Pyle, R.M. (2002) Eden in a vacant lot, in P.H. Kahn Jr. and S.R. Kellert (eds) *Children and Nature: Psychological, Sociocultural and Evolutionary Investigations.* London: MIT Press.

Reid, D. and Reid, F. (2004) *Insights into the Social and Psychological Effects of SMS Text Messages.* Plymouth: University of Plymouth.

Rennie, S. (2003) Making play work: the fundamental role of play in the development of social relationship skills, in F. Brown (ed.) *Playwork: Theory and Practice.* Buckingham: Open University Press.

Richards, D. and Rowe, W. (1999) Decision-making with heterogeneous sources of information. *Risk Analysis* 19(1): 69–81.

Richards, V. (2005) *The Who You Dream Yourself.* London: Karnac Books.

Richards, V. and Wilce, G. (1996). *the Person Who is Me: Contemporary Perspectives on the True and False Self (Winnicott Studies Monographs).* London: Karnac Books.

Rivkin, M. (1995) *The Great Outdoors: Restoring Children's Right to Play Outside.* Washington, DC: National Association for the Education of Young Children.

Roberts, R. (1995) *Self-esteem and Successful Learning.* London: Hodder & Stoughton.

Roco, M.C. and Sims, W. (2003) *Converging Technologies for Improving Human Performance: Nanotechnology, Biotechnology.* Guildford: Springer.

Roth, G. and Loudon, J. (1998) *Maps to Ecstasy: A Healing Journey for the Untamed Spirit.* Novato, CA: New World Library.

Royal Society for the Prevention of Accidents (2005) *Challenge to Make Play Safe but Still Exciting.* London: RoSPA.

Rugg, G. and Petrie, M. (2007) *A Gentle Guide to Research Methods.* Maidenhead: Open University Press.

Russell, W. (2006) *Reframing Playwork: Reframing Challenging Behaviour.* Nottingham: Nottingham City Council.

Ryan, S. (2005) Freedom to choose: examining children's experiences in choice time, in N. Yelland (ed.) *Critical Issues in Early Childhood Education.* Maidenhead: Open University Press.

Sabbatini. R.M.E. (2000) Are there differences between the brains of males and females? *Brain and Mind Electronic Magazine on Neuroscience* 11.

Sandberg, A. and Pramling Samuelsson, I. (2003) Preschool teachers play experiences: then and now. *Early Childhood Research and Practice* 5(1).

Sanjek, R. (1990/1998) *Fieldnotes: The Makings of Anthropology.* Ithaca, NY: Cornell University Press.

Saylor, C.F. (1993) *Children and Disasters.* New York: Plenum Press.

SCF (Save the Children Fund) (1998) *Working with Children of Prisoners.* London: SCF.

Schechner, R. (1988) Playing. *Play and Culture* 1(1): 3–27.

Schechner, R. (2003) *Performance Theory.* London: Routledge.

Scheflen, A.E. and Ashcraft, N. (1976) *Human Territories: How We Behave in Space-time.* London: Prentice Hall.

Schiller, F. (1965) *On the Aesthetic Education of Man.* New York: Frederick Ungar.

Scottish Executive (2006) *Pre-school and Childcare Workforce Statistics 2005.* Available from: www.scotland.gov.uk/Publications/2006/02/22115728/0.

Scottish Executive (2007) *National Review of the Early Years and Childcare Workforce: Analyis of Written Consultation and Workshop Responses.* Edinburgh: Scottish Executive.

SCYofBC (The Society for Children and Youth of BC) (2007) *Position Statement 8 on the Child's Right to Play, 2001.* Available from: www.scyofbc.org/qs/page/763/0/43

Sebba, R. (1991) The landscapes of childhood: the reflection of childhood's environment in adult memories and in children's attitudes. *Environment and Behavior* 23(4): 395–422.

Secretary of State for Social Services (1974) *Report of the Inquiry into the Care and Supervision Provided in Relation to Maria Colwell.* London: HMSO.

Secretary of State for Social Services (1988) *Report of the Inquiry into Child Abuse in Cleveland 1987*, Cm 412, London: HMSO.

Sibley, D. (1995) *Geographies of Exclusion.* London: Routledge.

SkillsActive (2002) *Assumptions and Values of Playwork.* London: SkillsActive.

SkillsActive (2005a) *National Occupational Standards for Playwork, Levels 2 and 3.* London: SkillsActive.

SkillsActive (2005b) *Skills Surve Analysis and Report for Northern Ireland: SkillsActive.* London: SkillsActive.

SkillsActive (2005c) *Skills Needs Assessment for Playwork.* London: SkillsActive.

SkillsActive (2006) *Quality Training, Quality Play 2006–2011: The First UK Strategy for Playwork Education, Training and Qualifications.* London: SkillsActive.

Smith, A. (1759/1976) *The Theory of Moral Sentiments.* Oxford: Clarendon Press.

Smith, F. and Barker, J. (2000) 'Out of school' in school: a social geography of out of school childcare, in S. Holloway and G. Valentine (eds) *Children's Geographies.* London: Routledge.

Smith, H. (1995) *Unhappy Children: Reasons and Remedies.* London: Free Association.

SNP (Scottish National Party) (2007) *SNP Manifesto.* Edinburgh: SNP.

Sorensen, C.Th. (1931) Open spaces for town and country, in Hurtwood, Lady (1968) *Planning for Play.* London: Thames & Hudson.

Sorensen, C.Th. (1947) Personal correspondence with the author, in Lady Allen of Hurtwood (1968) *Planning for Play.* London: Thames Hudson.

Spencer, H. (1873) Principles of psychology, in N. Hayes (1994) *Foundations of Psychology.* London, Routledge.

SPRITO (1992) *National Occupational Standards in Playwork.* London: Sport & Recreation Industry Lead Body.

Steckler, A. (1999) *Qualitative Evaluation and Research Methods.* [Internet] Available from: http://teach.Oit.Unc.Edu/script/hbhe201001ss199/scripts/serve_home> (accessed 14/02/00).

Stern, D.N. (1985) *The Interpersonal World of the Infant: A View from Psychoanalysis and Developmental Psychology.* New York: Basic Books.

Sturrock, G. and Else, P. (1998) The playground as therapeutic space: playwork as healing Proceedings of the IPA/USA Triennial National Conference, *'Play in a Changing Society: Research, Design, Application'.* Colorado. USA, June 1998.

Sturrock, G. and Else, P. (2007) See www.ludemos.co.uk

Sturrock, G., Russell, W. and Else, P. (2004) *Towards Ludogogy Parts l, ll and lll: The Art of Being and Becoming through Play.* Sheffield: Ludemos.

Suomi, S.J. and Harlow, H.F. (1971) Monkeys without play, in Bruner, J.S., Jolly, A. and Sylva, K. eds (1976) *Play: Its Role in Development and Evolution*. New York, Basic Books (original work published 1933, Soviet Psychology 5, 6–18).

Sutton, J., Smith, P. and Swettenham, J. (1999) Bullying and 'theory of mind': a critique of the 'social skills deficit' view of anti-social behaviour. *Social Development* 8(1): 117–27.

Sutton-Smith, B. (1978) *Die Dialektik des Spiels*. Schorndorf: Verlag Karl Hoffman.

Sutton-Smith, B. (1981) *A History of Children's Play*. Philadelphia, PA: University of Pennsylvania Press.

Sutton-Smith, B. (1997) *The Ambiguity of Play*. Cambridge, MA: Harvard University Press.

Sutton-Smith, B. (2001) Emotional Breaches in Play Narrative in *Children in Play, Story and School*, Goncu, A. and Klein, E. (eds) New York: Guilford Publications.

Sutton-Smith, B. and Kelly-Byrne, D. (1984) The idealization of play, in P.K. Smith (ed.) *Play in Animals and Humans*. Oxford: Blackwell.

Tamminem, B. (2000) Behind bars, in 'New Playwork New Thinking'. Proceedings of PlayEducation Conference, March 2000, Ely: PlayEducation.

Taylor, A.F., Kuo, F.E. and Sullivan, W.C. (2001) Coping with ADD: the surprising connection to green play settings. *Environment and Behavior* 33(1): 54–77.

Thomas, G. and Hocking, G. (2003) *Other People's Children*. London: Demos.

Thomas, G. and Thompson, G. (2004) *A Child's Place: Why Environment Matters to Children*. London: Green Alliance/Demos Report.

Thomas, T. (2002) Employment screening and the Criminal Records Bureau. *Industrial Law Journal* 31(1): 55-70.

Thomas, T. (2004) Sex offender registers and monitoring, in H. Kemshall and G. McIvor (eds) *Managing Sex Offender Risk*. London: JKP.

Thompson, K. (1998) *Moral Panics*. London: Routledge.

Thorne, B. (1993) *Gender Play: Girls and Boys in School*. New Brunswick, NJ: Rutgers University Press.

Trevarthen, C. (1996) How a young child investigates people and things: why play helps development. Keynote speech to the TACTYC Conference 'A Celebration of Play', London November 1996.

Trevarthen, C., Kokkinaki, T. and Fiamenghi Jr., G.A. (1999). What infants' imitations communicate: with mothers, with fathers and with peers, in J. Nadel and G. Butterwoth (eds) *Imitation in Infancy*. Cambridge: Cambridge University Press.

Trimble, S. (1994) The scripture of maps, the names of trees, in G.P. Nabahn and S. Trimble (eds) *The Geography of Childhood: Why Children Need Wild Places*. Boston, MA: Beacon Press.

Tucker, S. (2001) Community development: a strategy for empowerment, in P. Foley, J. Roche and S. Tucker (eds) *Children in Society: Contemporary Theory, Policy and Practice*. New York: Palgrave.

Turner, V. (1982) *From Ritual to Theatre: The Human Seriousness of Play*. New York: PAJ Publications.

UNICEF (1991) *United Nations Convention on the Rights of the Child*. Svenska: UNICEF Kommitten.

Voce, A. (ed.) (2006) *Planning for Play: Guidance on the Development and Implementation of a Local Play Strategy.* London: Big Lottery Fund and Children's Play Council.

Vygotsky, L.S. (1966) Play and Its Role in the Mental Development of the Child, in Bruner, J.S., Jolly, A. and Sylva, K. (eds) (1976) *Play: Its Role in Development and Evolution.* New York: Basic Books, (original work published 1933, Soviet Psychology, 5, 6–18).

Vygotsky, L.S. (1978) *Mind in Society.* Cambridge, MA: Harvard University Press.

Vygotsky, L.S. (1995) *Imagination and Creativity in Childhood.* Gothenburg: Daidalos.

Waiton, S. and Baird, S. (eds) (2006) *Cotton Wool Kids.* Glasgow: Generation Youth Issues.

Ward, C. (1961) Adventure playground: a parable in anarchy. *Anarchy* 7: 193–201.

Webb, S. and Brown, F. (2003) Playwork in adversity: working with abandoned children, in F. Brown (ed.) *Playwork: Theory and Practice.* Buckingham: Open University Press.

Weick, K. (1995) *Sensemaking in Organisation.* Thousand Oaks, CA: Sage.

Welsh Assembly (1998) *The National Childcare Strategy in Wales: A Consultation Document.* London: The Stationery Office.

Welsh Assembly (2002a) *Welsh Assembly Government Play Policy.* Cardiff: Welsh Assembly Government.

Welsh Assembly (2002b) *Integrated Children's Centres: Guidance Notes.* Cardiff: Welsh Assembly Government.

Welsh Assembly Government (2004) *Welsh Assembly Government Play Policy Implementation Group Recommendations.* Cardiff: Welsh Assembly Government.

Welsh Assembly Government (2006) *Play policy implementation group recommendations.* http://www.wales.gov.uk/subichildren/content/play/playpolicy-impgroup-e.pdf (accessed 19/04/2006).

Wheway, R. and Millward, A. (1997) *Child's Play: Facilitating Play on Housing Estates.* London: Chartered Institute of Housing.

Whitehead, J. (1993) *The Growth of Educational Knowledge: Creating Your Own Living Educational Theories.* Bournemouth: Hyde.

Wild About Play (2004) *Environmental Play Links.* Available from: www.playwork.co.uk/wildaboutplay/links.htm

Wilson, E.O. (1984) *Biophillia.* Cambridge, MA: Harvard University Press.

Wilson, R.A. (1995) Nature and young children: a natural connection. *Young Children* 50(6): 4–11.

Wilson, R.A. (2002) The wonders of nature: honouring children's ways of knowing. *Early Childhood.* Available from: www.earlychildhoodnews.com/early childhood/article_view.aspx?ArticleID=70.

Winnicott, D.W. (1949/1965) *The Maturational Processes and the Facilitating Environment: Studies in the Theory of Emotional Development.* London: Hogarth Press.

Winnicott D.W. (1956/1958) *Through Paediatrics to Psychoanalysis.* London: Karnac Books.

Winnicott, D.W. (1960) *The Maturational Processes and the Facilitating Environment.* London: Karnac Books.

Winnicott, D.W. (1963/1965) *The Maturational Processes and the Facilitating Environment: Studies in the Theory of Emotional Development.* London: Hogarth Press.

Winnicott, D.W. (1964) *The Child, the Family and the Outside World.* London: Penguin.

Winnicott, D.W. (1968/2007) Communication between infant and mother and mother and infant, compared and contrasted, in J. Abram (ed.) *The Language of Winnicott: A Dictionary of Winnicott's Use of Words.* London: Karnac Books.

Winnicott, D.W. (1971) *Playing and Reality.* London: Routledge.

Winslade, J. (2003). Storying professional identity. *International Journal of Narrative Therapy and Community Work* 4: 33–5.

Wood, A. and Kilvington, J. (2007) The gentle art of agonism: speculations and possibilities of missing female perspectives?, in W. Russell, B. Handscomb and J. Fitzpatrick (eds) *Playwork Voices.* London Centre for Playwork Education and Training.

Wood, D.J., Bruner, J.S. and Ross, G. (1976) The role of tutoring in problem solving. *Journal of Child Psychology and Psychiatry* 17: 89–100.

Woodhead, M. and Montgomery, H. (eds.) (2003) *Understanding Childhood.* London: John Wiley and Sons Ltd in association with the Open University.

Yeatman, J. and Reifel, S. (1992) Sibling play and learning. *Play and Culture* 5(2): 141–58.

Ylvisaker, M. (1998) *Traumatic Brain Injury Rehabilitation: Children and Adolescents.* Boston, MA: Butterworth and Heinmann.

Youlden, P. and Harrison, S. (2006) *the Better Play programme: An evaluation.* London: Children's Play Council.

Useful Internet References

Aid for Romanian Children – www.arccharity.org
The Association for the Study of Play – www.csuchico.edu/kine/tasp/
Children's Play Council – www.ncb.org.uk/cpc/
Children's Play Information Service – www.ncb.org.uk/library/cpis/
Fair Play for Children – www.arunet.co.uk/fairplay/home.htm
Fields in Trust (formerly National Playing Fields Association) – www.fieldsintrust.org
Leeds Metropolitan University – www.leedsmet.ac.uk
London Play – www.londonplay.co.uk
Ludemos – www.ludemos.co.uk
PlayBoard Northern Ireland – www.playboard.org/
Playeducation – www.xnd76.dial.pipex.com/
Play England – www.playengland.org.uk
Play Scotland – www.playscotland.org/
Play Wales – www. playwales.org.uk
SkillsActive Playwork Section – www.skillsactive.com/playwork
UKplayworkers – www.groups.yahoo.com/group/UKplayworkers/

Index

DEVELOPING MULTIPROFESSIONAL TEAMWORK FOR INTEGRATED CHILDREN'S SERVICES

Angela Anning, David Cottrell, Nick Frost, Josephine Green and Mark Robinson

Multiprofessional practice in the delivery of services is a central government imperative in the UK and other countries. This book offers a practical resource to professionals charged with conceptualising, planning, implementing and evaluating multiprofessional practice in children's services. The book:

- Exemplifies what multiprofessional work looks like in practice
- Examines real dilemmas faced by professionals trying to make it work, and shows how these dilemmas can be resolved
- Considers lessons to be learnt, implications for practice and recommendations for making multiprofessional practice effective

Discussion of dilemmas facing multiprofessional teams include organising and managing multi-professional teams, supporting professionals as they learn to adapt to new roles and responsibilities, and learning how to share professional knowledge and expertise.

Featuring useful guidance, theoretical frameworks and evidence-based insights into practice, this book is a key resource for students on courses studying early childhood and families, as well as social workers, teachers, support workers in children's centres, family support workers, health workers, and managers of a range of children and youth services.

Contents: *Part One: Researching and understanding multi-professional teams working with children – Working in a multi-professional world – Researching multi-professional teams – Organising and managing multi-professional teams – Part Two: Working and learning in a multi-professional team – Multi-professional perspectives on childhood – Changing roles and responsibilities in multi-professional teams – Sharing knowledge in the multi-professional workplace – Part Three: Planning, implementing and supporting multi-professional teams working with children – Making it work 1: Addressing key dilemmas – Making it work 2: Strategies for decision-making and service delivery – Taking multi-professional practice forward*

2006 156pp

978-0-335-21978-0 (Paperback)   978-0-335-21979-9 (Hardback)

CHILDREN, FAMILIES AND COMMUNITIES
Creating and Sustaining Integrated Services

Pat Broadhead, Chrissy Meleady and Marco Delgado

This book draws on the work of Sheffield Children's Centre, a well-known community cooperative which is recognized worldwide for its cutting edge approach and models of good practice that have emerged from community participation.

Gaining an insight into the work of the Centre contributes to a better understanding of the challenges, issues, difficulties and opportunities which confront integrated services for children and families. The authors illustrate how, through working closely with the local community and through hearing the voices of children and adults, service provision for children and families can meet needs and change lives.

The book:

- Looks at the alternative approach of Sheffield Children's Centre, where multi-professional working has grown through common principles and aspirations rather than through policy imperative and legislation
- Details innovative practices and approaches to holistic work with children and families
- Explores the challenges and celebrations of working with a wide range of children, families and communities both in the UK and internationally

It has particular resonance with the multi-professional agendas now required by Every Child Matters and the Children Act (2004) and is groundbreaking in terms of re-thinking support for communities perceived to be 'in difficulty', in fostering community cohesion and promoting active participation in community regeneration from a childcare perspective, working from grassroots upwards.

Children, Families and Communities is ideal for researchers, policy makers, practitioners and students training to work with children and families from a range of disciplines such as education, health and social services, including those pursuing the NPQICL (National Professional Qualification for Integrated Centre Leadership) qualification and the EYPs (Early Years Professional Status).

Contents: *The evolution of Sheffield Children's Centre; developing a project identity – Valuing children means valuing families – A community co-operative; growing and sustaining the services and the tensions in being a cutting-edge provider – Diversity as a cornerstone of centre development – International networks and global justice: A reciprocal highway for ongoing evolution – From cradle to grave for children, families and communities; understanding the holistic dynamic*

2007 136pp

978-0-335-22093-9 (Paperback)   978-0-335-22094-0 (Hardback)